SINCE
1854

MECHANICS' INSTITUTE
LIBRARY & CHESS ROOM

57 Post Street, San Francisco, CA 94104
(415) 393-0101

THE BUREAUCRAT KINGS

THE BUREAUCRAT KINGS

The Origins and Underpinnings of America's Bureaucratic State

PAUL D. MORENO

PRAEGER™

An Imprint of ABC-CLIO, LLC

Santa Barbara, California • Denver, Colorado

Library of Congress Cataloging-in-Publication Data

Names: Moreno, Paul D., 1965- author.
Title: The bureaucrat kings : the origins and underpinnings of America's
  bureaucratic state / Paul D. Moreno.
Description: Santa Barbara, California : Praeger, [2017] | Includes bibliographical
  references and index. | Description based on print version record and CIP data
  provided by publisher; resource not viewed.
Identifiers: LCCN 2016037769 (print) | LCCN 2016029585 (ebook) |
  ISBN 9781440839672 (ebook) | ISBN 9781440839665 (alk. paper)
Subjects: LCSH: Bureaucracy—United States. | Administrative agencies—
  United States. | United States—Politics and government.
Classification: LCC JK421 (print) | LCC JK421 .M56 2017 (ebook) |
  DDC 351.73—dc23
LC record available at https://lccn.loc.gov/2016037769

ISBN: 978-1-4408-3966-5
EISBN: 978-1-4408-3967-2

21 20 19 18 17   1 2 3 4 5

This book is also available as an eBook.

Praeger
An Imprint of ABC-CLIO, LLC

ABC-CLIO, LLC
130 Cremona Drive, P.O. Box 1911
Santa Barbara, California 93116-1911
www.abc-clio.com

This book is printed on acid-free paper ∞
Manufactured in the United States of America

*For my godsons, Harold Kenneth Birzer
and Vincent Pius Pestritto*

Contents

Preface: The New Ruling Class

The United States is ruled by an establishment nowhere mentioned in the U.S. Constitution. Once a federal republic, we have become a centralized bureaucracy run by an unelected administrative class. This class has consolidated power in Washington, DC, and combines the legislative, executive, and judicial functions that the Constitution separated. Congress has delegated its lawmaking power to this bureaucracy—and doing so makes Congress more powerful and less accountable. The president sometimes can use the bureaucracy to govern without Congress or to avoid responsibility, but no individual can control it. Like Congress, the president also often is happy to pass the buck to the bureaucrats. The unelected federal judiciary usually defers to the unelected administrators, but can choose to intervene to maximize its own power. The states often appear to have lost their constitutional powers, but are active partners in the construction of this new governing system. Those citizens who still vote rightly wonder why elections don't seem to make any difference. It is because elections have little impact on the administrative state. This book explains how this new state came into being and grew to what it is today.

The last few years—in the aftermath of the 2008 financial crisis and the Democratic party's surge in that year's elections—have seen the fourth wave of the development of the administrative state, after the progressive era at the opening of the 20th century, the New Deal of the 1930s, and the Great Society of the 1960s.[1] This fourth wave of modern liberalism produced three monumental pieces of legislation. In 2008, Congress enacted the Emergency Economic Stabilization Act which created the Troubled Asset Relief Program (TARP). TARP authorized the U.S. Secretary of the Treasury to send $750 billion to purchase any financial institution's assets they believed to be economically significant. Boston University Law Professor Gary Lawson described TARP as "a constitutional monstrosity and many of its problems are endemic to the modern administrative state."[2] Congress debated and rejected a bailout for the auto industry, but the U.S. Treasury decided that the industry was an eligible "financial institution" anyway. General Motors and Chrysler went bankrupt notwithstanding, and then the regular bankruptcy laws were waived to secure the interests of the United Auto Workers over other employees and creditors—especially the taxpayers who had funded the bailout.[3]

In 2010, Congress enacted the Wall Street Reform and Consumer Protection Act, known as "Dodd-Frank." The legislation created two new agencies—the Financial Security Oversight Council and the Consumer Financial Protection Bureau (CFPB)—to prevent the financial collapse that had led to TARP. These agencies can decide that a financial institution is "systemically important" or "too big to fail," and subject it to new regulations. The Dodd-Frank act is 2,300 pages in length, and required the further promulgation of 390 new rules, only about 60 percent of which were completed within five years. The CFPB can punish "abusive" lending practices, although this term is undefined. Bureau Director Richard Cordray told Congress that it would be inconvenient to define "abuse" in advance, and that he should be free to make up the definition as cases developed. Congress has no power to control the bureau by appropriations; it gets $400 million per year from the Federal Reserve—which is itself outside of congressional appropriations.[4] The act severely limited the power of the president to remove the director, and limited judicial review of the board's decisions.[5] Like earlier banking regulations, compliance costs for Dodd-Frank have driven small banks out of business, and it likely has made the financial system more vulnerable—not less—to systemic failure today.

The 2010 Patient Protection and Affordable Care Act (ACA) or "Obamacare" is the *ne plus ultra* of statism. It brought the American health care industry—already about half paid for by the federal and state governments—to the brink of full political control. House Speaker Nancy Pelosi famously derided a query about Congress' constitutional power to enact the ACA as "not a serious question." She further urged the American people that "we have to pass the bill so that you can find out what's in it."[6] The act is more than 2,000 pages long, and it refers to the secretary of Health and Human Services more than 2,000 times. There are more than 700 points on which the secretary "shall" do something, and more than 200 cases in which he or she "may" do something. "On 139 occasions, the law mentions decisions that the "Secretary determines." At times, the frequency of these mentions reaches comic heights. For instance, one section of the law reads: 'Each person to whom the Secretary provided information under subsection (d) shall report to the Secretary in such manner as the Secretary determines appropriate.'"[7] After enactment, it was found that the act required insurers to pay for contraceptives, and might impose occupational restrictions on health-club personal trainers.[8]

Perhaps most revealing of the nature of the modern administrative state, however, were the comments of Jonathan Gruber, one of the principal designers of the ACA. Gruber admitted that "the stupidity of the American voter" compelled the bill's drafters to hide its real costs. When his candid comments were publicized, the administration tried to conceal that Gruber was a major contributor to the bill, and that he was paid $400,000 for his work.[9] It is a recurring theme in progressive and modern liberal theory that the American people do not know what is good for them, cannot govern themselves, and thus need to be governed by an elite administrative class.

Another way to gain a perspective on the administrative state is to look at a random day's issue of the *Federal Register*, the bulletin of the regulatory agencies. The *Register* was established in 1935, as the New Deal was getting into high gear, and all the existing regulations published in its first issue totaled 2,619 pages. The 1980 *Register* added more than 80,000 pages. A typical year adds about 60,000.[10] It looks as if 2015 broke the record with more than 82,000 pages.[11] On the randomly selected day of August 4, 2015 (the birthday of President Obama and the author), we see 304 new pages (about the daily average), consisting of 126 notices, 5 proposed rules, 10 rules, 1 presidential document, and 3 "significant documents."

The National Credit Union Administration amended its regulation governing federal credit union ownership of fixed assets. The Department of Agriculture adjusted its appendices to the dairy tariff-rate import quota licensing regulation for the 2015 tariff-rate quota year. The Animal and Plant Health Inspection Service affirmed its revision of a treatment schedule for hot-water treatment of mangoes. Medicare and Medicaid proposed alterations in the schedule of payments. The Coast Guard established a "voluntary First Amendment area for individuals [who] desire to exercise their First Amendment free speech rights with regards to Shell [Oil Company] operations." There were additions and subtractions to the procurement list of the Committee for Purchases from People Who Are Blind or Severely Disabled. The Consumer Product Safety Commission published the Classification of Vacuum Diffusion Technology as an Anti-Entrapment System under the Virginia Graeme Baker Pool and Spa Safety Act.[12] The Department of Defense filed its environmental impact statement on its Mariana Islands training facilities. The Drug Enforcement Agency revoked the licenses of several physicians and licensed importers of controlled substances. The Economic Analysis Bureau released its "Quarterly Survey of Transactions in Selected Services and Intellectual Property with Foreign Persons."

This merely scratches the surface of one day of the *Register's* publication. Moreover, the *Register* is a record of only the formal, recorded rulings of administrative agencies. The bureaucracy does a lot more by informal means, including threats to sue, consent decrees, "memoranda of understanding," and other deals that leave no trace in the official record.[13]

Very few citizens have had direct contact with a federal bureaucrat, but we are affected by them behind the scenes of almost every activity in ordinary life. The statements—indeed, the mere verbal inflection or facial expressions—of the chairman of the Federal Reserve Board, perhaps the most powerful bureaucrat in the world, moves billions of dollars in global markets. If you have applied for a job, a mortgage, or college admission, or have sought any kind of medical care, the encounter has been significantly shaped by federal bureaucrats. The bankers, employers, colleges, doctors, and hospitals that each of us deals with all have to employ personnel to deal with the rules that those bureaucrats make. Many of us are more familiar with state-level bureaucracy, and usually do all that we can to avoid it. (Just think of your state Department of Motor Vehicles.) Additionally, much of what state governments do is dictated by federal bureaucrats, because the federal government provides an ever-greater share of the money for state programs.

The "fourth branch" of the administrative state feeds the other branches. The number of people directly employed by the federal government has not grown much since World War Two, because the centralized bureaucratic state uses state governments, contractors, and other third parties to do its work. The U.S. Treasury funds an ever-greater percentage of rapidly growing state bureaucratic systems, especially those of public-employee unions. Those who do business with the federal government—and this includes *every* major corporation in the United States—spend lavishly to lobby the source of their funding. Universities depend on federal funding, and retain counsel and consultants to help them deal with federal regulations. The media used to be called the "fourth estate." It now considers itself a fifth branch. All of this has made the DC metro area the home of seven of the 10 wealthiest counties in the country. Increasingly *The Hunger Games*, where the

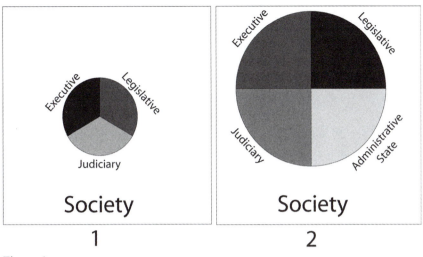

Figure 1

impoverished provinces pay tribute to the luxurious capital, looks more like a documentary than a fantasy.

It is important to recognize that the established branches of the federal government and the states might appear to have given power to the new "fourth branch," but their own power has grown in tandem with it. They could have a smaller *share* of political power, but they have a great deal more *total* power as government at all levels has grown. What could be described as once having been a small circle of a tripartite governmental power in a large square of private ordering is now a large circle with a new section in that square (Figure 1).

The new bureaucratic fourth branch also helps the president and the Congress to avoid responsibility. In 2013, when it was revealed that the Internal Revenue Service had targeted conservative organizations to scrutinize their applications for tax-exempt status, President Obama expressed his dismay. "The IRS as an independent agency requires absolute integrity," he said. The IRS is not independent, but an arm of the Treasury Department responsible to the President.[14] A while later, the president was widely regarded as having pressured the Federal Communications Commission, a formally independent agency, to impose his plan to regulate Internet service providers as public utilities.[15] The administration also delayed the issuing of controversial new rules on health, workplace safety, and the environment until after the 2012 elections.[16]

For its part, Congress gives the bureaucrats the power to make laws, but then tries to control them by a "legislative veto." In other words, the executive branch enacts laws, but the legislature can veto them—the complete inversion of the Constitution's processes. The Supreme Court ruled such vetoes unconstitutional in 1986, but Congress has ignored the decision and continues to enact them.

The procedures that these agencies follow show scant concern for citizens' rights. As a New York senatorial candidate remarked about the National Labor Relations Board in 1938,

> The Board files a complaint with itself. To hear and try out the complaint the Board appoints a trial examiner whose salary is paid by it. The trial examiner holds a hearing or trial and later reports his recommendations to the Board. The Board itself then reviews the record and makes the final decision on the complaint originally filed by it, prosecuted by it, and heard by its trial examiner. If the record produces any evidence it is binding on the courts.[17]

Or, as more recently observed by Professor Lawson,

> Consider the typical enforcement activities of a typical federal agency—for example, of the Federal Trade Commission. The Commission promulgates substantive rules of conduct. The Commission then considers whether to authorize investigations into whether the Commission's rules have been violated. If the Commission authorizes an investigation, the investigation is conducted by the Commission, which reports its findings to the Commission. If the Commission thinks that the Commission's findings warrant an enforcement action, the Commission issues a complaint. The Commission's complaint that a Commission rule has been violated is then prosecuted by the Commission and adjudicated by the Commission. This Commission adjudication can either take place before the full Commission or before a semi-autonomous Commission administrative law judge. If the Commission chooses to adjudicate before an administrative law judge rather than before the Commission and the decision is adverse to the Commission, the Commission can appeal to the Commission. If the Commission ultimately finds a violation, then, and only then, the affected private party can appeal to an Article III court. But the agency decision, even before the bona fide Article III tribunal, possesses a very strong presumption of correctness on matters of fact and of law.[18]

Today, this critical view of the new American state is mostly associated with conservatives and libertarians, but it extends across the political spectrum. After the defeat of constitutional opposition to the bureaucratic state in 1937–38, it was the New Left of the 1960s that first called attention to the system's defects.[19] Ralph Nader popularized many of these ideas when he began his career as a "public advocate" and consumer-protector and took them into the 21st century. Very recently, Harvard Law Professor Laurence Tribe—a longtime star of the liberal legal academy—argued that, however much he supported environmental controls, an attempt by the Environmental Protection Agency to impose them on the states without legislative sanction was illegitimate. "Frustration with congressional inaction cannot justify throwing the Constitution overboard to rescue this lawless EPA proposal," Tribe wrote.[20]

What scholars call "the administrative state" is a relatively recent phenomenon, emerging gradually in the late 19th century and reaching maturity in the New Deal. Foreign observers often noted that the Americans did not have a "state" in the European sense. Alexis de Tocqueville observed that the United States had a centralized government but decentralized administration. Most social needs were met by private, voluntary associations. America was a nation of joiners, whose vibrant civic culture was the sign of a healthy democracy. Prussian philosopher G. W. F. Hegel saw this as a sign of America's incomplete political development. It had not yet arrived at the state, which he worshiped as "the absolute Idea as it exists on earth."

The late arrival of the state was no accident. The Constitution of 1789 was designed to prevent the establishment of such a system, to preserve the rule of law against arbitrary government. Constitutional government or the rule of law is the antithesis of administrative government. As legal scholar Philip Hamburger has shown in his recent book, "administrative law" is an oxymoron; administrative law is unlawful.[21] The Founders were aware of this, seeing themselves as part of a long-running struggle to preserve constitutional government. This struggle was most prominent in 17th century English history, in the struggle to prevent the absolutist pretensions of the Tudor and Stuart kings, but is as old as human government.

It was not until after the Civil War that some Americans began to question the adequacy of a Constitution that did not provide for a modern state. The intellectual group known as the progressives, and then their followers in the New Deal, believed that the modern, urban, industrial world that had emerged in the 19th century required a new kind of government. Even as they built this state in the 20th century, it has never acquired complete legitimacy in the eyes of the American people, who continue to revere the Founders' Constitution.[22]

Some scholars have tried to revise the common historical view outlined above. There is a general animus against the idea of "American exceptionalism" among American academics, and many who hate American exceptionalism try hard to convince us that we are not and never were exceptional. Some have maintained that America had a powerful state throughout its history but that we have been unaware of it.[23] Others claim that the first generation of American statesmen, the Federalists, envisioned such a state but that it was undone by the Jeffersonians, Jacksonians, and Republicans after 1800, and that we should regard the progressives as neo-Federalists.[24]

These alternative histories are largely fanciful, showing that many scholars are eager to serve as shills for big government.[25] They tend to affirm rather than revise the traditional understanding of American hostility to statism. The progressives were indeed correct when they recognized the incompatibility of the Constitution and the modern state. Thus, they worked for decades devising a new political theory that would replace the constitutional principles of the Founders. Woodrow Wilson, years before he was president, elaborated the argument that the Constitution had been "outgrown" by 19th-century conditions. Others made the case for a "living Constitution" that would accommodate modern developments, and give the federal government whatever power it needed to meet new challenges.

We have no single narrative history of the rise of the new American state. Those that have been written on particular episodes of the rise have been by scholars sympathetic to it. This book aims to provide a critical synoptic account of its emergence. Although it focuses on the emergence of a bureaucracy, it must address the breakdown of the many constitutional safeguards intended to prevent such an emergence—the separation of powers and checks and balances above all, federalism and its related features (enumerated powers, the Tenth Amendment), and representation. Ultimately, American hostility to the bureaucratic state was rooted in a distinct philosophical and religious understanding of human nature and of government—"the laws of nature and of nature's God," as Jefferson put it.

Thus, this book can be called a "neo-orthodox" view of the rise of the administrative state. It argues that America was indeed exceptional and that the administrative state is incompatible with its Constitution, and tells the story of how the constitutional state was replaced by the administrative state.

For years, as I studied and taught American constitutional history, I avoided the question of the administrative state. What could be more tedious than bureaucratic rulemaking? The technical details of the business of government—of budgeting and accounting—lead one to read books such as *The Judicial Work of the Comptroller of the Treasury*, and articles with subtitles including, "The Bazelon-Leventhal Debate and the Continuing Relevance of the Process/Substance Dichotomy in Judicial Review of Administrative Action" (which begins at page 995 of the *Administrative Law Review*, meaning that there are nearly 1,000 pages of similar material preceding it).[26] As Supreme Court Justice Antonin Scalia put it, "administrative law is not for sissies."[27]

But state-builders recognize that they are strongest when they are most mundane. They love to emphasize that administration is a "science," a matter of great technical difficulty accessible only to highly trained experts. Much like the priestly classes of premodern civilizations, their power derives from their claim of possessing special knowledge. Though modern administrative theory was founded on the idea of a separation of "politics" and "administration"—the former being the *will* of the people, the latter the *mode* of executing that will, ends versus means, substance over procedure—they understand that great substantive policy decisions are made through the manipulation of procedure. The devil is indeed in the details. Elected representatives of the people are only too happy to hand over controversial political decision to the bureaucrats, as they often hand them over to judges.

I have tried to make all of that material comprehensible. This work is a synthesis of hundreds of books and articles that have been written about various parts and phases of the rise of the administrative state over the past century and more. I have tried to read and digest as many works as possible so that others won't have to—and have read many works that nobody should ever read. I also have tried to make it as concise and accessible as possible. As the anonymous Hellenistic Hebrew historian who wrote the Second Book of Maccabees put it,

> To collect all that is to be known, to put the discourse in order, and curiously to discuss every particular point, is the duty of the author of a history. But to pursue brevity of speech, and to avoid nice declarations of things, is to be granted to him that maketh an abridgement.[28]

So, as he concluded, "Here we will begin the narration. Let this be enough by way of a preface—for it is a foolish thing to make a long prologue, and to be short in the story itself."[29]

CHAPTER 1

The Roots of the
Founders' Constitution

The effort to limit human government under constitutionalism or the rule of law is the oldest problem in human political history. The first written law codes in the ancient world were efforts to take discretionary power out of the hands of a priestly or patrician elite, to be able to hold them accountable to the law by putting it in writing. This was the origin of the first Athenian Constitution, Draco's law code of the seventh century BCE. Similarly, the Twelve Tables of ancient Rome attempted to limit the arbitrary power of the patrician class.

The American colonists followed a similar pattern of insisting on the rule of law. The Puritan settlers in Massachusetts Bay demanded to see the charter that the colony's magistrates had taken with them. In 1641, they secured the *Body of Liberties* to limit the discretion of the magistrates. In response to these demands for a more democratic government accountable to the people, Governor John Winthrop warned that the rule of law could not mean a particular prescription for every possible contingency, that *some* degree of discretion was inescapable. "All commonwealths have had some principle, or fundamentals, from which they have framed deductions to particular cases, as occasion has required," wrote Winthrop in 1644. "No commonwealth ever had, or can have, a particular positive rule, to dispense power, or justice by, in every single case."[1] Chief Justice John Marshall and Abraham Lincoln later made similar points in their accounts of constitutional interpretation. As no constitution can completely do away with the need for political interpretation, no legislation can completely obviate the need for some administrative discretion.

The American Founders were most familiar with the great constitutional crisis of the 17th century, the English Civil War (1642–1649), and

Glorious Revolution (1688–1689), which were recent events for the Founders. In these conflicts Parliament and the common law courts resisted the attempt by the Tudor and Stuart kings to establish absolutism of the type that was emerging on the continent, particularly in France. They contested the king's power to rule by "proclamation," to raise taxes unilaterally, to declare crimes, or to suspend laws enacted by Parliament.

Sir Edward Coke—England's Attorney General, Chief Justice, and member of Parliament—was the most famous defender of the rule of law, or the rule of the common-law courts, in this 17th-century struggle. He considered the common law to be the greatest protection of the rights of Englishmen. Englishmen and colonial Americans would consider the common law—and trial by jury in particular—as the most important institutional safeguard of their liberties, along with the writ of *habeas corpus* and consent to taxation. Coke led the American Founders to believe that they, like their 17th-century forebears, were restoring a tradition of constitutional liberty. Coke was well-known to the colonists for his assertion of judicial control of arbitrary regulation.[2]

The English Civil War (1642–1660) established the principle of the "separation of powers" as the main political device to ensure constitutional government. The separation of powers, especially the division of government into three powers—legislative, executive, and judicial—was a relatively modern development. Aristotle used these three classifications, but most premodern theorists described two functions, making law and executing it—the judiciary was part of the executive, applying the general law in particular cases.[3] Strictly speaking, no human authority "made" law. Rather, all officials "discovered" the law that God or Nature had made. In medieval England, that law could be expressed by parliamentary statute, royal proclamation, or the judgment of courts. Liberty was preserved not by a separation of powers, but by the government representing the three social orders or classes. For Aristotle these were the one, the few, and the many; in England they were King, Lords, and Commons.

Separation of powers could be seen in the perennial conflict between secular and ecclesiastical power. Hebrew political history showed the separation of royal and priestly functions.[4] When King Ozias usurped the priestly function of burning incense, he was immediately smitten with leprosy.[5] Jesus's only definite statement on politics was to "render unto Caesar the things that are Caesar's and to God the things that are God's," to separate the sacred and the secular.[6] The first article of Magna Carta affirmed the independence of the church in England. The revolutionaries in the English Civil War fought not just for Parliament against the king, but for Protestantism against Anglo-Catholicism and "popery and arbitrary government," as the American colonists later expressed it.[7]

The Glorious Revolution of 1688 ended the threat of royal absolutism, establishing in its place the sovereignty of Parliament, or the "King-in-Parliament," as it came to be called. The English Bill of Rights of 1689 condemned the king's "assuming and exercising a power of dispensing with and suspending of laws and the execution of laws without consent of Parliament," the "levying money for and to the use of the Crown by pretense of prerogative," and the creation of courts by executive prerogative. The Act of Settlement of 1701 established life tenure for judges. The prerogative court of chancery or equity survived the 17th century, however, as the Whig reformers recognized the practical need for exceptions from the general law in unusual cases.

Political Theories of Constitutionalism and Absolutism

The most important philosophical work to come out of the Glorious Revolution was John Locke's *Second Treatise of Civil Government* (1689). It is best known for its statement of the social contract theory of government. Locke argued that human beings have rights in the state of nature that they establish governments to secure, and can alter or abolish governments that become destructive of these rights—as Jefferson paraphrased in the Declaration of Independence. Locke explained that legislature was "bound to govern by established *standing laws*, promulgated and known to the people, and not by extemporary decrees; by *indifferent* and upright *judges*, who are to decide controversies by those laws." The legislative power "being but a delegated power from the people, they, who have it, cannot pass it over to others." The people granted power "only to make laws, and not to make legislators, the legislative can have no power to transfer their authority of making laws, and place it in other hands."[8] This principle came to be called the "nondelegation" doctrine.

But Locke recognized that some measure of executive discretion was necessary. "The legislators not being able to foresee, and provide by laws for all that may be useful to the community," the executive "has by the common law of nature, a right to make use of [power] for the good of the society. . . . Many things there are, which no law can provide for and those must necessarily be left to the discretion" of the executive.[9]

Locke defended constitutional or limited government against the theorists of absolutism, or governmental sovereignty. He rejected the argument of Thomas Hobbes, who saw the disorder or anarchy in the English Civil War as akin to his theoretical state of nature, in which life was "solitary, poor, nasty, brutish and short," demonstrating the need for an ultimate, unlimited power. Hobbes's *Leviathan*, or all-powerful state, came to be a synonym for anti-constitutionalism or statism. Locke rejected the idea that the state of nature was so horrible as to necessitate absolutism. "This is to think that men are so foolish that they take care to avoid what mischiefs may be done them by pole-cats or foxes, but are content, nay think it safety, to be devoured by lions."[10]

Locke, however, acknowledged that the rule of law could not apply in foreign affairs as it did in domestic affairs. All sovereign states were in a state of nature with regard to each other, without a common judge, each having to enforce the law of nature and judge in its own case. Thus Locke identified a distinct "federative" power, "of war and peace, league and alliances." The person or group that held executive power—the power to enforce the law domestically—usually also held this federative power. The federative power, however, was "much less capable to be directed by antecedent, standing, positive law than the executive, and so must necessarily be left to the prudence and wisdom of those whose hands it is in."[11] The Glorious Revolution had severely curtailed the prerogative power in England, placing it under Parliament and the law; but prerogative persisted abroad. If some measure of discretion was inescapable in the enforcement of domestic law, foreign affairs left little room for the rule of law. It was difficult enough to have a Lockean, limited, constitutional government at home; it was perhaps impossible abroad. The world of sovereign nation-states was ruled only by the law of the jungle—it was genuinely Hobbesian. The great difficulty for constitutionalists would be to discern and maintain the boundary between domestic and foreign affairs.

The 18th-century French political philosopher Montesquieu provided the most extensive treatment of the separation of powers.[12] William Blackstone, the first English professor of law, borrowed liberally from Locke and Montesquieu in his *Commentaries on the Law of England* (1765) with added emphasis on the importance of an independent judiciary. Blackstone saw that the separation of powers during the English Civil War had produced a parliamentary despotism worse than the Stuart despotism that it had resisted. He called attention to the value of the checks and balances among king, lords, and commons since the restoration.[13] These three men—Locke, Montesquieu, and Blackstone—were the most influential thinkers for America's founding generation.[14]

Colonial Government in America

Americans believed that the principles of the Glorious Revolution applied to them as well as to Englishmen. The founding colonial charters all contained similar guarantees that the colonists had the rights of Englishmen—the common law, habeas corpus, trial by jury, representation, and consent to taxation. The colonists kept control of government primarily through their assemblies' control of taxation. Colonial governors—most of whom were appointed by the King—were thus unable to establish any effective system of administration because they lacked the "influence" of patronage. A governor's power to give out jobs and titles was one of the most important means of building a political machine. This was the chief difference between the English parliamentary system of the 18th century and the colonial system, which looked very alike on paper.

Most colonial government took place at the local level, in the townships and counties, and there the courts were the de facto administrative agencies.[15] There was no separation of powers at the local level, and no idea of "administration" as a particular function of government. "Administration" meant the administration *of law* (a very common phrase was "the administration of justice"), the application or enforcement of general law to particular cases. "What today would be an executive order to professional employees was then a judicial proceeding," a study of colonial Maryland observes.[16] Even in Roman- or civil-law countries, more conducive to state power, no administrative devices other than judicial process existed.[17] Local courts and justices of the peace dealt with licensing, taxation, poor relief, infrastructure, and the range of what later would be called "the police power"—regulation to protect the public health, safety, welfare, and morals.

The common law courts also provided the only means by which citizens could protect themselves against abuses of governmental power. Public officers were personally liable for offenses against persons and property they committed in the course of their duties. The remedy for an illegal search or seizure, for example, was to sue the police for trespass or false arrest. If a tax-collector took too much of one's property, one had to sue him to recover the excess. If the collector died in the meantime, one had to sue his estate, and not his successor.[18] Ordinary criminal and civil courts were sufficient to govern the colonies.[19]

The American Revolution

The Revolution repudiated British efforts to establish an administrative state in America, and rejected the British political theory of sovereignty—that absolute, unlimited power resided in the "King-in-Parliament." All of the founding-era documents display hostility to the idea of administrative power—of what 18th-century Americans called "arbitrary government."

The 1774 Declaration and Resolves of the First Continental Congress led with a condemnation of the 1766 Declaratory Act, which asserted that Parliament could legislate for the colonies "in all cases whatsoever," the expression of constitutionless sovereignty. It complained that Parliament had "established a board of commissioners, with unconstitutional powers, and extended the jurisdiction of courts of admiralty," just as the Tudors and Stuarts had extended the prerogative courts. The Congress expressed alarm "at these arbitrary proceedings of Parliament and administration."

The bulk of the Second Continental Congress's 1776 Declaration of Independence is a list of grievances against the King and Parliament, most of which can be described as administrative abuses.[20] The Declaration complains of King George III's harassment of colonial legislative assemblies, and his refusal to establish an independent judiciary in the colonies. With regard to what would come to be called "bureaucracy," the Declaration complains that "He has erected a multitude of new offices, and sent hither swarms of officers to harass our people, and eat out their substance." Though this was far from the case in 1776, the colonists envisioned this as the result of the imperial effort to gain an independent revenue, to establish a military, civil, and ecclesiastical establishment in America. The British did make offers of appointments to such offices to make the colonists more tractable.[21] Historian Gordon Wood has described the American Revolution as part of a long "assault on aristocracy," and certainly the revolutionaries saw the imperial establishment as the basis for introducing a British-style aristocracy here.[22]

The Declaration complains that the king had deprived "us in many cases, of the benefit of trial by jury." This was most pertinent in the Vice-Admiralty courts for the enforcement of the navigation acts and the proposed Stamp Act. These were prerogative courts, operating without the juries or other procedural safeguards of common-law courts.[23] Related to this was the complaint about the Quebec Act, "abolishing the free system of English laws in a neighboring province, establishing therein an arbitrary government, and enlarging its boundaries so as to render it at once an example and fit instrument for introducing the same absolute rule into these colonies." The Quebec Act did not provide a representative assembly for that colony and established the juryless civil law there, although it provided common law in criminal cases.

Eighteenth-century Americans adhered to the constitutional principles of 17th-century England, and the revolutionary and constitution-making period to a large degree repeated the history of 17th-century England.[24] Especially notable was the resort to an extreme version of the separation of powers, due to the Americans' belief that the influence of the king in Parliament had corrupted that body.

The separation of powers doctrine is implicit in the Declaration of Independence. Its first two complaints against the king concerned interference with colonial legislatures (the king had an absolute veto power). The complaints of lack of judicial independence reinforced this idea, and the Americans would take judicial independence further than the British did. Moreover, the Declaration appeals to God as legislator, executive, and judge in its references to "the laws of Nature and of Nature's God," "the protection of divine Providence," and "the supreme Judge of the World." God alone could be entrusted with all the powers of government, and human powers had to be separated.[25]

These oblique references to God penned by the more enlightened ran alongside more ardent and orthodox expressions of religious belief by ordinary colonists. The American Revolution reflected the Enlightenment philosophy of Locke and others, and also incorporated Christian beliefs, especially that of reformed and radical Protestantism. This was an important element in the colonial experience of local self-government. The Roman Catholic and Anglican Churches were centralized, bureaucratic institutions. Many English Reformed Protestants made no distinction between the Roman Catholic and English Catholic Churches on this point, and the Anglican authorities often agreed. "No bishop, no king," was how James I expressed the symbiotic relationship of civil and ecclesiastical authority. The Reformed Protestant denominations embraced local authorities—synods, presbyteries, and congregations. The radical Protestants verged on anarchic individualism. Local self-government in ecclesiastical life paralleled local self-government in civil life. This was most evident in New England—where congregation and town were coeval—but was recognizable throughout the colonies.

Historians, however, have underemphasized the influence of religion in the founding era.[26] The common 18th-century phrase, "Popery and arbitrary government," shows the connection. The colonies were founded by Reformed and radical Protestants, and shared hostility toward the Roman Catholic and Anglican establishments. The Whig man of letters and member of Parliament Edmund Burke observed that the Americans predominantly were Reformed Protestants. Even the southern Anglican colonies were largely locally controlled by lay vestries. Within the colonies, the more radical dissented from the Reformed, who dissented from the nominal establishment—Baptists and Quakers from Presbyterians, Congregationalists, and Anglicans. This colonial animus against ecclesiastical establishments extended naturally to a suspicion of civil or bureaucratic establishments. This made the imperial crisis resemble the 17th-century English Civil War. King George III and his ministers saw it as just another Presbyterian rebellion. This cooperation between religious zeal and rational political theory helped the American Revolution succeed.[27]

Of course, neither philosophy nor religion would have mattered had the colonists lost the War for Independence. The war and service in the Continental Army strengthened American unity more than any other forces did; war has been a nationalizing force throughout human history. As Washington wrote Hamilton, nothing did more than "the mixing of people from different parts of the United States during the War" to reduce provincial prejudices and jealousies. "A century in the ordinary intercourse, would not have accomplished what the seven years association in Arms did."[28] American hostility to European-style statism was most obvious, however, in the Americans' uneasiness about the army that they needed to win the war. An army is necessarily a bureaucratic, hierarchical institution. It was no surprise that the most advanced bureaucratic state in the 18th century was Prussia, which was said to be an army that constructed a state rather than vice-versa. The American revolutionaries initially hoped that they could fight the war for independence with their local militias and dispense with a professional army; but they came to see that amateur citizen-soldiers were no substitute for a regular army, with all of its rank, ceremony, discipline, and inequality. Many Americans regarded the need for a regular army as an indication that the people lacked the civic virtue upon which republics depended, and felt resentful rather than grateful for the services of the Continental Army. This sentiment expressed itself in disapproval of generous pensions for army veterans, and particularly in hostility toward the proposed "Society of the Cincinnati," a hereditary organization of Continental Army officers. These pensioned veterans and their descendants threatened to compose a new American aristocracy.[29]

The Confederation Period

The anti-administrative feeling of the Revolution was evident in the Articles of Confederation. The Articles did not establish a real government at all, but rather a "firm league of friendship" in which each constituent state retained "its sovereignty, freedom, and independence, and every power, jurisdiction, and right, which is not by this Confederation expressly delegated to the United States, in Congress assembled." The Confederation looked like one big legislature because it lacked a separate executive or judicial branch. Congress actually operated as a sort of executive committee of the states; John Adams called it "a deliberative executive body." Others regarded the unclear nature of the Congress as one of its principal defects.[30]

The Continental Congress had no power to legislate—the Articles do not contain the word "law." The Articles did stipulate that states could not interfere with "treaties" made by the United States. They also empowered Congress to "establish rules" in prize cases, and for "regulating the alloy and value of coin," and gave a few other specific regulatory powers. As James Madison observed, this suggested that the Articles were not a government at all, but instead more a plural executive committee concerned with the supervision of state and parochial—rather than general and national—affairs.[31]

Congress initially tried to exercise such powers as it had directly, through committees. In the early flush of republican enthusiasm, revolutionaries including Sam Adams believed that such a combination of legislation and administration was in keeping with republican principles, with a national government resembling a continental town meeting.[32] Congress established committees to borrow money, to supply and devise regulations for the Continental Army, and for more specific matters such as procuring saltpeter. When it became clear that the Congress could not administer directly, it established boards of outsiders, although it continued to interfere in their work by the establishment of ad hoc committees to oversee the boards. Just as the war showed that a centralized professional army was needed, more Americans—those who would lead the movement for a new Constitution and come to be called "Federalists"— saw the need for single-headed departments, especially in financial affairs. Near the end of its life, the Continental Congress set up such departments for Foreign Affairs, War, Finance, and the Marine.[33]

The nation had pressing needs, and the Continental Congress endeavored to meet these needs despite the inadequate grant of power in the Articles. The Northwest Ordinance provided a government for the common territories—an act "without the least color of constitutional authority" under the Articles, as James Madison pointed out.[34] A confederation that could not itself enact laws established a territorial government that could. Congress appointed a governor and judges who initially comprised the legislature. After the territory acquired 5,000 adult males, it got a representative assembly. The Northwest Ordinance included the standard list of the rights of Englishmen that had evolved from Magna Carta to the Declaration of Independence: liberty of conscience, habeas corpus, trial by jury, and consent to taxation. Its most celebrated provision prohibited slavery, the most arbitrary and despotic of human institutions. It also included a provision that "no law ought ever to be made or have force in the said territory, that shall, in any manner whatever, interfere with or affect private contracts, or engagements, bona fide, and without fraud previously formed." This was the first guarantee in a bill of rights that concerned the rights of individuals with each other, as opposed to those of individuals versus rulers. It protected private contracts and would be of enormous impact in the 19th century.

Upon independence, the new states wrote constitutions that took the separation of powers and hostility to administrative power to extravagant lengths. In accord with the principles of the Declaration of Independence, the states all established republican constitutions in which governments derived their powers from the people. The Continental Congress advised the colonies to revise their charters so that power derived "from the authority of the people."[35] States made their constitutions more responsive to the people. Pennsylvania's constitution established a unicameral legislature with no governor. A committee of the legislature provided the executive. Most states broadened the suffrage, lowering property qualifications. Annual or even semi-annual elections would keep legislators in touch with the people, and legislatures were reapportioned to make representation more equal.

The colonists thoroughly repudiated the theory of "mixed government" and adopted an extreme "separation of powers," wherein the executive branch would not influence legislation—for this was the mechanism of corruption in the English system. Virginia and Massachusetts had the most explicit statements of the separation of powers, but the practical result of this separation of powers was the concentration of all powers in the legislature, the branch most directly connected to the people, and the reduction of the executive and judiciary to nearly nothing. Most states reduced the powers of governors, such as the veto, the power to appoint officers, and the power to grant pardons. They especially denied what had been royal "prerogative" powers, including granting charters such as those that had established the American colonies. The revolutionaries sought to reduce the governors' powers to merely "ministerial"—simply carrying out the will of the legislature. Courts and judges, which the colonists had complained were dependent on royal patronage, became dependent on the legislatures.[36]

The fundamental problem with the revolutionary state governments was that the legislators forgot that they were the agents of the sovereign people and began to act as sovereigns themselves. Jefferson noted this in his *Notes on the State of Virginia*, written shortly before the Constitutional Convention. "All the powers of government, legislative, executive and judiciary, result to the legislative body. The concentrating [of] these in the same hands is precisely the definition of despotic government."[37] He told James Madison that "the tyranny of the legislatures is the most formidable dread at the present and will be for long years."[38] Madison built upon Jefferson's observation in *Federalist* 48, "The legislative department is everywhere extending the sphere of its authority and drawing all power into its impetuous vortex." It might not have been surprising that legislatures did not consider themselves limited by the state constitutions, for they were the authors and ratifiers of those constitutions. The Massachusetts Constitution of 1780 established more clearly that a constitution was a "higher law," the work of the people, created outside of—and superior to—the legislature. The legislature was the creature, not the creator, of the constitution.

The most common legislative abuses involved property rights. The United States endured an economic depression after the War for Independence, and distressed debtors demanded relief. The legislatures enacted "stay laws" that postponed the collection of debts and permitted debts to be paid with paper money of less value than the gold or silver money that had been lent. Many Americans saw these as violations of justice, using the force of numbers to redistribute wealth. More generally, the laws of the states changed rapidly, sensitive to shifts in public opinion, and this further undermined the security of private rights. In several cases where state judges attempted to protect fundamental or constitutional rights against legislative encroachment—usually involving judicial process and jury trials—they were intimidated by overweening legislators. The Rhode Island legislature compelled creditors to accept rapidly depreciating paper money in payment of debts, made violations subject to trial without juries, and forbad appeals to the state supreme court. A trial court refused to enforce the act against a butcher who refused to accept such payment. The legislature promptly impeached the judges.[39]

The Confederation "government" and the state governments exhibited opposite yet related pathologies. The Continental Congress had few powers, the states had many; both jealously guarded them. When a legislature with few powers refused to delegate, necessary work would not be done. Alexander Hamilton noted that "Congress have kept the power too much into their own hands and have meddled too much with details of every sort. Congress is properly a deliberative corps and it forgets itself when it attempts to play the executive." When Congress did not try to administer itself, it established multi-member bodies rather than single-headed agencies, which he considered no improvement.[40] As Joseph Story later put it, the Confederation government was "at once imbecile and arbitrary."[41] One of the principal effects of the Confederation experience was to show Americans that a stronger national government was needed to remedy the defects of overly strong state governments.

The Constitution

The Constitution of 1787 was meant to strengthen the central government, to render it "adequate to the exigencies of the Union," and also to deal with the abuses of excessive legislative power in the states. The latter, though not part of the explicit mandate given to the Convention by the Continental Congress, was essential to the former. Certainly the Federalists who wrote the Constitution intended to give the central government more "administrative" capacity than the Articles of Confederation, but they did not envision an unlimited, centralized bureaucratic state. Their Antifederalist opponents charged that they *were* creating a "consolidated" state, or at least that the new government would end up as one.

The Constitution's text says little about the administrative apparatus of the government. Most importantly, in contrast to the Articles it speaks of "laws" and "legislation," using these terms some 33 times, as well as of "rules" and "regulations" in other places.[42] It refers to "officers," "departments," and "heads of departments," but leaves these undefined under the larger legislative, executive, and judicial branches. Nor was there any significant discussion in the Constitutional Convention of these potential institutions. The type of state that the Constitution would establish would follow from its form and structure.

Perhaps the most important limitation on the power of the new government derived from its opening words, "We the People." The question of whether the power of the new government derived from the people of the United States, from the states, or from both, would be the chief constitutional controversy of the antebellum period, settled only by the Civil War. In either case, however, it was clear that the government itself was not sovereign. The chief defect of the old Confederation was that it derived none of its powers directly from the people—that it was, as the Articles said, a league or alliance rather than a real government. The chief defect of the state governments was that because they derived their powers from the people directly, they began to act as if they—rather than those people—were sovereign. The Constitution established that the people, not their representatives, were sovereign. As Publius put it in *Federalist* 71, "The representatives of the people, in a popular assembly, seem sometimes to fancy that they are the people themselves." Conversely, the sovereign people never exercised power directly, rather only through their representatives.[43] The Founders, as Hamilton put it, were "laying foundations of our national government deeper than in the mere sanction of delegated authority."[44] Like the Massachusetts Constitution of 1780, the federal Constitution would be ratified by the people, not by the state legislatures.

The most important structural feature of the Constitution was its perfection of the vital separation-of-powers principle by the addition of checks-and-balances.[45] Madison reiterated the importance of the separation principle, calling the combination of governing powers "the very definition of tyranny"; however, he also recognized that it was impossible to define the three powers precisely and neatly delineate them. "Experience has instructed us that no skill in the science of government has yet been able to discriminate and define, with sufficient certainty, its three great provinces," Madison wrote in *Federalist* 37, "or even the privileges and powers of the different branches." The revolutionary period showed the need to counterbalance the overweening legislatures.

Unlike several state constitutions, there is no explicit statement of the separation of powers in the U.S. Constitution, no admonition that the separate powers of each branch should never be exercised by any other. Madison proposed such language in the Constitutional Convention (and again as one of the Bill of Rights), but it was rejected as redundant.[46] As Madison noted in *Federalist* 48, such "parchment barriers" would not ensure the separation of powers and prevent the legislature from overwhelming the other branches as it had in the states. Rather, specific powers—impeachment, veto, and judicial review—were given to each branch to defend itself against the others, but these institutional checks did not mix or blend powers. The veto, for example, does not give the executive a legislative power, but enables the limiting of the legislature's legislative powers to ensure that laws are made only "in pursuance" of the Constitution, and especially to protect the president's executive power from legislative encroachment. The Senate's power to ratify treaties or to confirm appointments does not give it executive power, but curtails the executive power.

As Madison famously put it in *Federalist* 51, "Ambition must be made to counteract ambition. The interest of the man must be connected with the constitutional rights of the place." Here, the Constitution—like the Declaration of Independence—displays its foundation in a theory of human nature. Human beings are not angels; constitutional devices were necessary to check their innate desire for power. The Founders certainly had a "realistic" view of human nature—one, as the 19th-century journalist Horace White succinctly put it, "based upon the philosophy of Hobbes and the religion of Calvin."[47] The terms used to describe human nature are most often words such as "wickedness," "depravity," and "folly." But the Founders had not completely given up the ancient idea that republics depended upon virtue. "As there is a degree of depravity in mankind which requires a certain degree of circumspection and distrust, so there are other qualities in human nature which justify a certain portion of esteem and confidence," Publius wrote in *Federalist* 55. "Republican government presupposes the existence of these qualities in a higher degree than any other form." As Hamilton put it, a "supposition of universal venality in human nature is *little less* an error in political reasoning than the supposition of universal rectitude."[48] Similarly, American Protestantism, per Calvin, had emphasized original sin and the total depravity of man, but in the 18th century it began to open itself to Arminianism and even Universalism—the belief that man could at least contribute to his own salvation, and that in the end all might be saved. This was evident in the "first Great Awakening" of the 1730s and '40s, and would become more pronounced in subsequent awakenings.

The language of Article One also limits the power of the national government. "All legislative powers herein granted are vested in a Congress of the United States." Congress can exercise only such legislative powers as are "herein granted"—those enumerated in section 8, primarily—but not legislative power in general. This established that the national government was restricted to certain genuinely national ends or objects, primarily those having to do with foreign and interstate affairs. As Madison explained in *Federalist* 45, "The powers delegated by the proposed Constitution to the federal government, are few and defined. Those which are to remain in the State governments are numerous and indefinite." In saying that the legislative powers are "vested in a Congress," the Constitution confirms the Lockean doctrine of "nondelegation." Under the social contract theory behind the Constitution, "We the people" have delegated certain powers to a legislature; that legislature cannot delegate them to others.[49]

The bicameral nature of the legislature was meant to reinforce these limits. The upper house no longer represented an aristocracy or distinct social order. With fewer members serving longer terms, and concerned with particular matters such as treaties and appointments, it was hoped to introduce a superior wisdom and deliberative quality to the more popular house. It would, like the "extended republic" that Madison proposed, "refine and enlarge the public views," and prevent the precipitate and mutable legislation seen in the states. Additionally, the Senate represented the states *as states*, and would prevent the national government from usurping the powers reserved to the states.

The most important means of limiting the legislature was strengthening the executive and judicial branches. Article II established that "the executive power shall be vested in a President of the United States." Perhaps the most important word in this clause is "a," establishing one, unitary executive.[50] Alexander Hamilton explained in *Federalist* 70 that "decision, activity, secrecy, and dispatch will generally characterize the proceedings of one man, in a much more eminent degree, than the proceedings of any greater number." The weakness of plural executives in some states and (such as it was an executive body) in the Continental Congress, led the Federalists back to executive unity. Hamilton also explained that unity would promote *responsibility* in the executive. A unitary executive—one man—could not evade accountability to the people and the legislature. Later the progressives would confuse the principle of the concentration of power *in the executive* with an argument for the concentration of *all* government power in administrative agencies.[51]

One reading appears to give the president virtually unlimited power. Although Article I gave Congress only "legislative powers *herein granted*," Article II gave the president "*the* executive power," not "all executive powers herein granted." This led Hamilton to claim that the Constitution provided the president with all power that was not specifically withheld elsewhere in the Constitution. Conversely, subsequent clauses of Article II specify the president's powers, "to appoint ambassadors, other public ministers and consuls," to "give to the Congress information of the State of the Union," and to "receive ambassadors and other public ministers," undermining Hamilton's view that, although legislative powers are enumerated, executive power is assumed unless withheld. In between, Article II imposes duties on the president that left room for a wide discretion. The president takes an "oath or affirmation" to "preserve, protect, and defend the Constitution." The president is the commander-in-chief of the army and navy, and "He shall take care that the laws be faithfully executed."

The Constitution made no specific provision for administrative departments or officers other than the president. Motions were made in the Constitutional Convention to give the president a "council of state" or "privy council" composed of identified ministers, but these proposals were rejected. South Carolina delegate Charles Cotesworth Pinckney observed, in keeping with the unitary-executive idea, that a strong council would "thwart" the president, and a weak one would enable him to evade responsibility.[52]

Most relevant to the question of the administration of the new government, the Constitution gave the president the power to appoint "ambassadors, other public ministers and consuls, judges of the Supreme court, and all other officers of the United States." The Senate had the power to confirm or reject these officers, and Congress could "by law vest the appointment of such inferior officers, as they think proper, in the President alone, in the courts of law, or in the heads of departments." The Constitution said nothing about the tenure of federal officers, however, or how they could be removed from office other than by impeachment. Though Hamilton said rather matter of factly in *Federalist* 77 that "the consent of [the Senate] would be necessary to displace as well as to appoint," the term "displace" might have meant something distinct from "remove." Hamilton seems to argue that the requirement that the Senate confirm a replacement often would deter the president from removing incumbents.[53] This would quickly become another perennial problem in constitutional construction. Notably, America's official class was recruited politically. They were not chosen at random, as in the Athenian democracy, nor were they chosen according to any prescribed merit system, as in the imperial Chinese bureaucracy. The offices were open to all; the only specific provision as to eligibility was that "no religious test shall ever be required as a qualification to any office or public trust."

The Constitution established an unusually separate and independent judicial branch. The judges were to enjoy life tenure during good behavior, and their salaries could not be reduced. Although the strong presidency provoked great fears that it was an incipient monarchy, there was little opposition to the strengthened judicial branch. The courts had been on the Whig side during the 17th-century English constitutional struggle, as well as in the American colonies. Several state courts had stood up to legislative encroachments on individual rights, though to little effect, in the Confederation period. As Hamilton remarked in *Federalist* 78, the judiciary always would be "the least dangerous to the political rights of the Constitution," because the courts lacked the power of the purse and the power of the sword.

In the end, however, the legislature would be supreme.[54] It is clear that the Constitution meant to correct the overweening power of the state legislatures and to give a proper basis and limits to the national legislature, but not to displace them as the *primary* institutions in republican governments. Congress had the power to impeach and remove presidents and judges, and its power over the structure and jurisdiction of the courts indeed appeared to be significant. Only the Congress and the state legislatures were involved in the amending process. It was, as Madison noted, natural in republican governments for the legislature—as the branch most directly connected to the people—to be supreme. But the Constitution's safeguards intended that supremacy would not mean sovereignty.

Above all, the Constitution was an attempt to address the age-old problem of sovereignty, of how a human institution could limit the power of government in accord with human nature.[55] In the Constitution the people are sovereign, but they never govern directly—even constitutional amendment is a constitutional process. They can exercise their right to revolution, to "alter or abolish" their government, but this is an extra-constitutional action. The Constitution is a higher law made by the people; once made, it only can be unmade by revolution.[56] Congress can "make" law so long as it is "pursuant to the Constitution," not beyond constitutional bounds. The president and judges do not make law, but execute or enforce the law within constitutional bounds; they can hold the legislature to its constitutional limits through the veto and judicial review. The Court can appeal to the Constitution or to the principles of natural justice that inform the Constitution. If the positive law or letter of the Constitution conflicts with the spirit, then the Constitution prevails—ultimately, but not often, the positive law of popular sovereignty trumps natural justice. Slavery was of course the clearest instance of this outcome. Both the radical abolitionists and the secessionists were revolutionaries.

Thus, under the Constitution we do have a system where only the legislature "makes" law, and the executive and judiciary apply it. Clearly, however, the president and the courts in a way do make law. It can be said that all three branches make law *under* the Constitution, or discover constitutional powers, and the institutional structure of the Constitution keeps them within bounds. As Lincoln put it at the height of the crisis of popular sovereignty and constitutionalism, "A majority, held in restraint by constitutional checks and limitations, and always changing easily with deliberate changes of popular opinions and sentiments, is the only true sovereign of a free people."

A constitution's provisions for a limited national government might well prevent the establishment of a centralized bureaucratic state, but the specific provisions of the U.S. Constitution that withheld specific powers from the states seemed to do little to prevent the establishment of state-level administrative states. Article I, section 10, forbade the states to make their own polices with regard to foreign countries (even the Articles of Confederation did this) and other states. It prevented states from granting titles of nobility, issuing paper money, and impairing the obligations of contracts (virtually the same language is used in the Northwest Ordinance). But it left states with most of the powers of "internal police," which would come to be called the "police power," to regulate the safety, health, welfare, and morals of the people. This was a tremendous reservoir of power, which reservation would be reinforced by the Tenth Amendment's language that "The powers not delegate to the United States by the Constitution, nor prohibited by it to the states, are reserved to the states respectively, or to the people." Within the states, the Founding era saw very little change in the structure of local governments within which most "administration" took place. This left the states a lot of room to construct their own bureaucratic states if desired. However, the design of the Constitution did discourage bureaucratic oppression at the state level. The chief protection against it lay in what has been called "competitive federalism."[57] States that adopted oppressive regimes with heavy taxes, burdensome religious establishments, expensive economic regulations, and bureaucracies, would lose population and investment to other states.

The Constitution certainly established a government that was more effective than that of the Articles of Confederation. Congress under the Articles was not really a government at all, though it often acted as one.[58] The purposes of the government under the Constitution were largely the same as those of the old Confederation, limited to foreign and interstate matters. As Hamilton observed in *Federalist* 17, "The regulation of the mere domestic police of a state appears to me to hold out slender allurements to ambition." The states would remain "the ordinary administrators of criminal and civil justice."

CHAPTER 2

A Limited State: The American Government's First Century

The Founders had defeated the parliamentary threat to constitutional liberty, and the threats from their own state governments. The new Constitution showed that for more than a century a free people could enjoy effective government without a centralized bureaucratic state. The Founders' Constitution survived the first transfer of power between opposing parties in 1800, and accommodated the full democratization of politics in the following decades. It adjusted to the development of modern political parties—indeed, it turned what had been considered threats to constitutional government into assets. The Constitution also survived several wars and near-wars, especially the great crisis of the Union and the Civil War. War is the most common source of the growth of centralized bureaucratic states—armies are the quintessential bureaucratic organizations, and a struggle for survival leaves little room for constitutional quibbles. Although the United States did adopt some typically centralizing and bureaucratic measures to put down the rebellion, these measures were remarkably limited and temporary. By and large, the United States returned to antebellum forms and practices of government after Appomattox. Indeed, its unwillingness to adopt radically centralizing methods was one of the chief reasons why the postwar reconstruction of the South was so limited. Through this century the United States grew prodigiously in population and economic power. In the late-19th century, progressive critics would say that new social and economic conditions meant that the Founders' Constitution had been outgrown—but they did not see that the Constitution had *produced* that new world.

The Federalists

The Constitution established a framework for an improved government, but its effect only would be seen in practice. "All new laws," Publius wrote in *Federalist* 37, "though penned with the greatest technical skill, and passed on the fullest and most mature deliberation, are considered as more or less obscure and equivocal, until their meaning be liquidated and ascertained by a series of particular discussions and adjudications." In *Federalist* 82 he observed that "it is time only that can mature and perfect so compound a system, can liquidate the meaning of all of the parts"—"liquidate" meaning here to make clear and transparent. The Federalists did not, as House Speaker Nancy Pelosi did, argue that Americans needed to ratify the Constitution to find out what was in it, but there was necessarily a degree of interpretation or construction that would give meaning to the Constitution. Thus, the first years of the new government were especially important in providing the precedents.

The first great constitutional debate in the first Congress arose over the question of the president's power to remove officers from the congressionally created departments of War, Treasury, and Foreign Affairs. Hamilton argued that "the true test of a good government is its aptitude and tendency to produce a good administration," and added that "a judicious choice of men for filling the offices of the Union" was essential to good government.[1] The Constitution had provided for the appointment of officers but not for their removal. In the first Congress, the position narrowly prevailed that the president's removal power came directly from the Constitution, reinforcing the "unitary executive" idea that one person was responsible for the execution of the laws. This principle came to be called the "Rule of 1789" or the "Decision of 1789."[2]

The Rule of 1789 preserving the unitary executive was most easily defended in the departments of War and State, which had to do with foreign or "federative" affairs. The acts of the first Congress that established these departments did little more than continue offices operating under the Confederation. Even the most ardent Antifederalists agreed that the nation needed a more effective government for international purposes.

The Treasury Department was markedly different. The act creating the Treasury represented a compromise settlement. It suggested that in domestic affairs, unlike foreign affairs, Congress would leave less to executive discretion. The legislature could make domestic agencies responsible to itself as well as to the president, but preserving the president's removal power would curtail the type of legislative micromanagement that degraded government in the Confederation period. Legislative tyranny had been the chief problem of the 1780s and led to a separate and more clearly defined executive power under the Constitution. The opposite of legislative micromanagement was the wholesale delegation of legislative power.

One of the most celebrated congressional deliberations on the extent of delegation came in the 1791 debate of the establishment of postal roads. For more than a century, the Post Office would be the principal domestic activity of the federal government. For most Americans it would provide their only direct contact with that government. The postal service was perhaps the oldest institution of the Union, predating the Articles of Confederation and even the Declaration of Independence. The Constitution gave Congress the power "to establish post offices and post roads," but it was not clear whether this power was exclusive, prohibiting state postal systems or private competition. The Articles of Confederation had been more explicit on this point, giving Congress the "sole and exclusive right and power of . . . establishing or regulating post offices from one State to another, throughout all the United States."

Opponents of Hamilton's centralizing agenda coalesced around James Madison and Thomas Jefferson and came to be called "Republicans." The Republicans were not inattentive to the Post Office. Jefferson regarded it as a dangerous source of patronage, and argued that Congress could not lay out its own roads, but could only designate existing state roads for federal service. When the Second Congress took up the matter of choosing those routes, the question arose as to whether Congress could delegate that choice to the president or postmaster general. Members of Congress extensively debated the extent to which it could confer the power on the president. In the end, Congress retained its power to designate the routes. The debate illustrated that in cases in which the Constitution did not explicitly draw a line, the line must be determined by political practice and construction. In the House, James Madison noted that the delegation advocates' argument "appears to be drawn rather from theory than any line of practice." Although it might be difficult "to determine with precision the exact boundaries of the legislative and executive powers," the boundaries had to be drawn *somewhere*, to avoid "a blending of [legislative and executive] powers so as to leave no line of separation whatever."[3] An eminent scholar has observed that the members were more concerned about controlling postal patronage than about the constitutional principle of the separation of powers.[4] As Publius argued in *Federalist* 51, however, ambition was counteracting ambition.

Some advocates of an American administrative state argue that the Federalists meant to establish such a state, and that Alexander Hamilton was the true founder of administrative government.[5] There is some plausibility to this case with regard to Hamilton, at least, though it should not be exaggerated. In *Federalist* 27, for example, he argued that the federal government would become more legitimate as it became more powerful, "by its extension to what are called matters of internal concern," the reserved police powers of the states. The state governments would "be incorporated into the operations of the national government" but, he emphasized in italics, only "*as far as its just and constitutional authority extends.*" Hamilton also seemed to have had in mind something akin to the progressives' distinction between "politics and administration" when he argued that the people and their representatives understood the *ends* of government, but usually were incapable of understanding the *means* to achieve them.[6] Although Hamilton often sounded more skeptical about democracy than did other Founders, his statements about the human nature of both rulers and those ruled indicate an equal unwillingness to confide too much in a bureaucratic class.

It is especially important to recognize that however far Hamilton's administrative vision extended, he was unable to bring even most Federalists to follow him. His opponents charged that he sought by practice to establish the centralized constitution that he could not get at the 1787 Convention.[7] The most ambitious of Hamilton's plans, his *Report on Manufactures*, was fallow with regard to the development of a national "industrial policy" and infrastructure. The need for tariff revenue compelled the government to defer the use of import taxes for protection in its early years. The most controversial questions of government power in the Hamiltonian system centered on the national debt and especially the Bank of the United States (BUS).[8]

The bank, in turn, gave rise to the great debate between Hamilton and Jefferson on constitutional interpretation, with Hamilton's view of broad construction and implied powers prevailing over Jefferson's strict construction. It might well have promoted speculation and the rise of a financial elite, but the bank did not establish a large, bureaucratic regulatory apparatus. Some scholars have emphasized that the BUS was not a central bank; others claim that it did function as a central bank, and a markedly effective one.[9] The federal government had no formal role in regulating the bank; it was simply a 20 percent stockholder. The BUS was not the first "independent regulatory agency." It was independent because it was not a public "regulatory agency" at all. The government had not delegated broad powers to it as it would in the Federal Reserve

Act and other 20th-century acts.[10] It did not exercise monetary policy, still being constrained by the gold and silver standard.

Hamilton's Republican opponents accused him of abusing his discretion, particularly of using federal funds to bail out the Bank of the United States at the expense of paying the revolutionary war debt to France. In the course of defending himself, Hamilton pleaded that the management of foreign debt required a considerable degree of discretion on his part, which only further enraged his congressional opponents. In the end, a significant majority of the House of Representatives voted down a motion to censure him.[11] The Jeffersonian Republicans argued that this exoneration only proved that Hamilton had succeeded in corrupting the legislature, whose members owned shares in the Bank or held federal bonds. This was the final break between Jefferson and Hamilton; Jefferson resigned shortly afterwards and devoted himself to partisan organization. The accusation was severely unfair to Hamilton, whose financial program did great public service with no taint of personal aggrandizement. The Antifederalists' inordinate fears of a centralized bureaucratic state had nearly prevented the adoption of a Constitution which hardly could have been better crafted to prevent such a state. Jefferson's party also nearly repeated this work in the 1790s, when the nation's principal problem was too little—rather than too much—administrative power.

Disputes over foreign policy were the other principal source of partisanship in the 1790s, as the French Revolution engulfed Europe in nearly two decades of warfare. The Federalists opposed the French Republic and Empire and favored Great Britain, and the Republicans took the side of France. This conflict gave rise to additional conflicts between the legislature and the executive branches, most of which were settled on the side of executive discretion in foreign affairs. The decade established precedents in favor of the president's power to recognize foreign governments, declare neutrality, negotiate treaties in secret (which came to be called "executive privilege"), and to have treaty obligations paid for by Congress.

When the United States was on the brink of war with France during John Adams's presidency, the public saw the potential danger of the extension of foreign crises being used as a pretext to infringe domestic civil liberties. In 1798, Congress enacted several laws called "the Alien and Sedition Acts." The Alien Act permitted the president, for two years, to deport any alien whom he deemed dangerous. The Alien Enemies Act permanently allowed the president to arrest and deport enemy aliens in time of war. Most controversial was the Sedition Act which, also in effect for two years, made it a crime to say or publish anything false and malicious about the federal government. These acts led Jefferson and Madison to draft protest resolutions for the legislatures of Virginia and Kentucky which (Jefferson's especially) provided the basis for later arguments for nullification and secession.

However unconstitutional the Alien and Sedition Acts were in substance, they were more defensible on procedural grounds. The summary procedures of the Alien and Enemy Aliens Acts applied—as their names indicated—only to aliens (and still do, as the latter is still on the books). Jefferson pointed out that even aliens (all "persons") were protected from arbitrary detention by the Fifth Amendment, and noted that the acts gave judicial power to the president. Citizens prosecuted under the Sedition Act, however, enjoyed all the normal protections of the common law.[12] Indeed, the Federalists noted that the act provided greater protection for defendants than the common law had; however, Republicans argued that common-law forms did little to prevent the enforcement of an unconstitutional and unjust law. Partisan judges and marshals "packed" juries and conducted trials in a politically vindictive fashion. The redress for the Sedition Act and other acts of Federalist overreach came politically, in the election of 1800, in which Jefferson's Republicans won control of the presidency and Congress.

The Jeffersonian Republicans

The contrast between Hamilton as being the visionary of a centralized bureaucratic state and Jefferson as being the defender of a localist, agrarian, participatory democracy has certainly been overdrawn. The Jeffersonian Republicans, in power continuously from 1801 to 1825, left most of the Hamiltonian program in place, and after the War of 1812 brought back some of what had been undone. In 1792, Jefferson had proposed to Madison that Virginia could effectively nullify the Bank by making any Virginian who abetted the bank by "signing notes, issuing or passing them, acting as a director, cashier or in any other office relating to it" guilty of treason against the state "and suffer death accordingly."[13] Yet when Jefferson became president, he let the bank alone. Some scholars have gone overboard in the other direction, making the implausible claim that Jefferson was a "social engineer" and the first American national "planner."[14] This is another case in which progressive advocates of the new American state tried to establish a historical pedigree for their project.

The wars of the French Revolution brought Jefferson to adopt policies that threatened civil liberties even more than the Sedition Act had. Chief among them were the Embargo Acts of 1807–08, which prohibited Americans from trading with England or France. The policy, devised by Secretary of State James Madison, was designed to compel the European belligerents to respect American neutral rights without resorting to war. Jefferson was lukewarm about it, marking time toward his long sought-after retirement. The interpretation and enforcement of the act fell to Treasury Secretary Albert Gallatin, who had opposed it.[15]

The several embargo acts gave enormous discretionary powers to the president, who then delegated them to the treasury secretary and customs collectors. Congress allowed the president to give permission to ships to trade with the belligerents, but Jefferson was loath to exercise the power. The 1808 act allowed him unilaterally to suspend the embargo if he believed that it had achieved its purposes. Although it was largely successful in keeping American ships at home, it did not induce the British and French to change their policies about neutral rights.[16] The act provoked great resistance in New England, and especially on the U.S. border with Canada. Despairing of popular resistance to the embargo, Gallatin told Jefferson that "Congress must either invest the executive with the most arbitrary powers and sufficient force to carry the embargo into effect, or give it up altogether."[17] After a long period of neglect, Jefferson went to extremes in his effort to enforce the acts, including prosecuting smugglers for treason.[18] The embargo began to look like a campaign "to purify the republic by ridding it of corrupt commercial interests," particularly those in Federalist New England.[19] The Republicans were compelled to shift enforcement from common-law courts, whose juries were often hostile to the embargo, to the juryless admiralty courts.[20] Jefferson expressed admiration for local self-government in the New England townships, to whose vigilance he attributed the nullification of the embargo.[21] He agreed to the repeal of the unpopular embargo as he left office in 1809.

The nonintercourse and embargo policies that preceded the War of 1812 gave rise to the first Supreme Court foray into the questions of delegation and the separation of powers. The 1808 Embargo Act gave customs collectors the power to deny clearance to ships they believed might violate the act. In May, Secretary of the Treasury Albert Gallatin told all collectors to deny clearance to all vessels. The Charleston collector denied clearance to Adam Gilchrist, a shipowner, though he had no reason to believe that Gilchrist was likely to break the law. Gilchrist received a mandamus from the U.S. Circuit Court ordering the collector to let him depart. The treasury secretary's order, said Justice William Johnson, was "without the sanction of law" and was "not justified by the instructions" of the president. Jefferson, who had recently appointed Johnson to the court, was quite taken aback at this rebuke, which was the subject of great political controversy. Jefferson's attorney general published a letter condemning the decision, and Johnson responded publicly.[22]

In 1810, Congress enacted a law that opened American commerce with both Britain and France and let the president reinstate an embargo against *either* power 30 days after he determined that the *other* power had stopped violating American rights. In November, President Madison declared that France had complied and so an embargo would be applied to Britain as of February 1811. The *Aurora* left Liverpool in December 1810, and arrived in New Orleans in February 1811. There it was seized and sold for violating the embargo. The Supreme Court rejected the owners' factual claim that the ship had left Britain before the president's declaration had been publicized, as well as their constitutional argument that Congress could not give the president the legislative power to impose an embargo. Justice William Johnson saw "no sufficient reason why the legislature should not exercise its discretion . . . either expressly or conditionally, as their judgment should direct."[23]

The *Aurora* case concerned foreign policy where, as Locke theorized and history confirmed, constitutional limits are necessarily looser than in domestic policy.[24] A decade later the Court addressed the delegation question in a domestic matter, in what has become the most enduring statement on the question. In the Judiciary Act of 1789 and subsequent acts, Congress empowered the courts to make rules concerning judicial proceedings. The courts used this act to require that all court judgments be paid in gold or silver coin. This rule conflicted with a Kentucky law that made the paper notes of the Bank of Kentucky legal tender.[25] The defendants insisted that the national government could not override state law in this matter. Or, if Congress did have the power, they argued that it could not constitutionally delegate this power to the courts.

Chief Justice John Marshall upheld the courts' power, and Congress' power to delegate it. Congress could not delegate "powers which are strictly and exclusively legislative," he admitted, but it could delegate "powers which the legislature may rightfully exercise itself." Congress could have prescribed particular rules of judicial process, as it could amend rules adopted by the courts. Similarly, it could coin money itself, or let the Mint do it. He distinguished "important subjects, which must be entirely regulated by the legislature itself" and "those of less interest, in which a general provision may be made, and power given to those who are to act under such general provisions, to fill up the details." Marshall explained that the degree of legislative delegation was "a subject of delicate and difficult inquiry, into which a court will not enter unnecessarily."[26]

Marshall's decision did hold that there was a line beyond which Congress could not delegate, but did not offer much guidance as to how to define the line. As one scholar put it, his decision was a tautology, that "Congress must make whatever decisions are important enough to the statutory scheme in question so that Congress must make them."[27] It appeared to say that delegation was a "political question," one not justiciable, except perhaps in clear and egregious cases. This established the approach that the Supreme Court would take toward the question until the present day.

Jefferson's apparent hypocrisy on constitutional and administrative questions can be explained as deriving from foreign or federative necessities; the administrative weakness of the national government was revealed by the War of 1812. When the charter of the Bank of the United States expired in 1811, Congress narrowly voted down a renewal, and the country was left without the means to finance the war. The state militias proved unreliable, and the country's lack of roads and other infrastructure had strategic consequences. The war convinced most Republicans to return to the Hamiltonian system of national development. President James Madison dropped his constitutional objections to a national bank and signed a bill to incorporate a second Bank of the United States. Congress adopted a protective tariff in 1816, and reorganized the fiscal routines of the executive departments in 1817. But presidents Madison and Monroe drew the line at federal promotion of internal improvements without a constitutional amendment.

John Quincy Adams was elected president with a minority of the popular vote in 1824. He nevertheless called for an ambitious system of federal economic development including internal improvements such as roads and canals, but also wanted Congress to promote the "moral, political, and intellectual improvement" of the nation. He told Congress that "liberty is power," and that the "exercise of delegated powers is a duty as sacred and indispensable as the usurpation of powers not granted is criminal and odious." President Adams called for a national university, scientific explorations, and a national astronomical observatory. The legislature should construe its powers under the Constitution broadly and not be "palsied by the will of our constituents."[28] Adams's revival of Federalism caused a political reaction that brought about another return to Jeffersonian, minimal-government principles.

The Jacksonians

The new coalition, the Democratic Party, formed around Andrew Jackson, who in the election of 1824 had won the plurality of popular and electoral college votes but saw the House of Representatives award the presidency to Adams. It was the world's first modern, mass party and looked to some like a greater revolution than that of 1800.

Constitutional development in the states since the Revolution had given many more people the right to vote, and made more offices elective. Parties proved to be a necessary means of organizing the masses of newly enfranchised voters in a fully democratic age, a much-needed link between the individual voter and the government. The Democrats further popularized government by instituting "rotation in office." Rotation was often derided as the "spoils system," whereby the victorious party expelled the incumbents and gave those jobs to their supporters—"to the victor belong the spoils of war," as Jackson is said to have stated. Since the nation's founding, most federal officials had held their jobs for life, and many passed them on to their sons or other relatives. Though the president's power of removal had been established in 1789, it was almost never used except in cases of great dereliction. Before Jackson, presidents had steadfastly refused to use it to build personal followings. The initiative came from Congress, which enacted a four-year term for most federal officers in the 1820 Tenure of Office Act. The act purported to curtail executive use of patronage but, as Jefferson and Madison recognized, it actually threatened to introduce it. Madison believed that four-year limit was arbitrary, and the principle could allow Congress to limit terms to one day. Though initiated in Congress, the act gave more power to the president.[29]

Jackson was the first president to take advantage of the removal power and the Tenure of Office Act to open up the federal civil service to new men. There was a democratic logic to his approach. Jackson and his supporters believed that the federal civil service threatened to become an aristocratic class. As he stated in this first message to Congress,

> [O]ffice is considered as a species of property, and government rather as a means of promoting individual interests than as an instrument created solely for the service of the people. . . . Duties of all public officers are, or at least admit of being made, so plain and simple that men of intelligence may readily qualify themselves for their performance; and I cannot but believe that more is lost by the long continuance of men in office than is generally to be gained by their experience.[30]

The Jacksonian spoils system did not go as far as the ancient Athenian democracy, which distributed public offices by lot, but it did weaken the trend toward an entrenched bureaucratic caste. In time, the Whigs—which had formed as the anti-Jackson party—embraced the spoils system and settled in as the principal device of party competition for several decades. The federal Civil Service Act of 1883 began to tame the system, but it remained strong in the states for decades beyond. The system produced neither a great expansion in the numbers of federal officials nor any expansion in the functions of the federal government—quite the opposite. The Jacksonian Democrats remained committed to a strictly limited general government and opposed the Hamiltonian plan of national development taken up by Henry Clay and the Whigs. Democrats lowered the tariff, extinguished the Second Bank of the United States, and opposed especially the promotion of internal improvements. It is true that the influx of new men into federal service required new personnel policies and procedures. As Jackson had said in his first annual message to Congress, federal jobs should be "plain and simple" enough for ordinary citizens to perform. Making them plain and simple usually meant a degree of bureaucratic routinization and standardization, in the Post Office especially,[31] but this did not produce a "bureaucratic" system.

The importance of presidential control over subordinates can be seen in the dramatic conflict over the second Bank of the United States, one of many battles between the president and the Senate. Jackson raised hackles when he reopened the question of the constitutionality of the national bank, which Madison had accepted in 1816 and the Supreme Court had upheld in 1819. Jackson vetoed the bill to renew the bank's charter in 1832. He then determined to destroy the bank by removing the government's deposits, a decision which the charter said only could be made by the secretary of the treasury. When Treasury Secretary William Duane refused to remove the deposits, Jackson removed him and installed Roger B. Taney to do so.[32] The Senate howled and passed a resolution of "censure" condemning Jackson's abuse of executive power. Jackson responded that the Senate had no power to censure, only to try impeachments. When his party won control of the Senate, it "expunged" the censure from the Senate journal.

On the other side, Congress prevailed in its power to instruct federal officials in the execution of the law. Postmaster General Amos Kendall refused to pay a mail-carrying contractor, Stokes & Stockton, because the firm had obtained its contracts by fraud. Stokes got Congress to enact a law directing the solicitor of the treasury to arbitrate the dispute. The solicitor found for Stokes, but Kendall refused to pay the whole amount. Stokes secured a *mandamus* from a federal court ordering the postmaster to pay. Kendall disputed the court's power to issue the writ, claiming that this was a judicial usurpation of executive power. The Supreme Court affirmed the order, holding that Congress could prescribe—and the courts could compel the execution of—duties by executive officers regarding "mere ministerial acts."[33] This suggested a distinction between discretionary or political acts and administrative acts. If the president disagreed, then he could remove an official (such as William Duane) who believed that he was abiding by the law.[34] Presumably, if the president persisted in removing officers who refused to break the law, this would invite impeachment.

Reflections on the Antebellum State

By the 1840s the United States had become more democratized than any previous society in human history. Its central government was as limited and responsive to the people as it could be without threatening disunion or anarchy, which some observers feared. Most Americans, however, were proud of their constitutional democracy. As Georgia's William H. Crawford observed when he visited France in 1813, "I was now in a country where the rulers were everything and the people nothing. In the United States we are insensible of the existence of the Government except in the granting of benefits. Here the most ordinary act is subject to be, and absolutely is, inspected by some officer."[35]

To many European thinkers, the United States seemed to have no genuine government at all, to lack a "state" altogether. The philosopher G. W. F. Hegel, in his influential *Philosophy of History*, observed that America was still a developing nation, a "land of the future" which had yet to produce the centralized bureaucratic institutions of continental Europe. Hegel was the prophet of statism. He saw the state as the culmination of human development or evolution, nothing less than the expression of perfect rationality, "the divine Idea as it exists on earth." He had in mind the Prussian regime of his day, informed and reformed as it was by the Napoleonic French empire. Prussia had been the model of "enlightened despotism" in the 18th century, as seen in its civil code of 1794. Its government and society were a "well-ordered police state," operated like a well-oiled machine, like its army. To some, Prussia *was* an army—an army with a country, rather than a country with an army. Its defeat by Napoleon in 1806 caused it to absorb many of the methods of his enlightened despotism, but only to enhance the efficiency of its civil and military bureaucracy. To Hegel, America appeared to be far behind this continental path toward human perfection.[36]

Perhaps the best known analysis of the state of the American state before the Civil War came from Alexis de Tocqueville. In *Democracy in America*, Tocqueville noted the "compound" nature of the American constitutional system. He called it an "incomplete national government, neither precisely national nor federal." The old Confederation of sovereign states was no more, but "here things have stopped, and the word needed to express the new thing does not exist."[37] Though this made it sound like the United States was in a state of arrested development, Tocqueville more often praised the effects of American federalism. The chief thing that prevented the "tyranny of the majority" was that the U.S. Constitution provided for "centralized government" but "decentralized administration." "If, after establishing the general principles of government, it entered into the details of application . . . liberty would soon be banished from the New World," he warned.[38]

As Tocqueville observed, it was the strength of "civil society," of voluntary associations, that preserved American self-government. What the French turned to the central government to do, or what was taken up by the British aristocracy, the American people did for themselves. Tocqueville pointed out that religious associations were the principal movers of American civil society. "So religion, which among the Americans never directly takes part in the government of society, must be considered the first of their political institutions."[39]

Tocqueville also noted that America's democratic passion for equality might produce a new type of despotism. He prophesied that it would be "more extensive and milder and it would degrade men without tormenting them." Modern democracy would produce "not tyrants, but rather tutors . . . I will call it administrative despotism for lack of a better name"—what some today call "the nanny state." The government would provide the vulgar, material pleasures that democratic men seek. It would be "absolute, detailed, regular, far-sighted, and mild," like a parent who wanted to keep his children from growing up, to "remove entirely from them the trouble to think and the difficulty of living." What Hegel saw as paradise Tocqueville depicted as a stupefying hell. Tocqueville provided a memorable vision of this potential dystopia. "The sovereign power extends its arms over the entire society; it covers the surface of society with a network of small, complicated, minute and uniform rules, which the most original minds and the most vigorous souls cannot break through . . .; it does not break wills, but it softens them, bends them and directs them; it rarely forces action, but it constantly opposes your acting; it does not destroy, it prevents birth; it does not tyrannize, it hinders, it represses, it enervates, it extinguishes, it stupefies, and finally it reduces each nation to being nothing more than a flock of timid and industrious animals, of which the government is the shepherd."[40]

Tocqueville noted the exalted place of lawyers and courts in America, where they served as an important check on rampant democracy. The legal system also provided the chief substitute for a continental-style administrative state. To a large degree, as in colonial America, courts *were* the administrative branch. Nineteenth-century Americans administered their affairs through contract law. In an age of egalitarian democracy, individuals were assumed to be able to manage their own lives in private agreements, free from paternalistic government supervision. This was the most recent step in the liberation of individuals from traditional, medieval feudal ties, of the modern transition "from status to contract."[41] Contract law, which hardly existed in the 18th century, was elaborated and liberalized to encourage self-improvement and entrepreneurial activity.

Antebellum Self-Government

The security of the rights acquired by contract was among the most important contributions to American constitutional law made by John Marshall and the Supreme Court. The application of the contract clause limitation on state power was vital to preserving the independence of self-governing private associations. In the 1819 Dartmouth College case, the Court prevented the State of New Hampshire from taking control of a college—a purely "private and eleemosynary [charitable]" institution—by interpreting King George's 18th-century grant of a charter to the trustees as a contract that the state could not impair. Equally significant was the Court's recognition of business corporations as private enterprises, and their state charters of incorporation as contracts. The states themselves facilitated this development by enacting "general incorporation" laws that allowed almost any association of citizens to enjoy the benefits of the corporate form.

Americans governed themselves through state and local governments, and through non-governmental voluntary associations, especially religious ones. Tocqueville saw this as fending off a centralized bureaucracy, but antebellum religious developments also contributed to this threat by its promotion of the idea of human perfectibility.[42] The new denominations of the 18th-century First Great Awakening, such as the Methodists and the Baptists, turned away from Calvinism and toward Arminianism (the idea that an individual could determine whether he or she would be saved) and Universalism (the idea that all people could be saved). These tendencies became even more pronounced, explicit, and widespread in the Second Great Awakening of the early 19th century.[43] The new evangelical, pietistic denominations promoted a number of causes that would bring about the moral reformation of society—sabbatarianism, temperance or prohibition, prison reform (the program that brought Tocqueville to America), and education. Some of the more exotic sects embraced vegetarianism, communism, and free love. The most important of these reform movements would be the antislavery cause.

There was a strong current of "postmillennialism" in prewar American Protestantism, a belief that humans could bring about a 1,000-year reign of peace and justice *before* Christ returned to earth.[44] Although Hegel and the rationalists saw the moral perfection of the human race coming through the state, most antebellum Americans saw as it coming from the bottom up. Reformers debated how far their causes should become involved with government at any level—whether, for example, the abolitionists should rely entirely on "moral suasion" of the slaveholders, or try to restrict or abolish slavery by law. Some advocated the voluntary and individual approach to temperance, by having men "take the pledge"; others advocated the imposition of prohibition by the states—in 1851, Maine became the first state to adopt a prohibition law. One of Abraham Lincoln's first speeches was an endorsement of the voluntary rather than the statist approach to temperance.[45]

Although the federal government was retreating from active promotion of the national economy, there were countercurrents within the states. One of the most significant of these was the cause of public education. In the mid-19th century, the United States sent a greater proportion of its children to school and spent more money per pupil than England, France, or Germany.[46] In Massachusetts, Horace Mann led the movement to have the state take over the schools, heretofore run by townships and churches. He used the Prussian school system as his model.[47] Similarly, local boards of health began to exercise Prussian-style administrative power, bypassing traditional judicial process. As state legislatures moved from granting special privileges to establish banks to "general incorporation" or "free banking" laws, they also set up bank examination offices to make sure that the banks were sound.[48]

The Jacksonian state also was capable of expansion and adaptation when circumstances arose calling for national power. Congress addressed, for example, the problem of accidents and deaths caused by the explosion of steamboat boilers. In 1838, Congress enacted a law giving the federal district courts the power to appoint steamboat inspectors, with criminal penalties for steamboat operators whose vessels had not been certified to be safe. In 1852, Congress created a "Steamboat Inspection Service" in the Treasury Department and enacted more specific regulations. These included what law professor David Currie calls "what must have been the first federal law against sexual harassment—making it a crime for a member of the ship's crew to seduce a passenger by means of threat, promise or authority, or to visit a passenger's quarters for non-business purposes."[49] The act, however, was plausibly based on Congress' power to regulate interstate commerce and to the federal judiciary's admiralty and maritime jurisdiction. It left the technical details of safety standards to the inspectors, which seemed to be a reasonable delegation as Marshall described it in *Wayman*. The Service minded its own business and did not generate any serious complaints. It is not the tip of a forgotten antebellum administrative iceberg, but an anomalous island in a constitutional sea.[50]

The federal government was capable of exercising its limited functions before the Civil War. The United States was not "stateless," nor was it a "weak state."[51] It was largely what the founding generation expected it to be: a limited or constitutional state. Its powers were evident primarily on the periphery, in dealing with other nations or the territories.[52] As one scholar notes, when it came to dealing with the Native Americans, we see "big government Jacksonians."[53] It is significant that the territories were one of the places where the federal government could not avoid the most divisive issue of the antebellum period—slavery.

The Crisis of the Union

The steamboat inspection system was as far as America went toward a centralized administration before the Civil War. The Jacksonian Democrats —especially the southerners—always were fearful that an empowered federal government might threaten their "peculiar institution" of slavery. (Their arguments about the constitutional limits of federal power could be pretexts for slavery preservation, as John C. Calhoun confessed about his opposition to the protective tariff.[54]) Slaveholders, however, were willing to stretch federal power to protect their own rights. Secession was not a revolution against big government but against a government that did not do enough to protect slavery. Having dominated the national government through the Jeffersonian Republican and Democratic parties since 1800, the southerners left the Union when they could no longer rule it.

Chief among the slave-state complaints in their declarations of secession was that the Free States had not fulfilled their constitutional duty to return fugitive slaves. Congress in 1793 enacted a Fugitive Slave Act, though the Constitution did not expressly enumerate such a power. The act relied on state officers to enforce it, making it the duty of "any magistrate of a county, city or town corporate" to grant a certificate to a slave-catcher.[55] In 1842, The Supreme Court upheld the constitutionality of the act, but held that Congress could not compel state officers to help enforce this federal power. As northern states became more hostile to slavery, southerners demanded a new fugitive law with more federal enforcement. The Fugitive Slave Act of 1850 provided for federal "commissioners"—special court officers used to enforce unpopular acts—to enforce the law, and penalized federal officials who refused to enforce the law. It was a model of administrative rather than judicial process, instructing judges and commissioners to determine the status of alleged fugitives "in a summary manner."[56]

Its most innovative provision empowered commissioners "to summon and call to their aid the bystanders, or *posse comitatus*" of the county to help enforce the act, and it commanded "all good citizens . . . to aid and assist in the prompt and efficient execution of this law."[57] Southerners thus attempted to force northerners to recognize the legitimacy of slavery by actively participating in its enforcement, turning the ancient common-law institution of the *posse* into an agent of the national government. Abolitionists decried the act, in language echoing the Declaration of Independence, as creating an "army of new officials," and marking "the constant increase of power of the general government."[58] As South Carolina had tried to nullify the tariff, Wisconsin tried to nullify the Fugitive Slave Act.

Antislavery proponents saw the Fugitive Slave Act as a sign that the "Slave Power" controlled the government, and threatened constitutional self-government, even in the North. Slavery advocates had imposed a "gag rule" prohibiting congressional consideration of abolitionist petitions, censored the mails, violated the rights of free blacks, and expelled antislavery northerners from their states. After John Brown's raid, Illinois Senator Stephen Douglas introduced a resolution "to protect a state or territory against invasion" which Abraham Lincoln likened to a new Sedition Act. Its real object was "to put down republicanism, to prevent republican meetings, and to shut men's mouths."[59] The North fought the Civil War to preserve local self-government against the threat to it by a centralizing Slave Power.[60]

The United States was able to fight the War of 1812 and Mexican War in 1845–46 without the sort of mobilization that a great civil war required. Lincoln showed that the United States was capable of preserving the Union, in ways that have led many libertarian critics to claim that he established a Leviathan State, paving the way for 20th-century big government.[61] The Union built a million-man army and a world-class navy, and conscripted men into those armed forces (though most volunteered for patriotic or mercenary motives). It borrowed almost $3 billion to pay for the war, and taxed nearly everything imaginable. The Republicans revived the Federalist-Whig program of national mercantilism, establishing a protective tariff, creating a new national banking system, and distributing land and loans to construct railroads across the continent. It also granted federal lands for colleges and homesteads. The U.S. Treasury issued nearly a half-billion dollars of fiat paper money. These "greenbacks" had to be accepted at face value even though they depreciated to less than half the value of gold during the war's low points—exactly what had occurred in the states during the Revolutionary period, and an action which the Constitution forbad them to perform.

Most of these programs, however, were temporary and did not increase in national administrative power. The tariff introduced no new constitutional problems or bureaucratic apparatus. Most of the taxes levied during the war were repealed as quickly as possible. Congress also resisted calls for more inflation after the war ended, and the greenbacks returned to parity with gold by 1879.

The new national banking system in some ways was less centralized than the First and Second Banks of the United States. The National Currency Acts of the Civil War years copied the "free banking" system of many states. The federal government did not own stock in any bank. The "independent treasury" system continued, keeping federal deposits out of the banking system. The national banks had no discretionary monetary power; the currency was limited to the amount of bonds that the banks purchased. The act did provide for a system of bank examination by the Office of the Comptroller of the Currency (OCC). The OCC looks something like the first "independent regulatory commission." It was off-budget and funded by fees paid by the national banks. The comptroller was "appointed by the President, on the recommendation of the Secretary of the Treasury." He served a five-year term, "unless sooner removed by the President, by and with the advice and consent of the Senate"—the first attempt to limit the removal power since the Rule of 1789.[62] Herbert Croly, one of the most important promoters of the modern administrative state, recognized the limited nature of the OCC. Under the National Banking Act the government did not "interfere in the management of the bank, except when the management is violating certain conditions of safe banking—which have been carefully defined in the statute. As long as the banks obey the law, they need nave no fear of the Treasury."[63] To this day, the OCC would labor in obscurity, unknown to all but national bankers.[64]

The railroad and other land-distribution policies of the Civil War era did produce new bureaucratic institutions; these are discussed in the next chapter.

The North's animus against centralized, bureaucratic government shaped the Reconstruction dilemma. A century ago historians tended to depict this as a radical scheme to punish a conquered South, by long-term army occupation, redistributing land from whites to blacks, and imposing integrated schools and other institutions. Revisionist historians in the 1950s and 1960s showed that Reconstruction policy was dominated by moderate and conservative Republicans who did the best that they could within traditional constitutional limitations to accomplish the probably irreconcilable goals of restoring the southern states to the Union and ensuring justice to the freedmen. Today's "post-revisionist" view condemns the moderates for not having gone far enough—for not being the radicals that earlier historians claimed they had been. Reconstruction in this view is an "unfinished revolution." Some of them have seen the precursors of the modern welfare state—including race-based affirmative action—especially in the Freedmen's Bureau.

Having fought a war to preserve a constitutional, federal Union, the North would not sacrifice constitutionalism and federalism to protect the rights of the former slaves. In the immediate aftermath of the war, the army—the epitome of a centralized, bureaucratic institution—was highly regarded, and many reformers hoped to use it as a model for improving American government. As the Reconstruction process wore on, though, disillusionment set in and the traditional suspicion of standing armies and bureaucracy returned.[65] However unfairly, the Freedmen's Bureau and its military-bureaucratic traits was especially vilified.[66] The Bureau provided emergency relief for freedmen and white refugees, put abandoned land back into cultivation, arranged labor contracts for the former slaves, and operated hospitals and schools. Later it attempted to administer justice between blacks and whites and to assist in black voting.

Congress had opened the door to an unprecedented exercise of European-style state power in Reconstruction policy. The Bureau "represented the first broad effort in American history to build the apparatus of a modern administrative state." White southerners resented its extension just as antislavery northerners had objected to the Fugitive Slave Act.[67] Nineteenth-century Americans were simply not willing to turn the South into a police state to overcome white supremacy.[68] For all of its shortcomings, however, the limited Reconstruction policy might have been a better alternative for the freedmen than a long-term national supervision when one considers the record of the federal government supervising Native Americans.[69] Like the Freedmen's Bureau, the Bureau of Indian Affairs was part of the War Department. One historian calls it "arguably the first social program in U.S. history," the "first regulatory agency and social welfare bureaucracy." In the nineteenth century BIA bureaucrats undertook a "social reengineering project" to reconstruct Native American culture, with infamously disastrous results.[70] Many scholars have evaluated the Freedmen's Bureau as working against the interests of the freedmen, being principally concerned about providing an efficient workforce to restore southern cotton production.[71] Reconstruction helped transform the new term "bureaucracy" into a pejorative, and ultimately reinforced the nineteenth century animus against Statism.[72]

CHAPTER 3

The First Steps toward a Bureaucratic State, 1865–1899

The United States survived the Civil War with its original constitutional and political system intact, but it saw steps toward a national administrative state in the second half of the 19th century, and especially in its last two decades. Several federal agencies joined the First Congress' three original departments. Congress also began the process of reforming its personnel policies, challenging the antebellum era's Democratic Party–patronage system. These structural reforms, however, largely remained within the Founders' constitutional design.

A more profound challenge came from changes in political theory, education, and American religion. New assumptions about human nature, society, and the purpose of government came from a new system of higher education. The new universities produced both new theories about the role of government, and the scientifically trained expert administrators who would carry out those new roles.

The last decade of the 19th century saw significant breakthroughs in both the domestic and foreign policy of the U.S. government, as Congress created the first "independent regulatory commission" by the Interstate Commerce Act of 1887. Near the end of the century, the United States also became a world power with colonies to administer and new immigrants to assimilate. The popular and political reception of the new regulatory commission and the new empire, however, showed how uncertain and ambivalent Americans were about this alteration in their traditional system of government. The first steps toward a bureaucratic state were notably halting.

The Department of Agriculture, established in 1862, was an important addition to the American State. This was the first "client-oriented department," developed to provide information and benefits to farmers, and became a cabinet office in 1889. Leonard White—the preeminent historian of the 19th-century American bureaucracy—argued that the Agriculture Department "culminated a movement that in its early days had been resisted as a dangerous piece of class legislation, opening the door to demands of other economic groups" for similar preference.[1] White described the unique situation of such a client-based department. "The interests of the Treasury to the taxpayer did not always seem identical, particularly to the latter; the Post Office served the whole populace, not one group." The Pension Office was suspicious of pension applicants; it often was principally concerned with curtailing benefits. And "neither War nor Navy had a definite clientele whom it served or upon whom it could rely for support in time of need."[2] Even so, in the late-19th century, the U.S. Department of Agriculture (USDA) was a small, legislatively dominated, bottom-up "rural Santa Claus"; it was not until the 20th century that it developed into an executive-administrative, top-down harbinger of the centralized bureaucratic state.[3] Overall, however, the American State did not grow much in the 19th century. White concluded, "An old timer in Washington looking backward from the vantage point of the late 1890s would have found the government establishment bigger but not much different from its essential nature in 1870. Volume of activity had increased, but not new functions or activities."[4] But significant changes in the American political system, and in America's place in the world, would pave the way toward a new role for the federal government.

Civil Service Reform

The Pendleton Act often is seen as a first step toward establishing the administrative state that progressives soon would call for. To some degree this is true, as the system made the bureaucracy more independent and less politically accountable. Conversely, the civil service reformers were more backward- than forward-looking. They were trying to restore the personnel policies of the Founding era, based on "character" and "reputation" rather than partisan loyalty—but also instead of technical expertise. As one reformer put it, "The government, formerly served by the elite of the nation, is now served to a very considerable extent by its refuse."[5] The post–Civil War reformers were the scions of an old elite that had been pushed aside by the Jacksonian democratic arrival of the common man. They wanted to refine the *quality* of government personnel, but not to expand its *functions*.[6] Most of the reformers were classical liberals, advocates of "laissez-faire," who often wanted the government to do less rather than more.

Nevertheless the act was an important step in weakening Congress' influence over federal personnel, undermining the party system and increasing the power of the president. As historian William James Hoffer notes, it represented "a step toward a more powerful state because it separated the servants of power from the governed," taking a large step toward bureaucratic autonomy. Massachusetts Senator George Hoar said that future generations would regard the Pendleton Act "almost as the adoption of a new and better constitution."[7]

Political Science

At the same time that traditionalist patricians were reforming the civil service bureaucracy, a generation of scholars were importing European political theory to bring about a more fundamental change in American institutions.[8] Shortly after the Pendleton Act was adopted, the young political scientist Woodrow Wilson—who would become the most important theorist and politician of the progressive movement—wrote a book and an article that are usually seen as the beginning of academic study of administration in America. *Congressional Government*, his doctoral dissertation, was published in 1885 and analyzed the working of the American government. Wilson noted that his generation was the first to recognize that the original Constitution was no longer adequate to meet the needs of the nation. Wilson thus reflected the predominant trend of 19th-century political science, the rejection of the Founders' social contract and natural-rights philosophy—which claimed to be applicable in all times, places, and circumstances—in favor of an evolutionary, historicist view. The term "progress" or "progressivism" expressed this position. There were no self-evident truths, no fundamental or fixed principles by which humans could judge their customs and institutions. In short, there was no such thing as "human nature"; no "laws of Nature and of Nature's God." History had replaced Reason or Nature. Progressives often appeared to be perfectionists or utopians, and their perpetual-evolution outlook would account for this. That outlook, however, also could justify any existing conditions, because the "is" of History displaced the "ought" of Nature. Thus Wilson reflected that "I find myself exceedingly tolerant of all institutions, past and present," since historical conditions were the product of a larger, supervising force, of God working in History.[9]

Columbia University political scientist and progressive political activist Charles Merriam summarized these trends at the beginning of the 20th century. "The idea that liberty is a natural right is abandoned," he observed. "The individualistic ideas of the 'natural right' school of political theory, indorsed in the Revolution, are discredited and repudiated. . . . The doctrines of natural law and natural rights have met a similar fate." In the new political science, government did not *protect* rights that the individual possessed by Nature, but rather *provided* rights. Following German philosophy, American political scientists viewed the state as pursuing the goal of human perfection, far from the Founders' sober view of the limitations of government, which derived from the limitations of human nature. Merriam observed, "It appears that recent political theory in the United States shows a decided tendency away from many doctrines that were held by the men of 1776." Merriam recognized "that this is a scientific tendency rather than a popular movement."[10] Wilson was among the most important figures who would provide a bridge from political science to popular politics.

Wilson argued that Americans had no accurate analysis of how their government actually operated. For a century, the American people had been preoccupied with constitutional questions, particularly the nature of the Union. The Civil War settled those questions and made the United States a consolidated nation-state, marked by "federal omnipotence."[11] Wilson described a national state that "through its hundred thousand officers, carries into every community of the land a sense of federal power, as the power of powers, and fixes the federal authority, as it was, in the very habits of society." As a white supremacist, Wilson was particularly concerned about the presence of federal election supervisors who attempted to protect the right of the former slaves to vote. Wilson saw this as "the very ugliest side of federal supremacy."[12]

Much of this exaggerated description of the collapse of federalism betrayed Wilson's Confederate sympathies and the lingering of Reconstruction. He similarly exaggerated the degree to which Congress had "entered more and more into the details of administration, until it has virtually taken into its own hands all the substantial powers of the government."[13] He located the real power of the government in the committees of the House and Senate. This power was too dispersed and irresponsible, hidden from popular understanding and manipulated by parties. Much like the state legislatures of the Confederation period, Congress had combined legislative and executive powers, and neither legislated nor administrated competently. Wilson recommended something along the lines of the British ministerial system that concentrated political power in Parliament and delegated administrative power to outside experts. Congress should debate and revise laws drafted by expert commissions.[14]

Wilson dealt more specifically with the implementation of a modern administrative system in his 1887 article, "The Study of Administration." He observed that the recent Civil Service Act was just the first step toward a more thorough reform of American government. Post–Civil War America needed to address a new set of problems, those associated with the modern, urban, industrial world. Political or constitutional questions— disputes about *ends*—were settled. We now had to develop a system of administration to deal with questions of *means*. Yet we had not even begun to do so. Administration remained "a foreign science."[15] Oxford law professor A. V. Dicey made a similar point about the English constitution in his classic 1885 *Introduction to the Study of the Law of the Constitution.*[16]

Most Americans associated administration and bureaucracy with the despotic regimes of continental Europe—imperial France and Germany or, worse, Russia and China. Wilson recognized the deeply rooted suspicions of his countrymen about "a corps of civil servants prepared by a special schooling and drilled, after appointment, into a perfected organization, with appropriate hierarchy and characteristic discipline," amounting to "an offensive official class." Thus, Wilson asserted that "we must Americanize it, and that not formally, in language merely, but radically, in thought, in principle, and aim as well. It must learn our constitutions by heart; must get the bureaucratic fever out of its veins; must inhale much free American air." It was possible to adopt foreign methods of government without adopting foreign principles of government. "We borrowed rice, but we do not eat it with chopsticks," he observed. "If I see a murderous fellow sharpening a knife cleverly, I can borrow his way of sharpening the knife without borrowing his probable intention to commit murder with it."[17]

Wilson believed that it was possible to separate administrative means from political ends. Administration concerned only methods, it was "a field of business . . . removed from the hurry and strife of politics." Though the idea that administration could be politically neutral would become the most contentious of all the principles of public administration, Wilson blithely assured readers that "this discrimination between administration and politics is now, happily, too obvious to need further discussion."[18]

As with the question of the delegation of legislative power, it seemed undeniable that there was some difference between the political and the administrative. Some government jobs might be completely mechanical and routine, involving no questions of policy. Everyone could see that the highest offices involved political discretion. The Supreme Court had long recognized this distinction. As John Marshall put it in *Marbury v. Madison*, "By the Constitution of the United States, the President is invested with certain important political powers, in the exercise of which he is to use his own discretion, and is accountable only to his country in his political character and to his own conscience."[19] The Court reiterated this distinction in the *Kendall* case, in which it distinguished the discretionary or political powers of the executive branch from its "merely ministerial" or administrative ones. The first Civil Service Commission, however, recognized the difficulty of drawing the politics/administration line.[20]

Wilson saw the greatest obstacle to effective administration in the separation of powers, but more generally in the Constitution's bias against power in general. That Constitution was appropriate for a time in which political questions had not been settled, but was now an obstacle to the development of effective administration. "Large powers and unhampered discretion seem to me the indispensable conditions of responsibility. . . . There is no danger in power, if only it be not irresponsible."[21] One scholar has described this as a "frontal assault on the Madisonian doctrine of dispersed and fragmented power."[22] Wilson's essay was highly idiosyncratic and has given rise to a wide range of interpretations as to its meaning and impact.[23] Wilson did not develop its ideas, and changed his own views about American government during his academic career. As a politician, he often contradicted the academic ideas that he had expressed.

Columbia political scientist Frank J. Goodnow provided a more sustained and coherent theory of administrative government, and came to be considered the "father of American public administration." Goodnow also absorbed German political philosophy, especially the Hegelian view of the state. He depicted two functions of government: politics (the will of the people) and administration (its execution). These separate functions must be harmonized. The U.S. Constitution's separation of powers made this harmonization impossible. The political parties connected them, but the parties were corrupt and irresponsible, seeking only their own interests—especially the control of patronage. The parties, begun as *means* to coordinate politics and administration, had become self-seeking *ends*. They kept injecting partisan, patronage-based considerations into what should be an apolitical, neutral, scientific-technical administrative process. Goodnow looked especially to the states, many of which had begun to centralize their systems of education and public health.[24]

According to Goodnow, administration must be at once responsible to and independent of politics. He likened bureaucrats to judges, whose independence was based on the separation of politics and law. As courts became independent in the 18th century, so the bureaucracy should be made independent in the 20th century. As political scientists increasingly rejected the law/politics dichotomy, concluding that law *was* politics, the politics/administration dichotomy would take its place. The politics/administration dichotomy was problematic from the outset, however, obscuring more than it clarified. For one thing, it ignored the fact that the Constitution itself established the ends of government by its limitations of federal power, as Madison observed, in Article I, section 8.[25] The progressives—equating politics and ends—instead saw ends as being up for grabs, and determined by historical contingency or passing political moods. As political scientist John Rohr noted, the politics/administration dichotomy served as a way to empower bureaucrats without saying explicitly that politics—and thus democracy itself—was inherently corrupt.[26] And as political scientist Ronald Pestritto has said of Wilson's theory, his "separation of politics and administration becomes, then, a means for maintaining the democratic veneer of popular government while giving to unelected administrators the wide berth they need to manage the complex business of national progress."[27]

Sociologist Lester Frank Ward proffered a popular view of the scientifically administered state. Ward enlisted Darwin's theory of evolution for positive-government purposes. Whereas "Social Darwinists" such as Herbert Spencer and William Graham Sumner thought that government should not interfere in the natural process of evolution, Ward maintained that the development of the human mind enabled our species to shape its own evolution. He envisioned a "sociocracy" ruled by sociologists or experts in "social physics." He dismissed the American legislatures of the day much as Wilson did, and also advocated the drafting of legislation by committees of technicians who would be insulated from popular politics. Legislatures would "stand in the same relation to men in which a polytechnic institute stands to the control of nature," he wrote in his best-known work, *Dynamic Sociology.*[28]

Education and Religion

Most of the new class of academics represented by Wilson and Goodnow either had studied at German universities or were students of scholars who had. In the last quarter of the 19th century, American colleges began to remake themselves along the lines of German institutions.[29] Previously, most American colleges were religiously based liberal arts institutions, whose goal was to turn out well-rounded gentlemen for the learned professions. The German university model emphasized scientific research, and sought to train expert specialists to serve the state, and the state then would deal with the problems of modern, industrial life. This was the plan for Johns Hopkins University, established in Baltimore in 1876.

The Hopkins model spread to other institutions, especially Columbia, the University of Michigan, and the University of Wisconsin. Wisconsin progressives promoted the adoption of the German welfare state that Bismarck had introduced in Germany, with university faculty providing the ideas and personnel for the new agencies. Bismarck's Germany provided the model of the well-administered state, especially in the U.S. states of the upper Midwest with large German populations.[30] As Wisconsin historian Charles McCarthy, a leader of the progressive movement, said, "It was to the German scholar that Bismarck invariably turned for aid in the development of legislation . . . which has built it up from a country of poor peasants to a great nation."[31] As one scholar noted, in this view "the university was the fourth branch of government."[32] After the two world wars, the German sources of American progressivism became embarrassing and were quietly put away.

American religion also promoted the administrative state. The millennial perfectionism of the antebellum Second Great Awakening morphed into the "Social Gospel" or "Social Christianity" movement. Even more than the Second Great Awakening, the Social Gospel movement emphasized a shift from individual salvation and eternal life to social perfection in this life.[33] The Social Gospel responded to the challenges of the secular natural sciences by capitulating to them. The most prominent Social Gospel advocate, Walter Rauschenbusch, applied a Darwinian evolutionary model to Christianity, much as Wilson had applied it to the Constitution. (Wilson himself often appeared to be influenced by the Social Gospel movement.[34]) It was appropriate for premodern Christianity to look to the afterlife for perfection, but modern science made perfection attainable in this world. Sin was no longer an individual failing; "Sin is a social force," Rauschenbusch argued. Likewise, the love that Christ preached must be understood as "socialized love." The traditional Church role of seeking individual salvation was no longer the most pressing need. "Our inherited Christian faith dealt with individuals; our present task deals with society. Not the afterlife, the business before us is concerned with refashioning the present world, making this earth clean and sweet and habitable."[35] As historian Henry May put it, the Social Gospel marked "a complete break with the past," a rejection of American values and Protestant individualism. "The proposal that the Church's responsibility should cover not only moral issues but also issues of material welfare seemed to involve a change in basic spiritual values."[36]

The American Revolution saw a confluence of enlightenment-rationalist and evangelical trends. In the Gilded Age we see a convergence of secularism and the Social Gospel, but increasingly on the former's terms. The tension between science and religion had become so great that the late-19th century would be the last period before America saw a significant *Kulturkampf* of the type evident in Europe. In 1896, Cornell University President Andrew Dixon White wrote his *History of the Warfare of Science with Theology in Christendom*. As Rauschenbusch observed, socialism was hostile to religion in Europe, but need not be in America.[37]

Richard T. Ely, an academic economist and Social Gospel enthusiast, embodied the hope of a union of the new science and the old religion.[38] Ely studied at Halle and Heidelberg, and taught at Hopkins, where Woodrow Wilson was one of many prominent students. In 1892, he moved to the University of Wisconsin, and was one of the founders of the American Economic Association, which repudiated the dominant classical or "laissez-faire" orientation of the profession and called for more government regulation of economic and social life. Ely's argument for socialism echoed that of antebellum defenders of slavery—that it produced a more humane and harmonious social system. (In the progressive-historicist view, slavery itself was a necessary phase of socioeconomic evolution. Wilson implied this when he said that historicism made him "exceedingly tolerant of all institutions, past and present."[39]) Ely noted that socialists included many "preachers of the Gospel of Christ, 'the first Socialist,' as He is often called."[40] He saw American society torn between plundering plutocrats at the top and ignorant immigrants at the bottom.[41] It would take the new academic administrative class to bring about the Kingdom of God on earth.

In reading Ely's work, however, it is hard to believe that he was *any* kind of economist. He condemned the wastefulness of capitalism and economic inequality, but also praised the Mosaic Law and monastic poverty. "We Christians have well-nigh forgotten the existence of a cross," he wrote in 1889. "Christ meant that we should lead a life of renunciation."[42] Economics usually is regarded as a discipline that seeks to understand and reduce—not embrace—material scarcity. Moreover, if, as the new economists claimed, capitalism increased poverty, then it is hard to understand why Ely would want to reform it.

Ely represented the movement of many mainline Protestants into the emerging social sciences and ultimate absorption into the progressive movement. As Ely put it, religious studies should take up the social sciences; theologians should become sociologists.[43] Churches would not be rivals of the government providing educational, health, and other charitable services. The mainline churches would become arms of the state.[44] Their confidence in the state reflected their optimistic view of human nature and postmillennialism. In 1912, when Theodore Roosevelt led the progressives out of the Republican Party and ran as an independent, his campaign sounded a triumphalist tone. "We stand at Armageddon, and we battle for the Lord," was the Progressive anthem. The regular Republicans, on the contrary, stressed a view of the imperfect nature of man and the limits of government more in tune with the realism of the Founders. William Howard Taft warned that Roosevelt envisioned "a millennium." New York Senator Elihu Root, the chairman of the regular Republican convention of 1912, reminded the party that "We come from a God-fearing people, and we have learned the truth taught by religion that all men are prone to error, are subject to temptation, are led astray by impulse." He exhorted Americans to "keep the covenant that our fathers made."[45]

The Interstate Commerce Act

The centennial of the drafting of the Constitution saw Wilson's path-breaking essay on the need for administration, and also the creation of what usually is regarded as the first modern administrative agency, the Interstate Commerce Commission. A fully national railway system had been completed with the vast grants of public land and loans to the transcontinental roads during the Civil War. After the war, complaints mounted from shippers—especially farmers—about the railroads' abuse of power. States began to establish commissions to regulate them and set rates, but in 1886 the Supreme Court held many of these to be unconstitutional usurpations of Congress' power to regulate interstate commerce, compelling Congress to act.[46]

If any industry was engaged in "commerce among the states," it was railroading. It was a complex and technical network, exactly the sort of business that advocates of administrative government argued was too complicated for legislators, who needed to defer to the experts. The basic problem was that the railroads competed with one another on high-volume lines between major cities, which produced ruinous rate wars. Railroads charged extortionate prices ("all the traffic will bear") on low-volume short lines where they had no competition. The railroads needed to raise rates on the competitive lines via "pooling" to lower the short-haul rates. Voluntary pooling agreements were unenforceable and never lasted very long. Congress, however, would not make the clear choices that the problem required. Instead it declared that all rates must be "reasonable and just; and every unjust and unreasonable charge . . . is prohibited and declared to be unlawful." It prohibited pooling, but outlawed discriminatory rates only in cases of "substantially similar circumstances and conditions."[47] This significant loophole allowed the railroads to reap monopoly profits on their short-haul lines.[48]

After skirting clear legal standards, Congress muddied the waters of enforcement. Instead of ordinary judicial enforcement, it established a commission of five members serving staggered six-year terms, removable by the president only for cause. Initially housed in the Department of the Interior, Congress made it "independent" in 1889. (There was no discussion of this shift, but one scholar suggests that it was done to keep the commission out of the hands of incoming President Benjamin Harrison, who had been a railroad attorney.[49]) The commission could hear complaints about unreasonable or discriminatory rates. Congressman John Regan of Texas, the ardently anti-railroad sponsor of the House's bill, was afraid that the railroads would be able to control a commission—that the agency would be, as political scientists later put it, "captured" by the interest it was supposed to regulate. Conversely, the railroad-friendly sponsor of the Senate bill, Shelby Cullom of Illinois, pointed out the difficulties that small shippers would have in judicial appeals, and explained the benefits of cheaper and more efficient administrative procedures.[50] Richard Olney, President Cleveland's attorney general, saw such potential capture as a desirable feature of the act. "The commission," Olney told a railroad executive, could be "of great use to the railroads. It satisfies the popular clamor for a government supervision of railroads, at the same time that that supervision is almost entirely nominal." The regulators would come to "take the business and railroad view of things," and would help prevent unfriendly legislation. "The part of wisdom," Olney concluded, "is not to destroy the commission, but to utilize it."[51] Some historians argue that the railroads actually promoted the act to do just this.[52]

Some congressmen objected that the commission violated the principle of the separation of powers, combining legislative, executive, and judicial functions. Appointed by the president and confirmed by the Senate, the commissioners resembled traditional executive-branch officers, but rate-making was a legislative function and the commission's determination of particular cases seemed judicial. The commission could hear complaints, subpoena records and witnesses, and issue "cease and desist" orders if it found unreasonable rates, but the act did not explicitly give the commission the power to set its own rates. As one historian has noted, "Nobody really knew what the act meant or how it could be applied."[53]

But the federal courts ensured that the commission was limited to executive functions, making it more like an adjunct to the Justice Department. In 1889, a federal court indicated that the commission's findings of fact were not entitled to any judicial deference. The Interstate Commerce Commission (ICC) was not an inferior court; it was "invested with only administrative powers of supervision and investigation."[54] The Court regarded the commission as, at best, an advisory body, "in essence a master in chancery to the Court." The determination of whether a rate was "reasonable" was a judicial question, and the commission was not a court. The Supreme Court held that the commission had no power to fix rates after it had determined that a rate was unreasonable. The establishment of rates was a legislative power, and the commission was not a legislature.[55] The Court would not assume that Congress had given such power by implication. However, the Court did assume that Congress could delegate its rate-setting power to "some subordinate tribunal" if it chose.[56] The Court also held that commission attempts to compel shippers to testify violated the Fifth Amendment's protection against self-incrimination. Congress responded by providing for compulsory testimony with immunity, which the Court narrowly upheld.[57] In the late-19th century, the ICC generally tried to promote cooperation while the Court tried to promote competition. The commission largely ignored Congress' clear anti-pooling language and invited the railroads to pool if they did so in what the commission considered a "just and accommodating" way.[58] The Court also held that railroads were not exempt from the new Sherman Antitrust Act, further frustrating the commission's efforts to promote cooperation in the industry.[59]

Progressive state-builders roundly condemned the Court's "emasculation" of the ICC. They depicted it as an example of reactionary "laissez-faire" judicial activism. From another perspective, though, the ICC cases exhibited judicial restraint. In its earliest days, the Court had resisted taking on non-judicial tasks, and it would not interfere in purely legislative or executive tasks. Judicial review was "all or nothing"—either a genuinely judicial proceeding or none of its business.[60]

By the end of the 19th century, the ICC had been largely reduced to a statistics-gathering office, but this was a significant step in the development of the modern administrative state. Statistical data had always been an essential tool of government power—the term "statistics" derives from the term "state," especially in matters of finance and war. Premodern state power had been limited by the fact that states were unable to know very much about their territory and subjects.[61] The modern era's development of statistics was comparable in magnitude to the emergence of written languages at the dawn of civilization.[62] The first powerful bureaucratic states arose from their elites' control of that new technology. Ancient Egyptian dynasties and imperial China's "mandarin" classes derived their power from their command of the written language, and some of the earliest extant writing was employed for bureaucratic record keeping.[63] The mandarins' command of the language was certified by a series of civil-service exams. Maintaining the pictographic rather than the more accessible phonetic alphabet helped the mandarin bureaucracy to maintain its power. In the modern age, the spread of literacy accompanied the rise of political democracy, but alongside it came the development of modern science, whose language was high-level mathematics, the mysteries of which were open only to a few people.

The population census was a symbol of sovereignty. Thus, in the Old Testament, King David is punished for his presumption in taking a census of the Hebrews, as if they were his people rather than God's; and the New Testament begins with the Holy Family's return to Bethlehem to be counted in a census ordered by Augustus Caesar.[64] The U.S. government made its census more elaborate over the course of the 19th century. The Constitution required the federal government to "enumerate" the population to apportion representatives and direct taxes, but from the first census it began to collect additional data, first on sex and race, later on occupation and industry.[65] Government statistical reports focused first on the Indian tribes, then on the South after the Civil War, though the hopes of some reformers that Reconstruction would permanently establish a welfare-state role for the federal government were not realized. In the United States, as in other western states, official government data shaped the way that people understood themselves, their government, and their relationship.[66] Progressive social scientists, many of whom were suspicious of mass democracy, believed that statistics could help reduce the role of irrational, unpredictable human behavior in politics. "Statistical trends reveal objective laws and regularities that are independent of human existence and above ideological disputes," many of them asserted. Lester Frank Ward, the leading progressive social scientist, had worked in the Treasury Department's Bureau of Statistics.[67]

The Court also imposed limits on state legislatures and railroad commissions. In 1890, the Supreme Court held that if state authorities set rates that were too low, then they effectively deprived the railroads of property "without due process of law," violating the Fourteenth Amendment. In

1897, it decided that the states could not take railroad property for public use without just compensation, lest it violate the Fifth Amendment.[68] These doctrines, which came to be called "substantive due process" and the "incorporation of the Bill of Rights," would be the most important tools of judicial power in the coming century. The Supreme Court would use these to overturn economic regulations (such as maximum-hour labor laws) in the early 20th century, and to overturn morals regulations (restrictions on contraception and abortion) later in the century.

As the Court hobbled both federal and state railroad commissions as administrative agencies, also it adopted innovative means to expand its own administrative capacities. It allowed railroad managers to establish what were called "friendly receiverships" in bankruptcy. Populist railroad critics believed that these allowed rapacious manipulators like Jay Gould to profit from their mismanagement at the expense of creditors and the public. Congress, however, largely codified this mode of receivership in the 1898 Bankruptcy Act.[69]

Also prominent in railroad cases was the development of the "labor injunction" against striking workers. In 1894, the Supreme Court upheld the conviction of Eugene Debs, leader of the American Railway Union, for violating an injunction ordering him to stop interfering in railroad operations during the nationwide Pullman strike. Debs's union was engaged in a "secondary boycott" or sympathy strike, in which its members all over the country refused to work until a Chicago labor dispute was settled, which paralyzed the nation's transportation system. The injunction was an order issued by courts in equity cases, equity being a field of law historically separate from the common law. Equity was supposed to provide extraordinary remedies in extraordinary cases in which common law was inadequate. Most importantly, equity allowed judges to issue orders in a summary fashion, without notice or hearing from the defendants, and to act without juries. This was especially useful for cases in which local juries were likely to be biased against large, out-of-state corporations. (The use of the writ had been pioneered in state attempts to enforce locally unpopular prohibition laws.) The labor injunction was exactly the type of process which advocates of administrative government said that independent agencies should have without interference from common-law courts.[70]

The Federative Power and the Chinese

The Court was much more deferential in the regulation of foreign affairs. It provided the utmost latitude in immigration law enforcement, especially the Chinese Exclusion Acts, which showed some of the worst features of lawless and arbitrary government targeting unpopular minority groups.[71] Although the justices all agreed that Congress had plenary power to limit immigration, the Court was divided about what protections were due to those accused of being illegal aliens. Congress allowed federal officers to deport any person of Chinese descent who did not possess a certificate of legal residence, with none of the traditional protections of criminal defendants. (Deportation was not a criminal penalty, the government argued.) Justice Brewer echoed the observation of Senator John Sherman that the act resembled the Fugitive Slave Act, and warned that it could be extended to "other classes and other people."[72] When the federal courts in California insisted on extending legal protections to Chinese who challenged immigration officials, Congress stripped the courts of their power to hear appeals from the bureaucrats. By 1907, the consolidated Bureau of Immigration had, as one scholar puts it, been given the roles of "rulemaker, enforcer, and court of first and last appeal in all matters relating to aliens."[73] To make immigration restriction effective, summary administrative procedure had to replace the rule of law.[74]

Native-born Chinese-Americans continued to challenge the immigration system. Ju Toy claimed to be a native-born American citizen, but was held for deportation after he had returned from visiting China. A federal district court was satisfied by the evidence Ju Toy offered, and overruled the immigration officers. The Supreme Court reversed the lower court's ruling, however, and Ju Toy was deported. Justice Brewer in dissent said that he was unable to "see how anyone can read these rules and hold that they constitute due process of law."[75] But progressive academics held up these decisions as normal exercises of administrative discretion, and they became important precedents in the development of administrative law.[76] Many states had similarly given final authority to boards and commissions to determine what previously had been considered judicial questions.[77] The author of one of the first treatises on administrative law, Harvard Law Professor Bruce Wyman, called for broad deference by judges of official discretion.[78] Proponents of a stronger Interstate Commerce Commission, for example, called for what might be called "Ju Toy deference" by the courts to agencies.[79] One commentator considered the case the beginning of American administrative law.[80]

Although deferential on immigration, the Court could prevent excessive administrative discretion domestically. Anti-Chinese prejudice in California was potentially checked by the Reconstruction amendments, which prohibited the states from depriving any person—whether citizen or alien—of life, liberty, or property without due process, or from denying a person the equal protection of the law.[81] To get around these new constitutional guarantees, the city of San Francisco devised a clever scheme of delegation to harass the Chinese. The city prohibited the operation of laundries in wooden buildings unless the owners secured a license from the Board of Supervisors. The Board granted these licenses to all but one white applicant, and denied them to all Chinese operators. Yick Wo, who had operated a laundry for more than 20 years with the approval of the city fire warden, was fined for continuing to work without a license. The California Supreme Court and federal circuit court upheld the conviction, but the U.S. Supreme Court unanimously overturned it.

Justice Stanley Matthews wrote that the San Francisco ordinances conferred "not discretion to be exercised upon a consideration of the circumstances of each case, but a naked and arbitrary power." The law provided no standards for the supervisors—they could refuse licenses "without reason and without responsibility." This was not "discretion in the legal sense of the term, but is granted to their mere will. It is purely arbitrary, and acknowledges neither guidance nor restraint." It offended the fundamental founding ideal that we had "a government of laws and not of men." It practically invited discrimination against unpopular groups. Thus, although the law was neutral on its face, it still amounted to a denial of the equal protection of the laws.[82]

In *Yick Wo* the Court successfully resisted this effort to extend the unusually permissive standard of governmental power in foreign policy—what approached Locke's "prerogative" power—to domestic affairs. The state argued that the Chinese immigrants were actually foreign invaders, that they had extended Chinese law to the state, and had carved out an enclave where California's police power did not apply. The Court was willing to give a wide berth to the immigration officials because the admission of foreigners was an attribute of sovereignty, but it drew the line when California officials tried to extend that metaphor to legal aliens and citizens.[83]

Delegation and Foreign Trade

The last decade of the 19th century also saw important steps toward administrative discretion in the area of foreign trade. The McKinley tariff of 1890 sought "to secure reciprocal trade" with countries producing certain goods. It empowered the president to decide when a country producing these goods imposed duties "unequal and unreasonable," to take their goods off the free list and apply a prescribed tariff.[84] In 1897,

Congress passed an act "to prevent the importation of impure and unwholesome tea." It instructed the secretary of the treasury to appoint a board of seven men "expert in teas," who would provide him with samples of standard teas, which he would then give to the customs houses.[85] These acts reopened the old question of congressional delegation of lawmaking power.

The Court upheld these acts. On the reciprocal tariff act, it noted that Congress had frequently "conferred upon the President powers, with reference to trade and commerce," like this, emphasizing especially Chief Justice Marshall's decision in the *Aurora* case. The legislature could "invest the President with large discretion in matters arising out of the execution of statutes relating to trade and commerce with other nations." The act did not really give the president lawmaking power, but rather only executive power to apply a law when a certain factual situation arose.[86] Justice Lamar and Chief Justice Fuller dissented. This act, they argued, was "radically different" from the act upheld in the *Aurora* case. Earlier acts "entrust the President with the ascertainment of a fact therein defined upon which the law is to go into operation." But the reciprocal tariff act "goes further than that, and deputes to the President the power to suspend another section in the same act whenever 'he may deem' the action of any foreign nation . . . to be 'reciprocally unequal and unreasonable.'"[87]

The controversy over presidential power in foreign trade seemed to echo one of the first constitutional debates over foreign policy, President Washington's unilateral proclamation of neutrality when war broke out between France and Great Britain in 1793. Alexander Hamilton made the argument that, although the Constitution gave Congress the power to declare war, the president had the power to preserve the peace until Congress did so. Foreign trade was an important element of maintaining peaceful relations with foreign nations, and tariff adjustment might be seen as an alternative to war.

Law professor Edward B. Whitney agreed with the dissenters, noting that "It is impossible to formulate a rule, or anything nearer than a guess, as to the definition or the measurement of reciprocal unreasonableness. . . . The discretion does not concern details alone, but the broadest principles of action." He also, however, recognized that the courts would be loath to overturn the political branches "to take the side of the foreigner." Although one could make allowances in areas such as foreign policy, Whitney saw a larger danger, that both parties, "within a very short time, have shown a willingness and determination to grasp at authority without respect to the ancient traditions of our commonwealths."[88] The line between the foreign and domestic realms became blurred. Whereas a conservative like Whitney feared this development, progressive law professor Frank Goodnow was cautiously optimistic about it.[89]

Progressive Imperialism

The Spanish-American War presented an often overlooked watershed in the development of the modern American state. As wars almost always do, it strengthened the executive power and brought to an end the post–Civil War era congressional government. Woodrow Wilson, a rising academic star who became president of Princeton University in 1902, was notably impressed with the demonstration of presidential leadership by William McKinley. "No war ever transformed us quite as the war with Spain," he claimed. "We have witnessed a new revolution." Our involvement in world affairs was reviving the Hamiltonianism of the early republic, he noted, and "we are no longer strenuous about the niceties of constitutional law." He began to move his political theory from advocating an English-style parliamentary system to one focused on presidential leadership. Political scientist John W. Burgess, one of Wilson's teachers and the mentor of many progressives, later saw the war as a constitutional milestone.[90]

This war also marked the arrival of the United States as a global power, and indicated that it could no longer take for granted the almost free security that it had enjoyed for more than a century. Through the next century it would be drawn ever more deeply into world affairs, and this would exacerbate the always difficult task of drawing the line between prerogative and executive power—of preventing national security concerns (*raisons d'état*) from being used as pretexts to relax constitutional limitations at home. There was a great deal of symbiosis between imperialism abroad and progressive domestic state-building.[91] The bureaucratization of immigration policy accompanied the greater involvement of the United States in world affairs.[92]

The motive for the war—to liberate the oppressed peoples of Spain's decadent empire—signaled a fundamental change in American foreign policy. The Founders had focused on the development of American self-government, guarding America's national interest in world affairs while providing a model or example for others. John Quincy Adams said that America extolled freedom, "but she goes not abroad, in search of monsters to destroy. We wished freedom-fighters well, but guarded only our own."[93]

The foreign policy of the progressive era followed the progressives' historicism—their belief that no principles are timeless and immutable, but are contingent on historical circumstances. Progressives believed that America had a duty to extend its power to civilize less-developed peoples such as the Cubans and Filipinos, a revival of the "Manifest Destiny" idea of the antebellum period.[94] Republican Senator Orville Platt declared that the United States was carrying on the work of Providence, "part of the great development of the great force of Christian civilization on earth. . . . I believe that we have been chosen to carry on and to carry forward this great work of uplifting humanity on earth."[95]

The most important element in the progressive imperialist campaign that began with the Spanish-American War was that it gave voice to a repudiation of the founding principles of equality and natural rights. Like Stephen Douglas in the Lincoln-Douglas debates, the imperialists denied that the principles of the Declaration of Independence applied to all men. Indiana Senator Albert Beveridge regarded the Declaration as historically contingent, a "formula of words made only for enlightened, self-governing people." The more historically advanced races had the right and obligation to govern the less advanced. "We must never forget that in dealing with the Filipinos we deal with children." The principles of the American founding did not apply to them. "How dare any man prostitute this expression of the very elect of self-governing peoples to a race of Malay children of barbarians, schooled in Spanish methods and ideas?" Nor did Beveridge worry that the Constitution placed limits on the government's power to acquire an empire. Not all of the powers of the national government were stated explicitly in it. "The written constitution," he said, "is but the index of the living constitution."[96]

The imperialist movement thus represented a fundamental *reorientation* of American attitudes, from one that looked away to one that looked back toward Europe. Hamilton expressed the fundamentally anti-European view in *Federalist* 11. Europe, he argued, "by force and by fraud, has . . . extended her dominion" over Africa, Asia, and America. Europe now regarded itself as "Mistress of the World, and to consider the rest of mankind as created for her benefit." "It belongs to us," he wrote, "to vindicate the honor of the human race, and to teach that assuming brother, moderation. Union will enable us to do it." A century later the progressives discarded the Founders' plan to create a new world order and sought instead to join the old one in the imperial process. "If Germany can have foreign lands," Beveridge urged, "so can America."[97]

The Anti-Imperialist League opposed the campaign as a violation of America's founding principles. "All men, of whatever race or color, are entitled to life, liberty and the pursuit of happiness," the league declared. It condemned the "war against liberty, begun by Spain and continued by us. . . . The United States cannot act upon the ancient heresy that might makes right." The imperialist campaign had revived the Slave Power effort "to destroy [America's] fundamental principles and noblest ideals."[98] The Anti-Imperialists saw the rejection of our founding principles when the commander of American forces in Manila seized copies of the Declaration of Independence as an "incendiary document."[99]

E. L. Godkin, the founding editor of *The Nation*, the leading journal of American classical liberalism, lamented how the country had again repudiated its founding principles. As Lincoln had before the Civil War, he observed that "material comfort has blinded the eyes of the present generation to the cause which made it possible."[100] Reflecting the trends that Charles Merriam described, he wrote that

> the Declaration of Independence no longer arouses enthusiasm; it is an embarrassing instrument which requires to be explained away. The Constitution is said to be "outgrown"; and at all events the rights which it guarantees must be carefully reserved to our own citizens, and not allowed to human beings over whom we have purchased sovereignty.[101]

The rise of imperialism coincided with the end of any effort to secure the civil rights of blacks in the South, as segregation and disfranchisement took hold in the 1890s. "The great party which boasted that it had secured for the negro the rights of humanity and citizenship now listens in silence to the proclamation of white supremacy and makes no protest against the nullification of the Fifteenth Amendment," Godkin observed.[102] The Spanish-American War and imperialism began to popularize the anti-constitutional political theory that Merriam had regarded as limited to academics.

The Republicans won the election of 1900 while defending the cause of imperialism, although it is doubtful that the election was decided primarily on the issue, regardless of whether that election was a referendum on the issue.[103] The ugly suppression of the Filipino independence movement vindicated the anti-imperialists and effectively ended America's imperialist campaign. But the United States did have new territories to administer, and an important question was whether constitutional guarantees such as trial by jury applied in the territories. The popular question was "Does the Constitution follow the flag?" It would be very inconvenient for imperial administration if it did.

The Court rather deftly decided that in these new territories Congress must respect some, but not all, of the rights protected by the Constitution.

As Secretary of War Elihu Root pithily summarized it, "The Constitution follows the flag, but it doesn't quite catch up to it."[104] In a series of cases decided from 1901 into the 1920s—known as the "Insular Cases"—the Court held that not all new territory was "incorporated" or presumed to be on the road to statehood. The new doctrine meant that the United States could acquire territory on a temporary basis, allowing for what one scholar calls "deannexation." This would assuage anti-imperialists concerned about the curtailing of civil liberties, and also of racists alarmed at the addition of non-whites to the American polity. Above all, it provided room for administrative discretion, which the dissenters in the Insular Cases saw as a menace to constitutional government. We were on the verge, Justice John Marshall Harlan warned, of the end of the "era of constitutional liberty guarded and protected by a written constitution," headed toward the system of "legislative absolutism" that the American Revolution had been fought against.[105] The Court's treatment of the Interstate Commerce Commission showed its suspicion of centralized bureaucratic power. Although the Supreme Court was more deferential to the federal government in foreign affairs, it still displayed a healthy solicitude for constitutional limits.

CHAPTER 4

The First Wave of
the Administrative State:
The Progressive Era, 1900–1930

In the first third of the 20th century, the halting first steps toward a bureaucratic state became a regular stride. The activist presidencies of Theodore Roosevelt and Woodrow Wilson established important precedents in regulatory practice and laws establishing agencies including the Federal Trade Commission and the Federal Reserve Board. The Interstate Commerce Commission finally acquired the rate-setting power that Congress and the courts had withheld in its first 20 years of existence. The federal government devised new taxing and spending practices that enabled it to use the states as its regulatory agents. Although the United States did not become an imperial power, it made an important jump into world affairs by entering the First World War. Like every major war, this vastly expanded the power of the central government. Even the postwar decade—usually seen as a conservative reaction against progressive activism—saw significant extensions of regulatory power. The progressive ideology of statism had a firm hold in both political parties. Well before the Great Depression ushered in the next major wave of centralized bureaucratic government, conservative critics warned that an American Leviathan already had arrived.

Theodore Roosevelt and the Railroads

President Theodore Roosevelt also tried to establish federal control over the railroad industry. In 1901, financiers E. H. Harriman, James J. Hill, and J. P. Morgan established a $400 million holding company, the Northern Securities Company, establishing a virtual monopoly in the Pacific Northwest. Roosevelt then initiated an antitrust prosecution, which succeeded in breaking up the company. The Supreme Court narrowly upheld the government in 1904.[1] The suit was counterproductive, attempting to thwart the virtually inevitable consolidation of the American railway system.[2] Roosevelt, however, considered the economics of the issue to be beside the point. He primarily was concerned with showing the public that the federal government was superior to great business interests. Morgan implied that he was the equal of the president when he suggested that, if there were an antitrust problem, "Send your man to my man and we can fix it up."[3] "I do not care a rap what proportion [Morgan, Rockefeller, and Guggenheim] won of the industry," Theodore Roosevelt told William Jennings Bryan. "What I am interested in is getting the hand of government put on all of them—this is what I want."[4] Despite his reputation as a "trustbuster," Roosevelt actually was quite skeptical of antitrust law.[5] He recognized that bigness often was good for consumers. As his comment to Bryan shows, however, he was more concerned about political power than economic efficiency. He wanted the power to reward and punish in accord with his own sense of the public good.

Roosevelt pushed Congress to give the Interstate Commerce Commission (ICC) the power to set railroad rates in what became the Hepburn At of 1906. Though prominent economists had concluded that discriminatory railroad rates were necessary and actually beneficial, even to those small, isolated shippers who appeared to be victimized by them, the majority of economists and the public continued to insist that the rates were unjust.[6] For years the courts had frustrated the ICC's efforts to assume rate-making power that Congress had not explicitly granted, but after the Hepburn Act did so, the courts were notably deferential to the commission. It appeared that the Court took the Hepburn Act as the opportunity to bow out gracefully from its politically unpopular and apparently pro-railroad jurisprudence. This was an important step by the Court to give a wider berth to administrative agencies.[7] For the next decade, the ICC was dominated by the interests of small shippers. The profitability of American railroads rapidly declined, and the system was on the verge of collapse as the nation began to mobilize for the First World War, resulting in the federal government taking over the railroads and enacting a new regulatory system in 1920.[8]

Roosevelt also intervened to secure legislation regulating the manufacture and marketing of food and drugs. This was especially important because it helped to develop the idea that there was a "federal police power"—the power, traditionally reserved to the states—to regulate the safety, health, welfare, and morals of the public.[9] "Muckraking" journalists provided much of the impetus for this regulation in their exposés of adulterated and fraudulently sold food and drugs. The media or "fourth estate" would become an important factor in the development of the power of the government. By 1906, many manufacturers had come to welcome federal regulation. They believed that it would help American exports to have the government's stamp of approval. The cost of compliance would help eliminate competition from smaller producers.[10] Economic competition was moving from the market into the political sphere as businesses tried to control their markets, engaging in what has been called "rent-seeking" or "crony capitalism." Businesses increasingly invested resources trying to influence the government to help them or to burden their competitors.[11]

Also notable in the pure food and drugs campaign was the leading role played by the U.S. Department of Agriculture's (USDA) chief chemist, Harvey Wiley. Wiley appeared to be the type of technically trained, scientific expert that progressives hailed as being able to administer government without concern for political considerations. Wiley, however, was very active in promoting the work of the USDA by political influence and publicity. The USDA had been established in 1862 but was slow to attempt to extend itself from information gathering and advising into regulation and policy making. With Wiley it reached the point of "bureaucratic autonomy" or critical mass.[12] Regulatory agencies in the 20th century would begin to feed on themselves, and to move more clearly from the technical and scientific realm into the political one.

The Pure Food and Drugs Act, with the simultaneously passed Meat Inspection Act, was a significant step forward from railroad regulation into a more general regulatory role for the federal government. Progressive Republican Senator Albert Beveridge of Indiana called it "the most pronounced extension of federal power in every direction ever enacted."[13] It still had important limits that restrained its power, however, before it was strengthened in 1938. Like the original Interstate Commerce Commission, the FDA could not establish standards of purity or quality; it only could impose fines or seek prosecution for impure or adulterated food and drugs.[14] The agency tried to give its interpretive rulings the force of law, but courts often frustrated its attempts. The FDA decided, for example, that patent medicines not only had to list all of their ingredients, but also could not make extravagant claims about their therapeutic value. The Supreme Court overturned this decision in 1911 as beyond the scope of the act. The pushers of "B & M's External Remedy," for example, had to disclose that it was made of turpentine, ammonia, water, and eggs, but could still claim that it cured tuberculosis, pneumonia, cancer, diabetes, whooping cough, diphtheria, asthma, bronchitis, and laryngitis.[15] Congress amended the act in 1912 to overturn the Court's decision, but the agency still had to prove fraudulent intent in court. The agency's personnel and budget were limited, and its sanctions usually had little impact. Nobody ever was imprisoned under it, and many manufacturers chose to pay the modest fines the FDA imposed. The FDA succeeded more by cooperating with manufacturers, helping them to comply with the law and providing useful advice that would enhance the reputation of their products.[16]

Also notable during the Roosevelt administration was the role played by women's groups in the promotion of new social and economic regulation.[17] The increasing role of women in American politics accompanied the increase in federal administrative power. Columbia University political scientist John W. Burgess observed that American women were leading the movement to turn 19th-century "voluntary socialism" into compulsory socialism, with the state taking the place of the family.[18] As Hamilton put it in *Federalist* 17, "The regulation of the mere domestic police of a State appears to me to hold but slender allurements to ambition." Statesmen—assumed to be men—would be more concerned with war, diplomacy, and national greatness than with the economic order. The classical philosophers regarded the economic sphere as the woman's world—all economics was "home economics." Roosevelt often shared this view, fearing that American society was becoming soft and effeminate due to its great economic growth since the Civil War. But Roosevelt's domestic initiatives did enhance the allurements of internal administration for the future. In a 1910 speech articulating the need for greater federal power, he praised the new work of the USDA, saying

> And now a special word to the farmer. I want to see him make the farm as fine a farm as it can be made; and let him remember to see that the improvement goes on indoors as well as out; let him remember that the farmer's wife should have her share of thought and attention just as much as the farmer himself.

The Founders assumed that agriculture was a quintessentially local and particular matter—something that would be left to the states. Roosevelt, however, considered not just agriculture, but even farm home decor, to be his concern.

Taft and Conservation

William Howard Taft, Roosevelt's successor, usually is regarded as a conservative throwback between the progressive administrations of

Roosevelt and Woodrow Wilson. Lately, however, historians have recognized that Taft was in fact a progressive, albeit a conservative one.[19] The conservatives in the Republican Party were uneasy about Taft, Roosevelt's anointed successor, who genuinely wanted to maintain if not extend Roosevelt's policies. Although Taft had a robust view of presidential power, he had more scruples about constitutional limitations than did his predecessor.[20]

The first important dispute between Taft and Roosevelt arose out of the issue of bureaucratic discretion. It involved the withdrawal of federal timber lands for sale to private developers, part of Roosevelt's "conservation" program, in which progressives had been trying to apply the Prussian model of forest management to America. Conservation acts of the 1890s established the Forest Service and gave it a great deal of discretion. It was "a blank check . . . to manage these lands as it saw best."[21] Roosevelt very aggressively withdrew federal land from development, including some 16 million acres just before the 59th Congress prohibited any further withdrawals in six designated states.[22]

Taft was determined to impose the rule of law on the Forest Service. To a progressive congressman who complained that he was betraying Roosevelt's policies he said, "We have a government of limited power under the Constitution, and we have got to work out our problems on the basis of law."[23] When Taft took office he dismissed Secretary of the Interior James Garfield, whom he believed had exceeded his legal authority in conservation matters, and replaced him with Richard Ballinger. Ballinger regarded himself as defending the rule of law against paternalism and administrative discretion. He insisted that political decisions had to be made by politically accountable officials, not by irresponsible "experts." Decisions about the development of public lands—the construction of dams, power plants, and the like—were inescapably political. Progressives complained that the Interior Department was doing the bidding of large corporate interests but, in fact, the "conservation" of federal resources did more to aid the large current possessors of natural resources.[24]

Ultimately, Chief Forester Gifford Pinchot—a Roosevelt loyalist—led a campaign against the Taft administration. Pinchot was more of an evangelical believer in environmentalism than a scientist, although he manipulated science to alarm Congress into acting to conserve natural resources.[25] A land office agent, Louis Glavis, abetted by *Collier's* magazine, launched a sensational campaign accusing Ballinger of corruption in the leasing of Alaska coal lands. "It would be difficult to find magazine articles or editorials more replete with inaccuracies," wrote Taft's biographer. "Ballinger was the victim of an attack fostered by fanaticism and by bad journalism."[26] Taft fired both Glavis and Pinchot. A congressional investigation exonerated Ballinger, but he and the president lost the public relations battle—especially when Louis D. Brandeis, Glavis's counsel, showed that Taft had signed and antedated a report written by his attorney general. The rift between Taft and the progressive Republicans widened.[27]

The fight over conservation also produced a significant step forward for bureaucratic discretion. Congress gave the Interior Department the power to make rules concerning grazing on federal land, and made the violation of those rules subject to fines and imprisonment. The agency found that fines were not a sufficient deterrent to roving herdsmen, and thus tried to impose criminal penalties. In the debate over "nondelegation," the definition of crimes was considered the classic example of a legislative power that could not be delegated. Federal courts dismissed criminal cases brought by the bureau on this principle, and the agency abandoned the effort until Gifford Pinchot became the chief in 1905 and revived it. Pierre Grimaud was indicted for grazing without a permit, but a federal district court quashed the indictment on nondelegation grounds. The government appealed to the Supreme Court in 1910. The Court was divided 4 to 4 in the case (Justice Rufus Peckham's death having left a vacancy), leaving the lower court's dismissal of the indictment intact. The government asked for a reconsideration; meanwhile, three more justices died or retired. In 1911, the Court unanimously upheld the government.[28] "In the nature of things," Justice Joseph R. Lamar wrote, "it was impracticable for Congress to provide general regulations for these various and varying details of management." Bureaucrats now had the power to define violations of their regulations as criminal offenses.[29]

The Taft Courts

Grimaud showed that Taft's appointees to the Supreme Court were not hostile to administrative power. In 1910, the Court held that Congress could give rate-making power to the commission, and that it would only ask if the commission had exercised it reasonably—that it did not amount to a deprivation of property or a taking. The Court would not "under the guise of exerting judicial power, usurp merely administrative functions."[30] The Court appeared eager to restrain itself.[31] The early 20th-century Court relied on the due process clause of the Fourteenth Amendment rather than on separation of powers as a means of restraining government power. The Court of these years most often is associated with *Lochner v. New York*, in which it struck down a law that limited the number of hours that bakers could work. The conservatives' doctrine of "substantive due process" held that some fundamental rights, like the "liberty of contract" in the Lochner case, could not be abridged by legislation. This substantive conservatism was seldom invoked, however, and it accompanied an increasingly liberal view of the procedures of administrative agencies.[32]

In 1910, Taft appointed Charles Evans Hughes to the Supreme Court. As governor of New York, Hughes had fathered the most advanced state regulatory program, the Public Service Commission. Hughes warned that if the courts became involved in questions of administration, they would lose the independence and esteem which the Constitution and popular opinion gave them. "You must have administration, and you must have administration by administrative officials," he said in a 1907 speech, "in view of the wide extension of regulatory schemes which the future is destined to see."[33] Hughes himself essentially was an executive official.[34] He had been governor of New York, and would resign from the Court in 1916 to run for president. Hughes saw that judicial power depended on judges getting out of the business of overseeing administrative decisions. In the most famous line in this speech he said, "We are under a constitution, but the constitution is what the judges say it is." He seems to have meant that constitutional government depended on judicial power, and that judicial power depended on popular esteem—an esteem that would be undermined if the Court meddled in bureaucratic matters. Advocates of judicial power, then, had good reason to be deferential in matters of administrative law.[35] The Court's interpretation of the Hepburn Act in this period indicated that it was in accord with Hughes's admonition. Hughes rejoined the Court in 1930 as Chief Justice, when he would again be at the center of the political struggle over the administrative state.

Taft shared Hughes's fears that judicial prestige would be hurt by delving into administrative affairs. He was an essentially judicial figure whom fate drew into executive positions—president of the Philippine Commission, secretary of War, then ill-fated president—until he realized his lifelong dream of becoming chief justice in 1921. As president, Taft tried to ameliorate the railroad regulation problem by establishing a specialized "Court of Commerce" that would provide swifter and more uniform review of commission regulations. He got this in the enactment of the Mann-Elkins Act of 1910, which further strengthened the ICC. But the Commerce Court was unsuccessful and Congress abolished it in 1913. It became a by-word for judicial incompetence in administrative matters and an impediment to later calls for specialized judicial review of administrative action.[36]

The Wilson Presidency

Woodrow Wilson won the election of 1912 because the Republican vote split between its progressive and regular wings. Theodore Roosevelt challenged Taft for the nomination because he believed that Taft had sold out to the party regulars. Roosevelt claimed that he was the choice of the majority of Republican voters, but he was denied the nomination by the party bosses. This view was supported by his performance in those states that chose their delegates by direct primary election. Most delegates were not yet chosen directly, however, and Taft's control of the party machinery enabled him to be re-nominated. Roosevelt bolted and formed an independent Progressive (or "Bull Moose") Party.

Roosevelt's campaign was another blow to the party system, in decline since the Pendleton Act of 1883. The progressives believed that the party system was an impediment to the establishment of a modern state. Columbia political scientist Frank J. Goodnow in 1900 called for "greater centralization of our administrative system" and "subjugation of the political party." The parties had to be made responsible to the people, he argued.[37] The more democratic the parties became, however, the less the people participated in politics. Voter turnout in presidential elections, rarely below 75 percent in the late-19th century, would never exceed 75 percent in the 20th century. 1912 marked a record low, to that time, at 59 percent.

Taft, on the other hand, believed in the party system as a necessary guide and restraint on democratic politics. He thus refused to campaign personally after being nominated, allowing the party to manage the election. New York Senator Elihu Root, GOP convention chairman and Taft's spokesman, defended party discipline. "Without organized parties, having these qualities of coherence and loyalty, free popular government becomes a confused and continual conflict."[38] The regulars were especially concerned about Roosevelt's 1912 proposal to provide for the recall of unpopular judicial decisions. In one of the most influential analyses of 19th-century American politics, political scientist Steven Skowronek described the United States as a regime of "courts and parties."[39] Taft was defending both of the pillars of this regime.

Woodrow Wilson wrote the first significant American essay on administrative government, and his presidency would see a great leap forward in the bureaucratic state, but he campaigned in 1912 as an opponent of bureaucracy. Since Taft did not enter the fray, the real contest was between Theodore Roosevelt and Wilson, and the central issue was what to do about the "trusts." Roosevelt's position was that big business was here to stay, it often was beneficial, and that an administrative agency was needed to regulate the trusts to sort out the good ones from the bad ones. Wilson argued that all trusts were bad and should be broken up. Wilson severely criticized the view that government could regulate them. In 1912, he reiterated classical liberal themes that he had articulated in 1907 and 1908, lamenting "the perfect mania for regulation [that] has taken hold of us." "The less administrative government the better,"[40] he said. He drew Theodore Roosevelt's scorn when affirming that "liberty has never come from the government. The history of liberty is the history of the limitations of government power, not the increase of it." He warned that human nature, particularly the desire for power by men in government, had not changed. "What I fear . . . is a government of experts," he said. "God forbid that in a democratic country we should resign the task and give the government over to experts."[41]

Despite his anti-bureaucratic campaign talk, every one of Wilson's major legislative achievements augmented the administrative state. It is difficult to avoid the conclusion that candidate Wilson was dissembling, saying what he needed to say to win the nomination of the still relatively conservative Democratic Party and general electorate, but returning as president to his academic enthusiasm for bureaucracy. Wilson's éminence grise, Colonel Edward House, wrote a Utopian novel of the administrative state, *Philip Dru, Administrator: A Story of Tomorrow*. The protagonist leads a popular rebellion against the decadent plutocracy that has taken over his country. Dru does away with its obsolete constitution and reforms the republic along modern European lines. Ultimately, he conquers Mexico and reforms that country, too.[42] Wilson's Interior Secretary, Franklin Lane, said that it captured the spirit of the Wilson administration.[43]

The Wilson Agencies

The most straightforward Democratic position in 1912 was the reduction of the tariff. Congressional control of the tariff schedule was the antithesis of delegation and bureaucratic discretion. The legislature went into great detail specifying items and rates. The party had always inclined toward free trade, but when push came to shove, Democrats realized that many of their constituents benefited from the tariff, particularly small businessmen. The Democrats condemned the tariff as "the mother of the trusts," but protection actually permitted big business to tolerate competition from less-efficient small businessmen. If foreign corporations reduced prices for American consumers, then big American businesses could meet that new competition; their small American competitors would be ruined. The Underwood Tariff of 1913 did significantly reduce rates, but the complexities of the issue led Wilson to endorse an expert commission to set tariff rates.[44]

The Sherman Antitrust Act of 1890 was the counterpart of the Interstate Commerce Act. The difficult policy question at the center of the Sherman Act was whether Congress intended to maximize competition for the benefit of consumers, or to maximize the number of competitors to aid small business at the expense of consumers. It outlawed "every contract, combination in the form of trust or otherwise, or conspiracy in restraint of trade or commerce among the several states."[45] Read literally (the "per se" reading), this would outlaw every contract, for every agreement between two parties restrained trade from the perspective of a third party. The lower federal courts initially applied the "rule of reason"—only combinations that "unreasonably" restrained trade and harmed consumers were illegal. In 1897, a closely divided Supreme Court adopted the "per se" standard.[46] Fourteen years later, in the *Standard Oil* and *American Tobacco* cases, it reversed itself and adopted the rule of reason. This was the state of affairs during the 1912 campaign.

Wilson believed that Congress easily could make the Sherman Act more specific and explicitly criminalize anticompetitive business practices. This turned out not to be so easy, and the revised antitrust act (the Clayton Act of 1914) made no significant changes in the law. Instead, Wilson and his advisers shifted gears and created an agency—the Federal Trade Commission—to regulate competition. Rather than prosecuting businesses after they had become monopolistic, the commission would prevent them from becoming big in the first place. This would require a great deal more discretion than did enforcing the traditional common law standard of "unfair competition." Thus, Congress devised a new standard, outlawing "unfair methods of competition."[47]

The FTC succeeded Roosevelt's Bureau of Corporations. It looked much like the ICC, but had the entire American economy, not just railroads, within its ambit. Its framers' hope that it would prevent rather than punish monopolies was especially important, for it opened the door to a new kind of constant regulatory supervision in place of old-fashioned legal prohibition. This commission might become a part of the daily operations of businesses, intruding itself into ordinary operations, like a parent or guardian would. Vehemently populist antitrust was statist, not laissez-faire.[48]

The Federal Trade Commission was composed of five members—no more than three of whom could be members of the same political party—appointed by the president with Senate consent. The members served staggered seven-year terms, and could be removed for "inefficiency, neglect of duty, or malfeasance in office."[49] It was a potentially powerful independent regulatory commission. At the same time, members of Congress believed that the commission, unlike the courts, could be made to answer to the legislature. As Iowa Republican Senator Albert B. Cummins pointed out, agencies could be eliminated more easily than federal courts could.[50]

The FTC would never become the powerful regulatory agency that many envisioned. Much more powerful in the long run was the new Federal Reserve Board. The principal goal of banking reform in the 20th century was to control the periodic "panics" that resulted from the lack of an effective monetary reserve system—a place that banks could go to when there was a run on their deposits, a "lender of last resort." The money supply, limited to the amount of bonds that national banks purchased to secure their notes, was said to be "inelastic." Southern and western farmers, who had lost their campaign for monetary inflation in 1896, believed that they were being starved for credit and charged usurious interest rates by eastern banks. Others alleged that a Wall Street "money trust" needed to be broken up.

This variety of problems and interests produced the profoundly enigmatic Federal Reserve Act of 1913. Democrats were still opposed to a "central bank," so the act created a system that was more centralized than the old, Civil War–era National Banking Act system, but was still disbursed among 12 regional reserve banks, with a board of governors in Washington. The member banks were privately owned and elected members of the regional boards, but the president also chose some members of the regional boards and all of the central board members. The board would be "independent," its members serving 10-year terms and removable only for cause, but the secretary of the treasury and the comptroller of the currency were ex officio members. The notes of the new system—the Federal Reserve Notes that we have today—were backed by the federal government.[51]

The new banking system was significantly more public and centralized than earlier banking systems.[52] The money supply was still limited by the gold standard, but the Fed could issue notes more liberally than the National Banking system could. It did in fact have an inherently inflationary tendency.[53] Congress had delegated an enormous monetary policy to a new agency without any clear standards.[54] The Fed had more power over interest rates and reserve requirements than the comptroller of the currency had held. As the title suggested, the comptroller was an auditor and examiner, not a policy maker, and largely had stuck to his limited statutory mandate (the Treasury more often tried to act like a central bank). The Fed from the beginning manifested the "mission creep" characteristic of 20th-century agencies, by exercising questionable power to buy and sell federal bonds to influence the money supply.[55]

The Hidden Bureaucracy

In addition to establishing new regulatory agencies, the Wilson years saw important expansions of federal activity by taxation and spending. It often has been observed that much of American statism is indirect or invisible, carrying out policy by fiscal incentives and transfer payments, largely within the tax code.[56] The income tax provided the revenue for the modern American state. The Sixteenth Amendment had been ratified a month before Wilson was inaugurated.[57] The first income tax law was simple (six pages in length), with low rates that only the wealthiest Americans paid. From the outset, however, legislators recognized that they could make policy through the tax code. The first act, for example, allowed the deduction of interest payment on mortgages, to encourage home ownership. Theodore Roosevelt complained that it allowed only two child deductions, which would discourage procreation, especially among the upper classes. He called it "a premium on race suicide."[58] The Internal Revenue Service determined that employer-provided pensions were deductible business expenses. Similar decisions would encourage the peculiar American "private welfare state."

The Wilson years also saw the coming-of-age of the "grant-in-aid," federal subsidies to the states for them to execute powers that the federal government did not possess. In the 19th century, Congress distributed land to achieve its ends. It gave the states land if they used the proceeds to fund vocational colleges in the Morrill Land-Grant College Act of 1862. This grant came with no strings attached—the states did not have to comply with federal direction or regulation. In the Hatch Act of 1887 and the Second Morrill Act of 1890, Congress began to give the states revenue from land sales rather than giving the land itself, and began to supervise the proceeds more closely. Prominent progressive intellectual Herbert Croly looked forward to the dispensing of federal aid to the states by "disinterested [national] administrators."[59]

The Weeks Act of 1911 is usually considered the first modern grant-in-aid. Congress provided matching funds for states that adopted forest fire–prevention programs. In 1916, Congress passed the Federal Highway or "Good Roads" Act, to enable farmers to get their goods to market. States that took the aid had to comply with federal mandates. The act required states to centralize their highway administrations, which traditionally had been left to counties, thus accelerating the centralization of state government taking place in the progressive period.[60] The federal government also made states comply with progressive labor standards.[61] Similar grants imposed federal direction in agriculture, transportation, education, and health care. When the New Deal transformed federal farm policy in 1933, for example, it could draw immediately on the more than 3,000 county agents that had been established by earlier agricultural programs.[62]

World War One

Wilson's construction of the administrative government accelerated sharply during World War One. War again showed its historic tendency to empower central governments, and this finally produced a reaction that flattened the rising curve of bureaucratic government for a decade.[63]

War necessities extended many pre-war federal regulatory programs. In 1916, the country's railroad system was strained under the needs of the government to supply the Allies and prepare the nation for war, exacerbated by the last decade of pro-shipper ICC policy. Now the railroad unions threatened to go on strike unless their demand for an 8-hour day (with no reduction in daily pay) was met. Wilson got Congress to comply. After the war began, the government had to take over the railroads to assure that governmental mobilization needs were the railroads' priority. They were returned to private ownership in 1920, but under a fundamentally altered regulatory system. The Interstate Commerce Act had been administered chiefly with the interest of shippers in mind, at the expense of the railroads. The Transportation Act of 1920, however, intended to protect the railroads from competition. The ICC had been "captured" by shippers before the war; now it would belong to the railroads.[64]

The army introduced millions of Americans to bureaucratic regimentation. The World War One army was more conscripted than any previous American army. Besides the usual application of uniform standards of dress, food, shelter, hygiene, and labor, the authorities attempted to turn army camps into "national universities," in Secretary of War

Newton Baker's terms. The War Department applied prohibition to the camps and the areas around them, as well as stamping out prostitution. This was no small matter; some 30,000 women were arrested for immoral conduct, often according to how they dressed, danced, or walked.[65] The war transformed American policy about prostitution. Formerly, states and localities had tried to segregate and regulate "red-light districts" where prostitution would be tolerated but contained. If localities wanted the benefit of having federal army camps, however, then they had to comply with the federal standard of total suppression. This policy survived the war.

The Civil War was supplied largely by market mechanisms, but the government in World War One created a great number of public corporations to provide materiel for the war. This began with the Shipping Board, which built, operated, and regulated merchant ships. Its confused missions of acting as a shipper and regulating shipping produced a great deal of waste and corruption.[66] The United States was almost completely dependent on foreign sources of nitrates, necessary for munitions production, so it built hydroelectric dams in the Tennessee River Valley. For years after the war, progressives sought to keep the project going, to produce electricity and fertilizer and to guide the economic development of the region. This would come to fruition in the Tennessee Valley Administration during the New Deal.

Congress provided for the control of food and fuel prices under the Lever Act of 1917. Individuals could be jailed for charging "unjust or unreasonable" prices, but the Supreme Court struck down convictions under this unduly vague standard, one that delegated legislative power and invited arbitrary bureaucratic discretion.[67] Congress prohibited the manufacture of alcoholic beverages in 1918, putatively to preserve grain for the war effort, though the act passed after the armistice had been signed. This became the model for the Volstead Act of 1919, which stringently enforced the Eighteenth Amendment, the most drastic effort of federal regulation in American history.

The Great War also marked the first significant federal foray into propaganda and the first attempt to suppress dissent since the Federalist Sedition Act. More than a thousand people were convicted under the act and sentenced to prison terms for opposing the war. The Post Office censored the mails, denying mailing privileges to journals that were critical of the government. The federal government also undertook a propaganda campaign to cultivate public opinion by the Committee on Public Information. This was not just traditional criminal prosecution for disloyalty, but an attempt at social engineering.

For many progressives, such as Harvard Law professor Felix Frankfurter and Franklin D. Roosevelt who served in the wartime Wilson government, the war showed the great potential of administrative government.[68] Many hoped to continue it after the war.

Though it lasted barely 18 months, the First World War introduced millions of Americans to bureaucratic government for the first time since the Civil War. The popular reaction was markedly hostile, already expressing itself in the mid-term elections of 1918, which gave Republicans control of both houses of Congress. Although many progressives welcomed the opportunity that the war provided for building state power, the last thing that most Americans wanted was a permanent wartime regimentation. Most desired a return to "normalcy," a hiatus from progressive statism, that returned the Republican Party to control of the government in 1920.

The 1920s

For a long time, historians—predominantly sympathetic to the progressive-modern liberal tradition—depicted the 1920s as a reactionary decade that set back the movement to develop a modern American State. In more recent years they instead have emphasized the continuities between the progressive era and the 1920s. This is evident not only in the preservation of the federal regulatory apparatus of the previous three decades, but also in its extension.

The most overlooked expansion of progressive administration came in the Budget and Accounting Act of 1921. Congressional control over spending was the most important means that it had to control administration. In the 19th century, there really was no "budget," but instead a set of appropriations bills that came out of the congressional committees. Progressives had called for a centralized, "executive" budget as a means of reducing waste and promoting efficiency, but also to promote comprehensive "planning." In other words, budget reform would not just improve the means by which the federal government did its job, but would change the ends of that job, and make them more expansive. Government reformers began to look at the federal government not as a set of discrete agencies tied to Congress, but as an executive-centered bureaucratic whole.[69] It appeared to be a transfer of power from Congress to the president, but in fact expanded the power of both institutions.[70]

One scholar notes that executive budgeting was "at odds with the basic organizational precepts of the founding fathers," undermining separation of powers and checks and balances.[71] Cities and states began to adopt executive budgeting, and President Taft gave the cause a high priority when he established a Commission on Economy and Efficiency. The commission included important progressives such as Frederick Cleveland of the Bureau of Municipal Research, a leading local "think tank," and William Frank Willoughby, a statistician and economist and the first president of the Brookings Institute, the first national think tank.[72] A number of worrisome peacetime budget deficits in 1904–1905 and 1908–1910 gave the issue more salience. President Harding signed a budget bill in 1921, and called it "the beginning of the greatest reformation in governmental practice since the beginning of the republic."[73] Nevertheless, progressives were disappointed that the first budget director, Charles Dawes, used his new power not to increase the scope and power of government but to save money.[74]

The Radio Act of 1927 was a bolder step into federal regulation than anything in the progressive era. To ration the scarce commodity of radio wavelengths, Congress established an independent commission to award licenses on the basis of "public interest, convenience, or necessity." This phrase was even broader than the open-ended language of the Interstate Commerce or Federal Trade Commission Acts. It was the equivalent of the "police power" that states enjoyed to legislate generally for the "safety, health, welfare and morals" of the people." "It would be hard to find a case of the delegation of more drastic authority to an executive officer," political scientist Robert E. Cushman observed.[75] The Radio Commission reported that it would deny licenses to broadcasters whose programs were "uninteresting" or "distasteful."[76] It represented a decisive step away from the old system of common-law property rights, cutting off an effort by federal courts to deal with the wavelength issue along "homesteading," or first-come, first-served, lines. Scholars have variously argued that Congress was economically ignorant in its insistence that the market could not deal with the radio problem, that it deliberately chose to substitute political choice for economic choice, and that it genuinely believed that the public interest would be served by the prevention of monopoly in broadcasting.[77] Whatever the motives, an act handing the cutting-edge media of the day over to a federal bureaucracy was the brainchild of Commerce Secretary Herbert Hoover, passed by a Republican Congress and signed by President Calvin Coolidge.

Congress also enacted the Railway Labor Act in 1926, promoting organized labor in the railroad industry, which it had been trying to do since the Erdman Act of 1898. They key was to remove labor disputes from the common-law courts and to have an administrative agency (the

National Mediation Board in this case) oversee organization and disputes. This act was the precursor of New Deal labor legislation of the next decade.[78] States had taken similar steps in removing questions of liability for industrial accidents out of the courts and establishing workmen's compensation agencies.[79] More and more activity was removed from the judicial realm of contract and tort law into the administrative sphere.

The enforcement of national prohibition, however, stood out most prominently as the greatest effort yet undertaken to police the behavior of individual Americans. Efforts to limit the consumption of alcohol were deeply rooted in the American past. The first attempts, like those against slavery, relied on voluntary association and moral suasion. These were followed by state limitations and prohibitions, and culminated in the Eighteenth Amendment. It was thus a statist substitute for previously private, religious, and voluntary efforts, such as education, health, and welfare provision.[80] But popular resistance to prohibition was simply too deep and widespread to have submitted even to a massive and coherent enforcement campaign. In this respect it resembled the doomed task of the radical Republicans in Reconstruction, or the enforcement of the Embargo under Jefferson—impossible without arbitrary power. The national government never fully threw itself into the task. Prohibition was enforced through the Treasury Department, and then transferred to the Justice Department, but always by ordinary court proceedings. Indeed, insofar as it eliminated the licensing and taxing procedures of the old liquor system, it probably reduced bureaucracy.

The states also continued the prewar movement toward centralized administrative government. Some of this was funded by the continuation of federal grants-in-aid, though the more fiscally restrained administrations of the 1920s only initiated one new program (the Sheppard-Towner Act for maternal and infant health), which it ended in 1929. President Coolidge called these grants "insidious," because they "sugar-coat[ed] the dose of federal intrusion."[81]

The states undertook two significant programs of administrative government in the zoning and eugenic movements. These related campaigns illustrated progressive belief in governmental "social engineering," extending to the point that governments, rather than serving the people, could design and choose the people that they would manage.[82]

Congress did what it could to advance eugenics in the immigration restriction acts of 1921 and 1924. The federal government and the states both used the new social science "experts" to control what they regarded as inferior races. Their goal was, as progressive economist Richard Ely put it, to keep out "beaten men from beaten races, representing the worst failure in the struggle for existence."[83] The theory was another progressive application of Darwinism to social life, although their heirs would try to cover this up, as after the World Wars they tried to hide their enthusiasm for Prussian and German social policy.[84] Eugenics was a marvelous illustration of the reduction of individual human persons to statistical aggregates. The principal founder of the movement, Francis Galton, was a statistician and coined the term "eugenics" (from the Greek words for "good" and "genes" or ancestry). It was easy to argue that statistical correlation was causation, especially when the targets were socially unpopular groups. Thus, the New York Times dismissed it as "statistical gossip." State courts struck down legislation imposing involuntary sterilization of the "unfit" before the First World War, usually on the constitutional grounds of equal protection or "class legislation." After the war, the campaign was revived, and received the U.S. Supreme Court's approval in the 1927 case of Buck v. Bell.[85]

Carrie Buck provided a tragic illustration of how the bureaucratic state could victimize individuals. The state eugenic "experts" labeled her "a feeble-minded white woman, the daughter of a feeble-minded mother . . . and the mother of an illegitimate feeble-minded child."[86] The Bucks came from "the shiftless, ignorant and worthless class of anti-social whites of the South," and Carrie was "a typical picture of the low-grade moron." In fact, none of the people that Justice Oliver Wendell Holmes famously dismissed as "three generations of imbeciles" actually was feeble-minded. Her relatives committed Carrie to the state institution to cover up the fact that her illegitimate child was the offspring of a rape by a family member. The procedures used to commit her and to review her case were altogether summary. Her lawyer appeared to be more interested in having the Virginia act upheld than in defending his client.[87] State courts had struck down many eugenic laws in the preceding decade, but after Buck they stepped aside. Some 60,000 Americans would be sterilized against their will in the ensuing decades.

The Supreme Court usually is seen as having been taken over by conservatives in the 1920s, with Republican President Warren G. Harding appointing four justices, beginning with William Howard Taft as Chief Justice in 1921. The pre-New Deal Court, however, was quite accommodating to the growth of administrative government.[88] It did strike a blow at the Federal Trade Commission, holding that the cryptic phrase "unfair methods of competition," left undefined by Congress, would be determined by the courts, not the commission.[89] It was unwilling to allow the courts to review administrative decisions such as the Federal

Radio Commission's licensing choices, however.[90] It also upheld the president's power to adjust tariff rates upon the recommendation of the Tariff Commission. "If Congress shall lay down by legislative act an intelligible principle to which the person or body authorized to fix such rates is directed to conform, such legislative action is not a forbidden delegation of legislative power."[91] The "intelligible principle" standard would turn out to be almost impossible to fail to meet, seeming to put an end to the "nondelegation" limit to administrative power.

The Court also accepted state zoning ordinances as it had accepted eugenics.[92] It upheld grants-in-aid against individual taxpayer and state suits. An individual's interest in federal spending, putatively conservative Justice George Sutherland wrote, "is shared with millions of others, [and] is comparatively minute and indeterminate."[93] This meant that there were virtually no limits on the spending power of Congress, and no limits to what it could induce the states to do. It illustrated what economist Mancur Olson would later explain as the advantage of small groups who received concentrated benefits over large and diffuse groups of individuals who contributed small sums to those benefits.[94]

The Taft Court's best-known decision was the Myers case, in which it held that the president's power to remove executive officers was virtually unlimited.[95] The case involved Wilson's removal of a fourth-class postmaster under an act that gave him a four-year term. The Court was sharply divided, but a 6-to-3 majority held that the Constitution and the "Rule of 1789" prohibited congressional abridgement of the removal power. But *Myers* did not clearly address civil-service job protection, or the status of the "independent" agencies such as the ICC and FTC. It would not be the last word on the perennial issue of the removal power.[96]

"Administrative law" came into its own as a field of study in the 1920s, which saw an outpouring of academic literature in its defense, and popular works that attacked it.[97] Progressives who favored administrative government could not quite agree on how to define "administrative law," and especially how they could assure Americans that it need not produce arbitrary and tyrannical bureaucracy. Those influenced more by the continental tradition—particularly Ernst Freund—thought it should focus on the powers that bureaucrats exercised, and that these powers should be spelled out in detail by the legislature. This would give America a *rechtstaat*, or government limited by precise rules. Those who had more regard for the Anglo-American common law tradition—especially Felix Frankfurter—believed that administrators needed to be flexible and pragmatic, and relied on the judiciary to keep them within bounds. Frankfurter's Harvard colleague John Dickinson wrote an influential book in 1927 that hailed America's unique "appellate model" of judicial review of agencies.[98] Progressive legal academics recognized that judges need not be the rivals, but should be the partners—the senior partners—of the burgeoning bureaucrats. This view had the upper hand in the legal academy and would prevail in the long run, giving the United States a distinctly legalistic administrative state.[99]

Conservatives, however, continued to view the whole field of administrative government as illegitimate. The reaction against wartime interventionism helped them to depict progressivism as a threat equivalent to that of the Tudor absolutists in the 17th century, with the new agencies as latter-day Star Chamber courts.[100] The clarion was sounded in Great Britain by Gordon Hewart, the Lord Chief Justice, in his 1929 book, *The New Despotism*. Parliament had enacted laws that allowed ministers to alter the terms of the law. These officials made decisions in particular cases with none of the normal procedural protections of ordinary courts. In the United States, this critique was taken up by James M. Beck, the former solicitor general and now a representative from Pennsylvania. In *Our Wonderland of Bureaucracy* (1932), Beck claimed that the American situation was even worse than that of the British as described by Hewart, and that it was as bureaucratic and socialistic as the Soviet Union. Beck lampooned the Bureau of Home Economics as "Auntie Sam" distributing pamphlets to mothers on how to button boys' pants. He decried the waste of many wartime agencies that had survived the war. The agencies combined legislative, executive, and judicial powers; they both prosecuted and adjudicated. The regular courts refused to review questions of "fact," accepting any flimsy evidence as "substantial," when disputes were almost always matters of fact. The income tax provided the means by which the poorer states could get subsidies from the richer ones. He concluded that the Constitution had been "betrayed not only by the lust for power of the federal bureaucracy, but by the cupidity of the people of the states."[101]

Beck's book and similar works, such as Sterling E. Edmunds' *Federal Octopus* (1933), were at once overwrought and prophetic. In the panic of the Great Depression, it was likely that more rather than less government intervention would come about. Progressive political scientist Charles Beard made "The Case for Bureaucracy" against nay-sayers including Hewart and Beck. Bureaucracy, Beard claimed, "supplies from top to bottom an ideal, which this country needs, the true soldier's ideal—namely, that great deeds may be done without hope of profit."[102] It was "the one great moral stabilizer now operating in American society."[103] Like the First World War, the Depression provided an opportunity for progressives to show what government could do in time of crisis. President Herbert Hoover unavailingly adopted unprecedented programs to meet the economic collapse, but still had too many qualms about fascism and "regimentation" to do as much as progressives wanted. Democratic candidate Franklin D. Roosevelt did not tie himself down with any specific proposals, and his party's platform condemned "useless commissions and offices" and bureaucratic waste under the Hoover administration. But Franklin D. Roosevelt promised a "new deal," a fundamental reorientation of American governance. "The day of enlightened administration has come," he announced on the campaign trail.[104] After several decades of halting growth, the coming decade would witness the establishment of the mature administrative state in America.

CHAPTER 5

The Second Wave: The New Deal Era, 1930–1945

The New Deal marked the second wave of the development of an American bureaucratic state. It built on the progressive intellectual campaign to reconceive the purpose of government, providing a fuller articulation of the state as an entitlement-provider rather than a rights-protector. It established a host of new regulatory agencies (the "alphabet soup" of abbreviations and acronyms, from the AAA through the NIRA to the WPA), most of which empowered bureaucrats to manage and re-distribute economic resources, with special attention given to farmers and workers. In 1937, shortly after his landslide re-election, Franklin Delano Roosevelt (known as "FDR") and his New Deal ran aground due to his crackpot scheme to "pack" the Supreme Court, the labor union mayhem, and a depression within the Depression. This political setback frustrated Roosevelt's efforts to bring the sprawling bureaucracies under centralized White House control. At the same time, his conservative opponents were unable to roll back any of the New Deal, nor to subject it to more tradi-tional rule-of-law controls. American involvement in World War Two opened a new avenue for New Dealers to extend the bureaucratic state. The president, his advisers, and academic enthusiasts envisioned comple-tion of the stalled national welfare state when the war was won. The most that they were able to do, however, was to fend off a conservative reaction similar to that of the 1920s and lock in their earlier achievements.

The New Deal completed the movement begun by the progressives to redefine the purpose of government. The protracted economic depres-sion that began in 1929 gave the Roosevelt administration the opportu-nity to extend much of the bureaucratic system that had been temporarily or incompletely established in the previous three decades, and the Second

World War further entrenched it. The New Dealers proceeded on the theory that the Founders' constitution had been "outgrown," and that America needed a new kind of government—not one that merely *protected* individual natural rights, but one that defined and *provided* rights, or what came to be called "entitlements." Unlike the progressives, however, who often frankly stated their critique of the Founders, the New Dealers more often professed fidelity to the Founders and used their natural-rights language while transubstantiating it. In the 1930s, this advanced progressive program came to be called "liberalism," although it was a fundamental rejection of classical, founding-era and 19th-century classical liberalism, and so is better termed "modern liberalism."

Franklin D. Roosevelt most clearly expressed the new governing philosophy in two speeches, one before the Commonwealth Club in San Francisco during the 1932 campaign, and again in his 1944 State of the Union address to Congress. In 1932, FDR sounded like Woodrow Wilson, claiming that the Founders' definition of rights had been outgrown by modern economic developments. The simple agrarian world in which Jefferson had penned the Declaration of Independence no longer existed. Equality of opportunity was gone, Roosevelt argued, and "we are steering a steady course toward economic oligarchy, if we are not there already." New conditions called for "a reappraisal of values" and "enlightened administration." The old Bill of Rights needed to give way to "an economic declaration of rights, an economic constitutional order." The old right to life must give way to a right to "a comfortable living." Government no longer could be limited to protecting equality of opportunity; it must provide more equal outcomes.[1]

It was essential for the New Dealers that people understood the Great Depression as a "market failure" that required government correction. This was the argument for earlier regulatory interventions, such as the Interstate Commerce Act and the Federal Reserve Act. But many economic historians have interpreted the Depression as the result of inept government policy, particularly by the Federal Reserve Board. The Federal Reserve's inflationary monetary policy (more accurately, anti-deflationary) impeded economic growth in the 1920s. It did not prevent bank failures after 1929, perhaps from the desire to eliminate competition from non-member banks. Republican candidate Herbert Hoover only belatedly called attention to the Fed problem, however, and maintained his belief in the institution. The Federal Reserve would acquire greater power during the New Deal, leading some to observe that, in the federal bureaucracy, nothing succeeds like failure.[2]

Cartels

Roosevelt and Congress continued and expanded many progressive agencies that had been established in the previous three decades. They extended the most important agency of the Hoover years—the Reconstruction Finance Corporation, the original "bailout" program—which made loans to banks and utilities to keep them solvent. They gave the Food and Drug Administration control over cosmetics and strengthened its powers. The Radio Act of 1927 became the Federal Communications Act and moved telephone regulation from the ICC to the new Federal Communications Commission (FCC). The Federal Reserve System became more centralized and powerful under the Banking Act of 1935. Income taxes, already increased during the Hoover administration, rose higher. A vestige of the First World War effort to manufacture nitrates, the Tennessee Valley Authority became the prototype of comprehensive regional "planning," to bring progress to a backward province.

The centerpiece and most original act of the "first New Deal" or the first "hundred days" of the Roosevelt administration was the National Industrial Recovery Act (NIRA).[3] The act invited industry groups to devise "codes of fair competition" that would avoid wasteful or "cutthroat" competition, to stabilize prices, profits, employment, and wages. Such agreements would be exempt from the antitrust laws. Essentially, the NIRA invited businessmen to establish "cartels," or agreements not to compete.[4] Every code had to guarantee collective bargaining for organized labor, so that labor cartels (unions) could balance employer cartels. Employers got around this guarantee by recognizing their own employee representation plans or "company unions." If an industry could not devise an acceptable code, then the president could impose one, and could require that businesses obtain licenses to operate. The act would be enforced by the National Recovery Administration (NRA). The NIRA's farm equivalent—the Agricultural Adjustment Act (AAA)—similarly tried to cartelize American agriculture, getting farmers to agree to limit production to raise prices. If prices did not rise enough, then farmers would receive a subsidy from a tax on farm product processors. States also promoted industrial and agricultural cartels in their "little New Deals."

The NIRA often was likened to Prohibition—impossible to enforce in such a vast and diverse nation without establishing a police state. The sheer number and complexity of American industries was baffling. Codes were written for the Powder Puff Industry, the Academic Costume Industry, the "Industry Engaged in the Smelting and Refining of Secondary

Metals into Brass and Bronze Alloys in Ingot Form," and the "Fluted Cup, Pan Liner, and Lace Paper Industry." The code for the Burlesque Theatrical Industry said,

> By reason of the peculiar nature of this Industry, it is impracticable without further data, to be furnished by the Code Authority, to set the maximum hours for actors and chorus. Therefore, the Code Authority shall investigate the hours of labor, wages, and working conditions of actors and chorus, and . . . shall report thereon to the Administrator.

In due course "Izzy" Hack, the executive secretary of the Burlesque Code Authority, decreed that New York theaters were limited to four strip-tease acts per day.[5]

Organized labor felt cheated by the company-union loophole, which allowed employers to keep out their "independent" unions and substitute bogus management shills. Small businessmen especially complained about "racketeering and bureaucratic imperialism."[6] It seemed that the NRA was trying to insulate larger, established firms from competition from newcomers who offered consumers more for less—"chiselers," the respectable producers called them, as union members called workers willing to work more efficiently "scabs." New Jersey's dry-cleaning code, for example, imposed a price floor of forty cents to press a suit. Jacob Maged was fined and imprisoned for pressing a suit for thirty-five cents. Similarly, Rochester grocer Leo Nebbia was fined for getting around the New York Milk Control Board's minimum-price edict by throwing in a loaf of bread with the mandated eighteen-cent purchase of two quarts of milk.

Recognizing its constitutional vulnerability, the NRA tried to avoid a legal defense of the codes for as long as possible. Upon Roosevelt's inauguration, the U.S. Supreme Court was composed of four reliable conservatives (Sutherland, McReynolds, Butler, and Van Devanter), three reliable liberals (Brandeis, Stone, and Cardozo), and two swing Justices (Chief Justice Hughes and Justice Roberts). The Court's early decisions on New Deal and similar state legislation had been relatively congenial, but became more hostile in 1935. In that term, the Supreme Court struck down section 9(c) of the NIRA, the "hot oil" clause that allowed the president to outlaw the interstate shipment of oil produced in excess of that state's production quota. The object of this regulation was to limit production and raise the price of oil. (Before World War Two, the United States produced twice as much oil as the rest of the world combined. In

World War Two, the United States would provide 7 billion of the 8 billion barrels of oil consumed by the Allies.) The Court returned to the constitutional question of the "delegation" of legislative powers, and for the first time explicitly held that Congress had violated the nondelegation principle.[7]

Section 9(c), the Court held, "does not state whether or in what circumstances or under what conditions" the president could act. "It establishes no criteria to govern the President's course. It does not require any finding by the President as a condition of this action." Congress had declared no policy—it did not lay out any "intelligible principle." The act simply "gives to the President an unlimited authority to determine the policy . . . as he may see fit."[8] Worse still, the code authorities had not published the rule. This made the government appear to be acting, as John Locke had put it, by "extemporaneous decrees" rather than by "known and standing laws."[9] Despite its ideological divisions, the Court decided this case with only one dissent.

The Court unanimously struck down the entire Recovery Act in May 1935, in a case that neatly illustrated the pathology of bureaucracy. The A.L.A. Schechter poultry company—a wholesale butcher shop owned by four brothers—had violated several provisions of the NIRA live-poultry code. In addition to wage and hour violations, the brothers were accused of the "sale to a butcher of an unfit chicken," which made *Schechter* go down in constitutional history as the "sick chicken case." The brothers also violated the code's prohibition on "straight selling," or allowing customers to choose particular chickens. The NRA code required customers to purchase whatever birds happened to occupy a coop or half-coop. "Well, suppose that all the chickens have gone over to one end of the coop?" asked Justice Sutherland in oral argument, which provoked peals of laughter in the courtroom.[10] The goal of the experts who devised the code was to force customers to buy poor chickens along with good chickens, lest the inferior chickens glut the market and depress poultry prices.

Chief Justice Hughes noted that the NIRA in the extent of its regulation and its lack of due process went further than the Federal Trade Commission Act or any other act. "Congress cannot delegate legislative power to the President to exercise an unfettered decision to make whatever laws he thinks may be needed or advisable for the rehabilitation of trade or industry."[11] The NIRA "supplies no standards for any trade, industry, or activity. It does not undertake to prescribe rules of conduct to be applied to particular states of facts determined by appropriate administrative procedure. Instead of prescribing rules of conduct, it authorized the making of codes to prescribe them."[12] The act also exceeded Congress's power to regulate interstate commerce, because the Schechters bought and sold only in Brooklyn. The Court found it unnecessary to consider whether the act also violated the Due Process Clause of the Fifth Amendment. Even Justice Cardozo—the most liberal member of the Court and the sole dissenter in the "hot oil" case—concurred. "This is delegation running riot," he concluded.[13]

In its next term, the Court struck down the Bituminous Coal Conservation Act, a specialized version of the NIRA for the coal industry. The act established a Bituminous Coal Conservation Commission to oversee production, prices, and labor relations in the coal industry. It allowed those operators who produced two-thirds of the coal or employed half of the workers in any district to set production and labor policies. The act attempted to establish a cartel or "bilateral monopoly" between the owners and the United Mine Workers Union, to raise prices and wages—which would ultimately be paid by coal consumers. Political scientist Robert Cushman said that it was "an interesting experiment of industrial self-regulation without precedent in the field of federal control."[14] "The power conferred upon the majority is, in effect, the power to regulate the affairs of an unwilling minority," Justice Sutherland said for the majority. "This is legislative delegation in its most obnoxious form, for it is not even delegation to an official or an official body, presumptively disinterested, but to private persons whose interests may be and often are adverse to the interests of others in the same business." Such reckless delegation amounted to a deprivation of due process of law.[15]

The Court also issued a sharp rebuke to the Securities and Exchange Commission (SEC), which had been established in 1934 to replace the FTC in the administration of the preceding year's Securities Act. The SEC was supposed to protect investors by compelling stock-issuers to provide full and truthful information about their companies. Though the Court sustained the constitutionality of the act itself, it insisted on the rule of law in its administration. J. Edward Jones had notified the SEC of his intent to sell securities. The commission questioned the accuracy of Jones' filing, prohibited the issue, and ordered him to appear before it with records related to the proposed offer. Jones then told the commission that he was withdrawing his proposal, and pleaded that the commission had no more power to investigate him. The Court agreed, holding that "the right to dismiss is unqualified unless the dismissal would legally prejudice the [commission] in some other way than by future litigation of the same kind."[16]

In the Jones case, Justice Sutherland gave an extended statement on the rule of law that horrified advocates of administrative discretion. "To the precise extent that the mere will of an official or an official body is permitted to take the place of allowable official discretion or supplant the standing law as a rule of conduct, the government ceases to be one of laws and becomes an autocracy." He acknowledged that "the increasing complexities of our modern business and political affairs" would produce new agencies such as the SEC, but warned against "encroachments—even petty encroachments—upon the fundamental rights, privileges, and immunities of the people." In this case, the SEC was embarking on "what Mr. Justice Holmes characterized as 'a fishing expedition . . . for the chance that something discreditable might turn up.'" If Jones had violated any laws, the ordinary legal processes of criminal and civil prosecution were open to the government. The Court, however, could not allow administrative discretion that violated constitutional guarantees against self-incrimination and unreasonable searches and seizures. Such methods, Sutherland noted, were "among those intolerable abuses of the Star Chamber."[17] Justice Cardozo, writing for the dissent, warned that Sutherland's interpretation of the SEC Act made "the statute and its sanctions . . . the sport of clever knaves," and predicted that "historians may find hyperbole in the sanguinary simile" of his likening of the commission to the Star Chamber.[18]

SEC Chairman James Landis made a broader argument against the Court. Its decision treated the act like an ordinary law-enforcement statute. It resembled the Federal Trade Commission that it succeeded; its goal was not to root out monopoly *after* it had occurred, but to regulate competition to *prevent* monopoly from arising. Even more, the commission's job was not merely to prosecute or even prevent fraud, but to provide "guidance and supervision of the industry as a whole."[19] Modern administrative agencies needed all the powers of government, not only those of the executive branch, if they were to provide direction and planning for the New Deal State. Critics saw Landis championing the combination of powers that Publius in *Federalist* 47 had called "the very definition of tyranny." Commissioner (and future Supreme Court justice) Abe Fortas added that the agency could not be bound by rules, but required discretion to gain "bargaining power." The administrator "must have sanctions or desired favors which it can trade for changes in practices." The commission might expedite its approval of a proposed issue of securities, for example, in exchange for an agreement by the promoter "to amend its practices in accordance with the administrator's conception of equity and justice." This he regarded as "an earmark of wise and effective administration," one condemned by the Court.[20]

Piecemeal Cartelization

Congress and the president responded to these Court reversals by reenacting the comprehensive legislation of the first hundred days in more detailed and focused form or under new constitutional guises.[21] Farmers continued to receive the subsidies of the first Agricultural Adjustment Act out of general revenues rather than from the tax on processors, and the AAA was repackaged as a "Soil Conservation Act," an Agricultural Marketing Act, and then as a second AAA. The Bituminous Coal Conservation Act had been a similar attempt to devise a special code for that industry. The Motor Carrier Act of 1935 put trucking under the Interstate Commerce Commission, to prevent competition within the trucking industry as well as to relieve railroads from truck competition. Many of these New Deal regulatory agencies would be "captured" by the industries they regulated, which replicated in retail fashion the wholesale design of the NIRA.

The most important attempt to revive the first New Deal in 1935 was the National Labor Relations Act, called the "Wagner Act" for its sponsor, Senator Robert Wagner of New York. Though the "labor relations" title sounded quite expansive, the act really intended only to promote labor unions, or cartels (agreements not to compete) among workers in the labor market as other New Deal legislation had promoted cartels in product markets.[22]

Like many other regulatory statutes, the Wagner Act's rationale was unclear if not contradictory. On the one hand, it claimed that a special system of labor regulation was necessary to ensure the "industrial peace" necessary for the free flow of interstate commerce. On the other hand, the act declared that it was necessary to give workers "full freedom of association or actual liberty of contract"—in other words, that its goal was justice for exploited workers rather than industrial peace. The act's sponsors tried to reconcile these goals by claiming that employers' anti-union tactics caused strikes that impeded interstate commerce: "No justice, no peace," as a later generation would put it. The act outlawed "unfair labor practices" by employers, forbidding them to "interfere with, restrain, or coerce employees in the exercise" of their rights to organize independent unions and bargain collectively. The Wagner Act compelled employers to bargain collectively with whatever organization was chosen by a majority of their employees. It established an independent agency, the National Labor Relations Board (the NLRB or Labor Board), to determine what "unit" would be "appropriate for such purposes" under the act, and to make rules and adjudicate disputes under the act.[23] Labor relations had heretofore been regulated by common law courts and contract principles. The Wagner Act replaced these legal norms with administrative rulemaking and adjudication.

The Court's May 1935 decision in *Schechter* seemed to doom the Wagner Act that was passed a month later. Employers opposed to the bill dropped their effort to prevent Congress from enacting it, now sure that it would not survive a court challenge. The American Bar Association went so far as to advise employers that they could safely ignore the act. Many congressmen voted for the bill on the assumption that the Court would strike it down—thus they could placate organized labor but avoid living with the consequences of the act. Thus, one of the most radical pieces of federal legislation passed the House of Representatives without a recorded vote. Roosevelt had opposed Wagner's bill until *Schechter*. Like many progressives, FDR was suspicious of independent labor unions. He had more of a paternalist, *noblesse oblige* view of government providing for the welfare of workers, rather than letting labor organizations fight for them. He, too, seems to have assumed that the Court would strike it down. Some members of his administration welcomed such an outcome, which would allow him to sharpen the conflict between the popular will and the judiciary and enable him to bring the latter to heel.[24]

Roosevelt won an overwhelming victory in his 1936 reelection, and in February 1937 he boldly asked Congress to allow him to appoint a new Supreme Court Justice for every incumbent justice older than the age of 70 who did not retire. This would expand the size of the Supreme Court to 15 members, and would allow FDR to add six new justices right away. Though Roosevelt claimed that it was the age of the justices that was the problem, it was obvious that he was asking to "pack" the Court with members who would support the New Deal.

Congress, heretofore largely subservient to the president, rose in opposition to the Court-packing plan, about which it had not been consulted. Key Democratic interest groups and the public generally opposed the plan. The Republican minority shrewdly kept quiet and let the Democrats fight among themselves. Roosevelt's attack on one branch of the government had stirred up a fight with another branch of the government. Whatever was the popular animus against a reactionary Court in 1937, it was superseded by a fear that the president had become a potential dictator.[25] Though it was doomed from the outset, Roosevelt kept up the fight into the summer of 1937, squandering the unprecedented majority that he had won the previous November. The political backlash largely ended the New Deal.

In April 1937, the Court suddenly reversed course and surprised nearly everyone by upholding the Wagner Act.[26] Scholars remain divided over whether the liberal and swing justices were responding to the political pressure that Roosevelt had applied, but it certainly appeared that the justices were doing just that.[27]

Many of those who maintain that the Court did not switch in response to political pressure argue that the Wagner Act—and other pieces of "second New Deal" legislation—had been more carefully drafted than the sloppy and reckless NIRA.[28] This is true to some extent, but not enough to explain such a sharp doctrinal shift as that demonstrated by the Labor Board cases. Chief Justice Charles Evans Hughes offered a tortured interpretation of the Court's precedents defining interstate commerce and due process. Although the Court had become more sympathetic to administrative agencies, the Wagner Act appeared to share the nondelegation problem that the Court had identified in 1935 and 1936. The dissenters in the Labor Board cases did not emphasize this point, because they believed that Congress could not itself have exercised the power that it gave to the board. In the Wagner Act, Congress delegated power that Congress itself did not possess.[29] The act's "definitions" of "unfair labor practices" were so vague as to give the Labor Board the power to legislate.[30] The Labor Board also would prosecute and adjudicate, thus completing the bureaucratic trifecta.

The Labor Board, which almost nobody expected to survive, soon became the poster-child of bureaucratic abuse. That employers would complain was to be expected, but the board also aroused opposition within the ranks of organized labor. The American "labor movement" long had been dominated by the "craft" or skilled unions of the American Federation of Labor (AFL). These unions claimed to rely on their economic value, their unique skills, or their strategic place in the industrial system to obtain what they wanted. What they wanted was simply "more"—higher wages, shorter hours, better working conditions. The AFL maintained that all that it asked from the government was to be left alone, and to stop being picked on by the courts especially. This ethos of "privatism" or "voluntarism" was always something of a sham. What the AFL really wanted was privileged exemption to engage in activity that would be illegal for others, to be exempted from the antitrust laws and from court injunctions in particular.[31] The federation got this in the Norris-La Guardia Act of 1932. The AFL was somewhat ambivalent about going further. It wanted the Labor Department, which it considered its own, to administer the Wagner Act, but industrial union partisans insisted on an independent board.[32]

Congress, in section 7(a) of the NIRA, had inspired the unskilled workers in the mass-production industries to demand more than the AFL offered. Led by John L. Lewis's United Mine Workers, insurgent laborers formed a "Committee on Industrial Organization" within the AFL, and in 1937 many unions broke off and formed a rival federation, the Congress of Industrial Organizations (CIO). Many of these unions went beyond the simple wages-and-hours, "bread-and-butter" agenda of the AFL unions; a good number of them were controlled by Communists. The United Auto Workers (UAW) had devised the radical new method of the "sit-down strike," occupying the plants of General Motors in Flint, Michigan. The Labor Board had the all-important power to decide what would be the "appropriate bargaining unit" whom the employer had to recognize. Would workers be represented by the AFL craft unions or the CIO industrial unions? The Labor Board became an ardent advocate of the new CIO industrial unions, and the AFL joined Labor Board critics.

1938: High Noon for the Administrative State

President Roosevelt's attempt to get the Supreme Court under control coincided with his effort to bring the bureaucracy under the White House. On the same day ("Black Monday," as New Dealers called it) that the Court struck down the NIRA, it also held that the president had acted illegally when he fired a member of the Federal Trade Commission, William Humphrey, a Republican whom progressives regarded as a pro-business partisan. The FTC Act limited presidential removals to cases of "inefficiency, neglect of duty, or malfeasance," but Roosevelt had urged Humphrey to resign because he was out of step with administration policy. "I do not feel that your mind and my mind go along together on either the policies or the administering of the Federal Trade Commission," FDR appealed to Humphrey before firing him. The Supreme Court's last word on the subject, in the *Myers* case of 1926, suggested an unlimited presidential removal power. The Court, however, surprised observers by holding that members of the "independent regulatory commissions" could be insulated from removal. Justice Sutherland writing for a unanimous Court held that the postmaster in the *Myers* case was an executive officer, but that FTC commissioners were not. The commission was "neither political nor executive, but predominantly quasi-legislative and quasi-judicial." He observed that the commission "is to be nonpartisan and it must, from the very nature of its duties, act with entire impartiality." It was "called upon to exercise the trained judgment of a body of experts."[33] When Justice Sutherland—the leader of the conservative bloc on the Court—had been in the Senate, he denounced the FTC Act as "utterly void" because it combined legislative, executive, and judicial powers. He now confirmed its special constitutional status in a way that sounded naively progressive.[34] Although the decision was unanimous, it looked to many New Dealers that Sutherland and the conservatives on the Court had designed the opinion to spite the president.

Roosevelt appointed a Committee on Administrative Management to help give central direction to the sprawling bureaucratic apparatus of the New Deal. It was known as the Brownlow Committee after its chairman, Louis Brownlow, a prominent progressive political scientist, who was assisted by Luther Gulick and Charles Merriam, also esteemed progressive academics. The committee report in January 1937 made the case for the "unitary executive," a centralization of presidential control over the bureaucracy. It was especially contemptuous of the independent regulatory commissions that the Court had protected in the *Humphrey* case. Commissions such as the FTC were a "headless fourth branch of government, a haphazard deposit of irresponsible power. They do violence to the basic theory of the American Constitution that there should be three major branches of the government and only three." The diffuse arrangement of agencies impeded the comprehensive planning that modern liberals sought from the federal government.[35]

The Brownlow Report provoked opposition among those with investments in the congressional-agency relationship when it initially was submitted to Congress, but opposition acquired a new intensity after Roosevelt proposed to pack the Supreme Court the next month. His opponents were able to depict the president as a budding dictator, trying to push a compliant Congress to cow the courts and bureaucracy. Particular interest groups also lined up to preserve the relationships that they had formed with the agencies and their congressional partners. The Court fight consumed most of 1937 and was followed by an economic collapse that only added to the administration's woes. Congress finally enacted a very minor reorganization act in 1939.[36]

The Court's decision in *Humphrey* and the failure of the Brownlow Committee meant that, for the foreseeable future, the United States would have a peculiarly bifurcated administrative state. The "fourth branch" was not really independent, but was able to maintain something like independence as the president and Congress fought over it. Congress had the power to create, abolish, and alter the funding of the agencies. Congressional committees could also investigate and exercise "oversight." Conservatives in Congress were already doing so, especially with regard to the Labor Board. Presidents would continue to shape the agencies through appointments, the veto, and other means of influence.[37] It looked like Congress had successfully defeated the unitary executive and substituted a plural executive, intruding itself into the administration of its laws—or the administration of its delegations of legislative power. Conservative critics of the New Deal charged that the legislature and the executive branch had both lost sight of the limited ends and purposes of government under the Constitution, and created an expansive bureaucratic apparatus that neither could direct. The federal government was doing too many things, and could not do them well. Madison hoped that his scheme of the separation of powers would prevent such a state from arising. Once it had arisen, it appeared that the separation of powers either contained it or kept it from working effectively.

While the Brownlow Committee was trying to promote an effective executive-led administrative state, the American Bar Association (ABA) was leading a campaign to rein in the bureaucracy and to subordinate it to the regular law courts. The ABA was dominated by established law firms that opposed the New Deal on ideological grounds and also saw the rise of administrative government as a threat to their practices. There was also an ethno-cultural element to the ABA's position as well, as the Democratic Roosevelt administration had opened opportunities for Catholic and Jewish lawyers who had been excluded from the Ivy League WASP establishment that the ABA represented and served. The old legal regime fought a new political regime that was creating new kinds of legal practice and staffing it with new men.[38]

In 1933, the ABA established a Special Committee on Administrative Law to evaluate the growth of the bureaucratic state. Roscoe Pound became its chairman in 1938. Pound was the dean of the Harvard Law School and probably the most prominent progressive legal academic of his day. He is the father of "sociological jurisprudence," and was critical of the classical natural-law philosophy of the founding era. Natural-law theorists held that judges "discovered" eternal, immutable principles of law and applied them in particular cases. Instead, Pound argued that law grew and changed as society changed, and that judges did and should "make" law to keep up with socioeconomic developments. In his famous essay on "liberty of contract," for example, he argued that early-20th-century judges adhered to an antiquated view of labor relations, one that treated employer and employee as legally equal, blind to the fact that the industrial revolution had created such vast inequalities of bargaining power that rendered formal, legal equality meaningless.[39]

By the 1930s, however, Pound had become a leading critic of the New Deal and administrative law. As early as 1907 he had warned of the rise of what he called "executive justice," or the disposition of cases by particular ad hoc decisions rather than by general rules of law. American legislatures had ceased passing such acts as bills of attainder, divorces, and private bills. "We had achieved in very truth a *rechstat*," he said. But too much reliance on general principles had paralyzed practical administration, and made necessary the agencies' use of flexible—and potentially arbitrary—administrative power to deal with new social and economic problems. Such executive justice, Pound said, "is always an evil," but it was preferable to injustice.[40]

Pound also was alarmed at the rise of "legal realism," a philosophy considerably more radical than his own sociological jurisprudence, promulgated by scholars who claimed to be following in his footsteps. Revolutionary where Pound was evolutionary, the Realists denied that there was any distinction between law and politics at all. Law was either completely arbitrary, or the tool of the dominant classes in society. Pound became increasingly concerned as he saw many Realists take administrative posts in the Roosevelt administration.[41]

Pound was not prepared to follow the progressives' repudiation of the traditional distinction between law and politics that was at the heart of American constitutionalism—the idea that the Constitution represented a "higher law" that could control and limit ordinary politics.[42] They saw the Constitution—especially its structural features like federalism and the separation of powers—as impeding the ability of the government to meet the needs of modern society. In its place they had offered the distinction between politics and administration, which Woodrow Wilson had first articulated in his 1887 essay.[43] By the 1930s, though, most political theorists recognized that the "politics/administration dichotomy" was naïve, to say the least, and that administration was inescapably political.[44] The collapse of the law/politics and the politics/administration dichotomies left nothing but politics. This is what alarmed Pound and other critics in the 1930s.

Pound expressed these misgivings in the ABA Special Committee's 1938 *Report*. It condemned the trend toward "administrative absolutism," which came from theories of unrestrained government power that were becoming prevalent in American law schools. These theories were fundamentally Marxist or at best French or continental but fundamentally opposed to the Anglo-American tradition of the rule of law. They removed government from popular institutions such as legislatures and juries and confided them to unelected elites. "Administrative bureaus and agencies are constantly pressing upon legislatures for increased jurisdiction, and for exemption from review, and in the nature of the case encroach continually on the domain on judicial justice."[45] The biggest problem was the combination of powers in the agencies. Pound repeated an earlier observation by Arthur Vanderbilt (that year's ABA president), that a commission lawyer

> drafts rules and regulations for his commission, directs an investigation, files a complaint in the language of an outraged plaintiff, presents evidence to the commission to support the complaint, writes the opinion of the commission sustaining the complaint of his outraged plaintiff in judicial language adapted to the pertinent decision of the court of last resort, and in event of appeal, moves heaven and earth to prevent a review of the facts.[46]

Nobody, Pound said, advocated a return to 19th-century standards of review, but the growing imbalance of government power and individual rights needed to be redressed.[47]

The ABA report became the basis for a congressional effort to curb the New Deal bureaucracy, the Walter-Logan bill, which Congress passed in December 1940, but was successfully vetoed. Then the war allowed Roosevelt to kick the can of bureaucratic reform down the road, as Congress was preoccupied with war mobilization, creating new bureaus rather than corralling old ones. It was certain to return, however— especially when the war exacerbated the problem. Roosevelt had tried to put off the Walter-Logan effort by commissioning a report on the problem from his attorney general. Divisions within the president's official family caused this committee's report to be delayed until 1941, and the attorney general could not prevent the minority members from appending their view that the majority did not go far enough on the problems of the separation of prosecution and adjudication, the scope of judicial review, and of procedural fairness.[48]

The middle of FDR's second term showed that the New Deal had reached a dead end, having provoked a significant political opposition. At the same time, the reaction was unable to do anything more than stop the progress of the New Deal, not roll it back. The administrative state had taken a long and permanent step forward. One sign of this was SEC Chairman James Landis's Storrs lectures at Yale University, which were published as *The Administrative Process* in 1938. In 1921, New York Court of Appeals Justice Benjamin Cardozo had given the Storrs lectures that became *The Nature of the Judicial Process*, a classic in the emerging movement of Legal Realism.[49] In the lectures Cardozo said that the traditional distinction between law and politics was outmoded. Judge-made law was a fact of life, here to stay, but was nothing to be overly worried about. Landis made a similar argument about administration in 1938. He ridiculed the Brownlow Committee's orthodoxy on the trinity and separation of powers. Bureaucrats needed a maximum of flexibility and discretion if the benefits of administration—expertise, speed, affordability, and all those things that the judicial process lacked—were to be enjoyed. For decades, American progressives had called for "industrial democracy," bringing American political principles into the economic realm. Landis inverted this, saying that we needed to bring the principles of industrial organization, unity rather than separation of powers, into the political realm. Landis boasted that "one of the ablest administrators" that he knew "never read, at least more than casually, the statutes that he translated into reality."[50] Although his own agency had been sharply rebuked by the Court, he saw that the judiciary was becoming increasingly tolerant of bureaucratic power. For all the recent "chorus of abuse and tirade," he said, "the growth of the administrative process shows little sign of being halted. Instead, it still exhibits the vigor that attends lusty youth."[51]

World War Two

The New Deal was a sharp growth spurt in the lusty youth of Landis's administrative state, curtailed by the domestic political reaction of 1938, following Roosevelt's Court-packing blunder, the sit-down strikes, and renewed depression; but the Second World War would provide another. Scholars usually depict the war as the betrayal or derailing of the New Deal, "the end of reform," in historian Alan Brinkley's words.[52] Federal policy moved from a welfare state to a warfare state and, when the war was over, toward a policy that promoted consumer spending rather than public investment. It is true that some New Deal programs were ended, especially make-work ones such as the Works Progress Administration and the Civilian Conservation Corps, because the war ended unemployment. Many important programs were continued, however, and became more powerful during the war.

The Second World War looked much like the First World War in the government's control of the economy. Federal economic regulation already had heartily encouraged large-scale, bureaucratic corporations at the expense of smaller business. As many historians have shown, this is why big business often welcomed federal regulation that would drive their marginal competitors out of the market. The enormous needs of the military required that the government turn to big business. Both the

Wilson administration in the First World War and the Roosevelt administration in the Second World War abandoned their antitrust efforts.[53]
Two-thirds of Second World War contracts went to 100 firms; half went
to 36 firms. General Motors alone absorbed 10 percent of war spending.
The population also became more centralized and urbanized, as millions
of Americans moved from rural areas to urban defense-production
centers.

Like the First World War, the Second World War also strengthened
organized labor, which was in a much stronger prewar position due to
the Wagner Act. The government's policy was that only firms in good
standing with the Labor Board, and who agreed to bargain with unions,
would receive government contracts. This brought even the most dog-
gedly anti-union employers including Henry Ford to heel. The government adopted a "union shop" policy, in which employees were compelled
to join and pay dues to the union that represented them. Union membership grew from 9 million to 15 million during the war.[54] In time, government contracts such as the state grant-in-aid would become an important
means of expanding the power of the federal government.[55]

The war also raised taxes. The income tax became a "mass tax" during the war, with millions more Americans paying it. Only 5 percent of
Americans paid income taxes before Pearl Harbor; 65 percent did by V-J
Day. The government also introduced withholding to make the tax less
noticeable. Heretofore citizens had to pay their annual tax all at once.
Now tax would be deducted from every paycheck, and if too much was
withheld then the taxpayer would be entitled to a refund—often giving
people a feeling that they were getting something *from* the government,
not that they were receiving something that initially had been taken
from them. This was a stroke of bureaucratic genius.[56] The top tax rate
rose to more than 90 percent, and remained there until the 1960s.
Current taxes paid for about half of the war's cost, a far greater proportion than any previous war. World War Two made the income tax—the
engine of the bureaucratic state—unprecedentedly powerful.

In addition to the economic controls used in World War One, the
government imposed rationing and price controls of scarce consumer
goods during World War Two. This was meant to curb inflation and to
equalize the burden of war shortages. The speed limit was reduced to
30 miles per hour to conserve gas and rubber (by some estimates, this
saved more lives than were lost in the war). No automobiles were produced during the war and there was almost no private construction.
Restrictions on nylon—needed to make parachutes—made stockings
almost unattainable. The government prohibited double-breasted suits

and cuffs on pants. These restrictions produced a "black market" and many ingenious schemes to evade the restrictions. Employers, with wage controls making them unable to attract workers by offering more money, began to offer new "fringe benefits" instead. One of the most important of these was health insurance. This wartime adjustment would shape the American health-care system to the present day.

These controls were enforced by the Office of Price Administration, which historian Alan Brinkley has called "the most intrusive federal bureaucracy ever created in America."[57] Its most ambitious members were trying to carry over the economic "planning" or social engineering functions of prewar agencies including the NRA and National Resources Planning Board.[58] It was one of the most heavily staffed of the civilian agencies created during the war (federal civilian employment grew from 1 million to 4 million), with 60,000 officers by 1943. It also enlisted local volunteers to check on prices.[59] Its opponents called it "a kitchen gestapo reminiscent of the block warden policing tactics of Nazi Germany or the Soviet Union."[60] The OPA was the face of bureaucratic government for millions of American civilians.

The armed forces were a more stark exposure to bureaucracy for the 12 million men and women who served in uniform. Americans have remembered World War Two as "the Good War." The attack on Pearl Harbor and the extraordinarily evil nature of the Nazi regime provided many good reasons for that view. There was no significant opposition to the war, something unique in American history. Most Americans regarded the war as something necessary rather than heroic, however—a task that they wanted to complete as soon as possible. They fought the war with stoic endurance, and many veterans maintained a laconic attitude after the war. As years went by, more people began to appreciate the tragic aspects of the war, such as the alliance with the Soviet Union, the internment of the Japanese-Americans, and the strategic bombing campaign that culminated in the nuclear attacks on Hiroshima and Nagasaki. The victory left them at once proud of what their government had accomplished (confidence in government was never greater than at the end of WWII), but also suspicious of it.[61]

The war forced the United States to adopt some of the methods of bureaucratic tyranny, and create an alliance with a communist bureaucratic tyranny, to defeat a fascist bureaucratic tyranny. One can see this ambivalence in the 1946 film, *The Best Years of Our Lives*, and in Joseph Heller's later novel, *Catch-22*, which joined the ranks of anti-bureaucratic literature.[62] Walter Lippmann, a progressive public intellectual who had turned against the New Deal, had warned of this trend in his 1938 book, *The Good Society*. James Burnham, another intellectual who had repudiated his earlier Marxism, argued similarly in his 1941 book, *The Managerial Revolution*. Burnham and other Trotsky followers believed that the Stalinists had betrayed the socialist revolution for the sake of their own bureaucratic power.[63] One could say the same of the American Revolution's repudiation by the progressives. Perhaps the best-known version of the argument that the western democracies were following the totalitarian trend was economist Friedrich A. Hayek, who wrote the surprise best-seller *The Road to Serfdom* in 1944. Liberals responded by likening their critics to fascists. As FDR put it in his "second bill of rights" address, "If history were to repeat itself and we were to return to the so-called 'normalcy' of the 1920s—then it is certain that even though we shall have conquered our enemies on the battlefields abroad, we shall have yielded to the spirit of Fascism here at home."[64]

However Americans felt about the war, it is safe to conclude that most of them did not bring back a favorable view of the army experience—including rank, privileges for officers, discipline, orders, uniforms, red tape—all of which were military versions of traits common to bureaucratic institutions. Certainly almost none of them wanted to make a career of military service. Yet one of the results of World War Two, the strengthening of the Soviet Union and the bipolar Cold War, meant that a generation of Americans could expect to serve in the armed forces as the country adopted conscription from 1948 (just a few months after the wartime draft ended) until 1973. Nearly 6 million American men, or 250,000 annually, were drafted in this period.

The Postwar Administrative State

The New Dealers tried to convince the public that their wartime sacrifices were for the sake of a new social order. President Roosevelt outlined the postwar agenda of modern liberalism in his 1944 State of the Union address which elaborated the ideas that he broached in his 1932 Commonwealth Club address. He explained that rights articulated in the Declaration of Independence and protected by the Constitution, our "rights to life and liberty," had become "inadequate to assure us equality in the pursuit of happiness." Thus, we had come to embrace "a second Bill of Rights" that would provide economic security. Among the new economic rights were the right to a job, the right to adequate farm prices, the right to a decent home, the right to health care, and the right to a good education. The task of the New Deal administrative state was to secure these rights.[65]

Part of Roosevelt's political genius was to use the vocabulary of the Founders while fundamentally transforming the substance of their political philosophy. His new "economic rights" were not rights at all in the Founders' definition of rights—natural rights that existed before governments were formed to protect them. Rather, they were "entitlements" that the government provided. There was a basic difference between a government that protected the *pursuit* of happiness and a government that provided happiness itself. The right to work was fundamentally different from the entitlement to a job—the latter obliged somebody else to employ you. The right to pursue an education was not the same as an entitlement to an education, which required the provision of teachers, buildings, and books. Indeed, the provision of entitlements often requires the curtailing of rights. Roosevelt's obfuscation of the difference between rights and entitlements has been carried on by his successors in their effort to implement his agenda. One of these, law professor Cass Sunstein, advises that "the best response to those who believe that the second bill does not protect rights at all is just this: unembarrassed evasion."[66]

Political scientist Dwight Waldo outlined the vision of the new order in his 1948 book, *The Administrative State*. He described the philosophy and values behind what he called "the heavenly city of the twentieth-century administrators." The last vestiges of religion had disappeared from political thinking. "Planning" had become the new faith. "Once it is realized that there is no natural harmony of nature, no divine or other purpose hidden beneath the flux and chaos of present planlessness, it becomes immoral to let poverty, ignorance, pestilence and war continue if they can be obliterated by a plan."[67] Planning was premised on scientific naturalism or materialism; it viewed human happiness in Epicurean or hedonistic terms. "The Good Life is chiefly a matter of the possession or enjoyment of tangible things," Waldo argued. The administrators' job was to provide as much of these things to as many people as possible. The equal distribution of material goods was "the chief ingredient of their sense of justice." Liberty and democracy had to take a back seat to equality and be curtailed for its sake. The administrative state shared the postmillennialism of the old Social Gospel movement. Public administration expected "to 'engineer' for Heaven an earthly locus."[68]

The Administrative Procedure Act

The postwar Congress returned to the issue of administrative procedure that had been deadlocked by Roosevelt's veto of the Walter-Logan Act in 1940. It enacted the Administrative Procedure Act (APA) of 1946. The act prescribed the steps that agencies had to take in rulemaking and adjudication. It divided these functions into "formal" and "informal" categories, telling agencies when they had to notify affected parties of new rules, allow them to "comment" on them, and how much time was required before the new rules took effect. Although the act did not entirely separate the roles of prosecution and adjudication, it did strengthen the office of "trial examiners" (now "administrative law judges"), increasing their salaries and making them more independent. Section 10 of the act provided for what appeared to be extensive judicial review of agency decisions. Courts could overturn any act that they found "arbitrary, capricious, an abuse of discretion, or otherwise not in accordance with law; contrary to constitutional right, power, privilege, or immunity; in excess of statutory jurisdiction, authority, or limitations, or short of statutory right; without observance of procedure required by law; unsupported by substantial evidence." The court should "review the whole record or such portions thereof as may be cited by any party, and due account shall be taken of the rule of prejudicial error."[69]

The APA is most often seen as an achievement of opponents of the New Deal, a moderated version of the Walter-Logan Act.[70] Despite the triumphal claims of groups such as the American Bar Association, the APA was more of a confirmation of New Deal administrative practice than a reform of it.[71] A Democratic Congress and a Democratic president accepted the APA in 1946 because they wanted to lock in current administrative rules in the increasingly likely event that the Republicans would take control of the electoral branches and start staffing the bureaucracy.[72] Insofar as the APA curtailed bureaucratic discretion, it would secure policies made in the previous decade and hobble Republican appointees' efforts to change them. If the act really augmented judicial review, there were very few federal judges who were not reliable New Dealers. (FDR was the first president to choose lower-court federal judges on ideological grounds.) After more than a decade of conflict, the APA was "a cease-fire armistice agreement that ended the New Deal war on terms favorable to New Deal supporters."[73]

The APA was often called something like "the Bill of Rights for the administrative state," a wonderfully ironic expression. In the 20th century—especially under the post-New Deal Court—the Bill of Rights became the principal means by which judges curtailed the police powers of the states and imposed a national standard of civil liberties. In its first century and a half, however, the Bill of Rights changed very little, and largely was declaratory of the original, unamended Constitution. The APA similarly did almost nothing to alter the path of administrative government. When Congress was serious about curtailing administrative power—as it was with the National Labor Relations Board—it enacted specific statute (e.g., the 1947 Taft-Hartley Act) to do so.

In 1948, Harry S Truman was reelected and the Democrats regained control of Congress. Congress, however, continued to be controlled by a conservative coalition of southern Democrats and Midwestern Republicans that had taken shape in 1937. So, little of Truman's "Fair Deal," let alone Waldo's Heavenly City of the Twentieth-Century Administrators, was achieved. American politics seemed to have settled into a mixed system that political scientists called "interest-group pluralism." Politics was simply the constant competition among various interest groups, with no overall "public interest" standing above it all. The government's job was to provide the arena in which this contest took place, and to ensure that no single group acquired overwhelming power. In the progressives' and New Dealers' view, big business had acquired this position, and they corrected it by measures such as the Wagner Act. The new bureaucratic agencies that the New Deal established were the overseers of this new, more-level playing field.[74] Economist John Kenneth Galbraith described this as a system of "countervailing power."[75] Mid-20th-century political science held that America had transcended the problem of faction that so concerned Madison and the Framers—some even attributed their theory to Madison.[76] Faction no longer was a problem whose effects had to be contained, the problems were now embraced as a positive good. For 20 years after the end of World War Two, the New Deal system of "interest-group liberalism" would settle into place before it met serious challenges from both left and right, and would be superseded by a new wave of statist expansion.

CHAPTER 6

The Third Wave: The Great Society and the New Social Regulation, 1945–1975

The deadlock in American politics between New Deal liberalism and a conservative reaction, noticeable since 1937, endured through the 1950s. The nation neither advanced nor retreated from the welfare state and international commitments that it had made under Franklin D. Roosevelt. Liberals could not enact very much of Truman's Fair Deal; conservatives could not undo much of the New Deal. In the midst of this containment of liberalism, the administrative state that the New Deal had established matured—indeed, it seemed to advance rapidly into senescence.[1] The new system began to demonstrate costly inefficiency and corruption. By the end of the decade a rising chorus sang of a crisis in the American bureaucracy. What followed, however, was a new expansion of the administrative state. This time the movement was led, rather than impeded, by a resurgent judiciary.

Hiatus: The Truman and Eisenhower Years

Truman's surprise reelection in 1948 showed the strength of the New Deal coalition and the political theory of interest-group liberalism. Truman's second term unraveled mostly due to the stalemate of the Korean War. He left office with the lowest public-approval rating of any president, but his presidency also had been weakened by many "corruption" cases associated with the new bureaucratic state. Truman had come to Washington in 1935 as a senator who popularly was regarded as being the tool of the Kansas City Democratic machine run by "boss" Tom Pendergast. Even if exaggerated, there was substance enough to the allegations.[2] In the Senate, however, Truman made his reputation as chairman of the Special Committee to Investigate the Defense Program, exposing waste and corruption in government contracting. The urban machine chieftains insisted that he replace the ideological liberal Henry Wallace as FDR's running mate for his fourth term.

As president, Truman was embarrassed by his personal confidant, General Harry H. Vaughn, who continued to engage in the sort of "constituent service" that he had done while Truman was a legislator. Once his boss became the head of an expansive bureaucratic state, however, Vaughn's activity appeared improper. Symptomatic was the case of James V. Hunt, who established a lucrative business helping those who sought government contracts to "cut through the red tape"—for a fee and 5 percent of the value of the contracts. Others sought to curry favor with federal officials by giving gifts such as deep-freezers and fur coats. Officials of the Reconstruction Finance Corporation took jobs with corporations to whom the RFC had made loans. The Internal Revenue Service became a showcase of patronage and favoritism that resulted in several dismissals and the indictment of a cabinet officer and a high-level member of Truman's staff. As historian Alonzo Hamby notes, although exploited by the Republicans these episodes actually were more of "a natural outgrowth of government-business relations in the 1930s and 1940s carried on by members of both major parties."[3] Eisenhower's chief of staff, Sherman Adams, was forced to resign for similar influence-peddling.[4]

Most of the Truman scandals smacked of old-fashioned political machines such as Boss Tweed's Tammany Hall, Richard Daley's Chicago, or Pendergast's Kansas City. Progressives and New Dealers had long been battling these urban machines, although they often were forced to cooperate with them. Woodrow Wilson and Franklin D. Roosevelt both had made their political names in New Jersey and New York, respectively, as opponents of the machines. A new type of bureaucratic-regulatory manipulation was replacing the old party-patronage system, and the new centralized bureaucratic welfare state slowly was eroding the power of the machines and of the political parties in general. This was the theme of Edwin O'Connor's 1956 novel, *The Last Hurrah*, one of the best-known works of American political fiction. The book described the end of (what most reviewers assumed to be) the Boston Democratic machine of James Michael Curley.[5]

Clark Clifford, one of Truman's advisers, represented the new mode of machine politics—a more sophisticated, professional, and credentialed variety. When the lawyers who had built the New Deal agencies left public office—especially in 1952 when their party was swept out— many established private law firms and recruited clients whom they could help deal with the regulatory agencies that the lawyers had helped create. Clifford and others—including FDR's legislative architect Tommy Corcoran, Interior Undersecretary Abe Fortas, and SEC Chairman James Landis—became the Washington-insider "super lawyers" who anchored a growing body of lobbying activity centered on K Street in Northwest Washington, DC. Clifford became the first Washington attorney to earn more than $1 million, the kind of money previously associated with white-shoe (elitist) Wall Street corporate lawyers. (Clifford had declined Truman's offer of a Supreme Court appointment because it paid only $12,000 per year.) His clients included General Electric, AT&T, Du Pont, and Standard Oil.[6]

There were significant economic costs associated with this byproduct of the New Deal state. Americans had to pay not only the direct costs of big government, but also the costs that the private sector incurred when dealing with the state. Former President Herbert Hoover estimated in the 1950s that more people worked as advisers helping to deal with government than worked for government itself.[7] Economists called these costs "rent-seeking"—the wasteful diversion of resources from the production of goods and services to the seeking of government favors.

The new class of Washington lawyers represented a type of crony capitalism or "clientism," influence-peddling that did not differ fundamentally from James V. Hunt and the "five-percenters."[8] The "revolving door" of government service and lobbying apparently made many participants feel like they were above the laws that they had drafted and interpreted. This was perhaps a predictable result of progressive administrative theory. Old-fashioned laws enforced by judges were supposed to be uniform and universal, but rules made and applied by administrators had to be flexible and malleable. Human nature suggested that the administrators would be especially flexible when applying rules to themselves and their friends. Many of the super lawyers ended their careers mired in scandal. Landis was imprisoned for income-tax evasion in 1963; Fortas was forced to resign from the Supreme Court in 1968 due to revelations of his association with a crooked financier; Clifford was indicted for bank fraud in 1992.

The new mode of New Deal politics did not change much under the Eisenhower administration. Eisenhower accepted the premises of New Deal liberalism; he had entered politics in 1952 to keep the Republican Party out of the hands of those he considered laissez-faire and isolationist reactionaries.[9] As Eisenhower wrote to his brother in 1954,

> Should any political party attempt to abolish social security, unemployment insurance, and eliminate labor laws and farm programs,

you would not hear of that party again in our political history. There is a tiny splinter group, of course, that believes you can do these things. Among them are H. L. Hunt (you possibly know his background), a few other Texas oil millionaires, and an occasional politician or business man from other areas. Their number is negligible and they are stupid.[10]

President Eisenhower believed that the Republican Party had to live with what the New Deal had established, espousing the variety of "Modern Republicanism" as laid out by his speechwriter and Undersecretary of Labor Arthur Larson in his 1956 book, *A Republican Looks at His Party*.[11]

Truman is reported to have pitied Eisenhower for having to make the transition from the military to the presidency, saying, "He'll sit here, and he'll say, 'Do this! Do that!' And nothing will happen. Poor Ike—it won't be a bit like the Army. He'll find it very frustrating."[12] In fact, Eisenhower's military background was an ideal preparation for the modern presidency. His greatness as a general arose not from being a great strategist or tactician, let alone a battlefield leader, but from his organizational and managerial ability. Twentieth-century warfare, total war or "GNP war," was warfare conducted by mass bureaucracies and requiring mobilization of the entire national economy. Eisenhower turned out to be very prepared for the leadership of the post-New Deal State and—as scholars have recognized since the 1980s—was a more engaged and effective president than his contemporaries and early interpreters recognized.[13]

Although there certainly were no significant extensions of the welfare state along the lines of Truman's Fair Deal in the 1950s, the decade did see the tendency for established bureaucracies to grow. The most important of these was Social Security. Social Security began in 1935 as a very limited federal old-age pension system, with the Treasury providing grants to the states for other "welfare" programs, especially the Aid to Dependent Children program. Franklin D. Roosevelt insisted that Social Security be depicted as "social insurance," whose beneficiaries received what they had paid in, and not as a handout or "dole."[14] The economic reality did not matter to him. He told Luther Gulick, a critic of the payroll-tax financing of the system,

> I guess you're right on the economics. But those taxes were never a problem of economics. They are politics all the way through. We put those payroll contributions there so as to give the contributors a legal, moral, and political right to collect their pensions and their

unemployment benefits. With those taxes in there, no damn politician can ever scrap my social security program. Those taxes aren't a matter of economics, they're straight politics.[15]

The bureaucrats of the Social Security Administration (SSA) pushed for its expansion into a fuller welfare program from the outset. They influenced Congress to extend benefits in 1939 to survivors and dependents, even before the first benefits were paid in 1940. No additional taxes (technically "contributions") were exacted to fund the new benefits. The first recipient, Ida Mae Fuller, had paid in $25 and had collected $25,000 over her lifetime. Although this was an extreme case, most early recipients received 10 to 100 times what they contributed. A 64-year-old farmer could contribute to the program for 18 months and then retire on his Social Security benefits. The SSA ignored the actuarial realities of the program, which was possible in the early years when benefits were concentrated on a fortunate few elderly citizens and costs were diffused among millions of younger taxpayers. Real spending on Social Security increased 800% over the decade.[16] In 1956, despite the opposition of the White House, Congress added disability "insurance" to Social Security. This helped turn what had once been a minimally staffed income-transfer office into a major bureaucratic office. By the end of the century, the Social Security Administration's Board of Hearings and Appeals was the largest adjudicative system in the western world.[17]

By mid-decade, it was liberals rather than conservatives who were complaining about the administrative state. It increasingly seemed that the regulatory agencies had lost their drive for reform and had become too comfortable in their relations with regulated industries—indeed, that they had been captured by the industries. The idea of "regulatory capture" was as old as regulation itself; populists had warned that the Interstate Commerce Commission was designed to be dominated by the railroads.

The idea began to attract more scholarly attention in the 1950s, notably with Princeton professor Marver Bernstein's 1955 volume, *Regulating Business by Independent Commission*. Bernstein argued that regulatory agencies have a natural "life cycle," beginning with a zeal for reform but, as they mature, becoming dependent on and sympathetic toward the industries they regulated.[18] Samuel P. Huntington, who would go on to be one of the most important political scientists of the 20th century, described what he called "the marasmus [severe malnutrition] of the Interstate Commerce Commission"—once dominated by shippers, the commission had become a "railroad agency," protecting a declining industry from competition.[19] In labor, agriculture, telecommunications, transportation, and energy, agencies conspired with industries to insulate them from the discipline of the market. Congress was the source of the problem, its members benefiting from these favors. Ever since the New Deal court-packing crisis, the judiciary also was complicit in what one scholar called "an abdication of judicial responsibility" to defend the public interest.[20] Harvard professor Louis L. Jaffe echoed this critique, and noted the ironic fact that liberals, who in the 1930s had castigated the Supreme Court for its activist attack on the New Deal, were thus loath to call upon the courts to reform the bureaucracy.[21] By the end of the decade, law professor Bernard Schwartz claimed that "We have been seeing in our own day a renaissance of administrative justice of the type which prevailed in the common-law world in Tudor and Stuart times."[22] The bureaucratic managers of the New Deal's crony capitalism threatened the rule of law.

Beside this business-as-usual problem there also were cases of gross corruption. The Federal Communications Commission drew fire for protecting established broadcasters from competition, for the deteriorating quality of television, and for the "quiz show" scandals. Congressional investigations revealed that commissioners had had numerous "ex parte" or informal, off-the-record meetings with broadcasters, and had enjoyed their favors in return for licenses and renewals. Several FCC members were forced to resign.[23] Arkansas Senator John McClellan chaired sensational hearings about the prevalence of organized crime in organized labor. The special privileges of unions were practically an invitation to such abuses. Congress responded with the Landrum-Griffin Act of 1959, requiring more public disclosure of the internal financial affairs of unions. Additionally, although the days of wildly violent strikes and lockouts had ended and labor relations were generally peaceful, 1959 did see a nationwide steel strike that was the industry's longest in American history—a sign that the Labor Board had failed to secure "industrial peace."

The regulatory burden of the New Deal certainly contributed to the mediocre performance of the American economy in the 1950s. Regulation insulated the "big unit economy" of the postwar years, dominated by the companies and unions that had grown during the war. Many of these firms had established a "private welfare state" for their employees, with generous health and pension benefits. International Business Machines (IBM) characterized this era—a secure, bureaucratic organization with an implicit guarantee of life tenure, and a dress code (blue or white shirts only). The financial sector also illustrated the regime. It was hemmed in by securities and banking regulations that made finance a sober and conservative industry. There virtually were no bank failures in the 1950s. This was the era of "3–6–3 banking"—bankers borrowed at 3 percent, lent at 6 percent, and were on the golf course by 3 p.m.[24] The big picture would be managed by the experts in the Treasury Department and the Federal Reserve, which could "fine tune" the economy by fiscal and monetary policy to ensure full employment and low inflation.

The economic torpor of the 1950s added to the public sense that the Eisenhower administration had become exhausted. The president's age and ill health contributed to the image. The Soviets' apparent superiority in satellite technology with their launch of Sputnik in 1957 suggested that the United States was falling behind in the Cold War. The Democratic Party made significant gains in the 1958 midterm elections, and its 1960 campaign theme was "get the country moving again."

The Democrats' presidential nominee, John F. Kennedy, was not the ardent liberal that liberal journalists and historians usually depict.[25] He took for granted progressive/modern liberal assumptions about the nature of government, however. He believed that the United States had outgrown its founding political (liberals called it "ideological") principles, and that the country only faced technical, managerial problems. "Every past generation has had to disenthrall itself from an inheritance of truisms," Kennedy said in a 1962 speech, and he lamented that "we hold fast to the clichés of our forebears." He also warned against being "bound by traditional labels and worn-out slogans of an earlier era," and that "our rhetoric has not kept pace with the speed of social and economic change." The ends of government he assumed were those of the New Deal welfare state—Kennedy pointed to postwar Western Europe as a model for America. We need only consider the means or methods of achieving it. These, he said, were practical, technical matters, subtle and complicated problems for experts to solve, "basically an administrative or executive problem."[26]

As president-elect, Kennedy had recruited the dean of American regulators, James Landis, for advice on regulatory reform. Landis had not been reappointed as chairman of the Civil Aeronautics Board by President Truman, a decision that he attributed to the hostility of the airlines that he disciplined. Facing unemployment, Landis had his super-lawyer friend Tommy Corcoran fix things with Joseph Kennedy, who hired Landis to manage "Kennedy Enterprises, the holding company that delivered the profits for the trusts designed to ensure that the children could devote their lives to public service." His new job duties were "never defined." Landis was understandably grateful to the elder Kennedy.[27] He tutored JFK, and was one of the ghostwriters of Kennedy's 1956 book, *Profiles in Courage.*

In his regulatory report, Landis reiterated the progressive shibboleth that bureaucracy was an inevitable product of modernity. "The complexities of our modern society are increasing rather than decreasing," he told the president-elect. "The advent of atomic energy, of telecommunications, of natural gas, of jet aircraft, to cite only a few examples, all call for greater surveillance by the government."[28] Landis argued that the administrative state needed more independence, though he also occasionally sounded as if he had moved closer to the position of unitary-executive advocated by the Brownlow Committee, which he had objected to in 1938. The old concerns of the New Deal era—especially of the combination of powers in agencies—were shown to be exaggerated. The Administrative Procedure Act had only made the bureaucrats less effective. Excessive judicial review had produced "stagnation." The agencies suffered from inadequate funding and unqualified staff, and were vulnerable to legislative and executive as well as industry manipulation. Under the Eisenhower presidency, the Bureau of the Budget was "quietly and unassumingly becoming in essence a Bureau of Administrative Management." Landis called for another round of executive reorganization, concentrating power within the White House's Executive Office of the President, which had been established after the Brownlow Committee's report was released.[29]

The most striking feature of the Landis Report was its avoidance of matters of the ends and purposes of the administrative state. Like Kennedy, he assumed that the political question of the ends and purposes of government had been settled, and that only questions of expert administrative management needed to be considered. Landis sought to "galvanize a moribund sector of national governance into some degree of action," as one law professor observed. "And there, of course, is the rub. What action? For whose benefit? Who will be hurt?" Landis's recommendations were "an ingenious catchall with palliative for perennial problems."[30] The new president did very little on the issue; he was usually preoccupied with foreign rather than domestic affairs, and often made relatively conservative policy choices.[31] When he was assassinated in November 1963, President Kennedy left the country on the verge of its greatest substantive expansion of liberal statism since the New Deal.

The Great Society

It was Lyndon Johnson's dream to complete the New Deal, to complete the agenda of the "economic bill of rights" that FDR had articulated. He was an apt figure to do it, being in many ways the product of the New Deal state. He headed the Texas branch of the National Youth Administration, an educational-employment program of the early New Deal (Congress abolished it, labeling it superfluous during the war). Johnson entered Congress in 1937, defeating a crowded field in the Democratic Party by being the only candidate to endorse Roosevelt's court-packing plan. Johnson made a personal fortune in radio and television, an industry in which political influence with the Federal Communications Commission was extremely valuable. He worked to bring agricultural subsidies to the large farm interests in Texas. The state's oil and aerospace industries also depended on federal spending. One biographer calls him a "highly successful entrepreneur," but this was entrepreneurship of a peculiarly public kind.[32] Johnson had done well for himself by state favors, and sought to do good for others by them.

The most important piece of Great Society legislation might have been the Civil Rights Act of 1964. It is especially notable because the issue of black civil rights affected so many other groups and areas of policy. The so-called "rights revolution" of the 1960s grew out of it, with a great number of other groups—including women, Hispanics, the elderly, the disabled, and homosexuals—adopting the vocabulary and tactics of the movement. It also is notable that the legal and political movement for civil rights was launched by the Supreme Court in the 1954 *Brown* decision. One of the most important developments of the American state in the Great Society era was the revival of judicial power. By the 1970s, the courts had reasserted their primacy over the bureaucracy, and had gone far toward becoming the chief administrative agents of the country.

After avoiding the issue for as long as possible, in June 1963 President Kennedy called on Congress to pass a Civil Rights Act. Lyndon Johnson turned Kennedy's assassination later that year into a public appeal to honor his memory by passing the Civil Rights Act. After the longest debate in the history of Congress, the act was passed on July 2, 1964. The centerpiece of the act, Title II, which used Congress' power to regulate interstate commerce to outlaw segregation in "places of public accommodation"— hotels, restaurants, theaters, and the like—was widely and immediately accepted by white southerners and required little enforcement. Other sections of the act, however, produced a permanent enlargement of the federal administrative state and provoked controversies that continue to this day. The most important of these was Title VII, which outlawed racial and sex discrimination in the labor market.

The act repeatedly proscribed "discrimination based on race," but did not define the term. In this respect, it looked a great deal like the broad delegation of legislative power seen in the Interstate Commerce Act ("just and reasonable rates") and the Federal Trade Commission Act ("unfair methods of competition"). Like those progressive-era acts, it established an "independent commission"—the Equal Employment Opportunity Commission (EEOC)—to enforce Title VII.[33] Many congressmen pointed to the danger in this lack of definition, and warned that it might lead to the imposition of "racial balance" in public schools and the adoption of racial quotas by employers. This is exactly what happened. Bureaucrats in the Department of Health, Education and Welfare (HEW) and in the EEOC adopted the "disparate impact" definition of discrimination. Any device for admitting students to school or choosing employees was considered to be discriminatory if it produced statistically disparate racial outcomes. There was no need for the school or employer to intend to discriminate, nor was there any need for an individual minority-group member to prove that he had been treated differently. All that mattered was the statistical outcome.[34] This transformation from consideration of individual persons to statistical aggregates was perfectly suited to the movement from the rule of law to bureaucracy, for it is the essence of bureaucracy to reduce individuals to statistics. As the great sociologist Max Weber put it, dehumanization is the supreme virtue of bureaucracy.

As historian Hugh Davis Graham concluded, affirmative action was developed through "a closed system of bureaucratic policymaking, one largely devoid not only of public testimony but even of public awareness that policy was being made."[35] Alfred W. Blumrosen, a law professor and consultant to the EEOC, was the man most responsible for the adoption of the disparate impact definition. He explained its adoption by the courts as an illustration of the "law transmission system." Congress set a broad goal, left it to administrators to devise the means of reaching that goal, and courts confirmed them.[36] Another pair of scholars see the Civil Rights Act as a "super statute," something more than an ordinary law, something equivalent to a constitutional amendment that allows room for administrators and judges to make pragmatic adjustments in dealing with complicated problems such as antitrust or antidiscrimination. Such super statutes are necessary because the original Constitution did not provide room for the provision of entitlements and is too difficult to amend formally.[37]

The federal courts not only accepted the bureaucrats' definition of discrimination, but opened up new judicial routes for race-based affirmative action. The Civil Rights Act was one of the first significant applications of the idea of the "private attorney general"—the idea that private lawsuits could help enforce public policy. Ironically, this was largely due to

Republicans in Congress, who expected the antidiscrimination agencies to be "captured" by civil rights organizations, and wanted to give employers the benefits of legal process. They imagined that the new agencies would be like the National Labor Relations Board in the early administration of the Wagner Act. Liberals, conversely, wanted the agencies to have the independence and enforcement power of the NLRB; they still regarded the courts as enemies of vigorous administration. Both sides were haunted by memories of the 1930s.

The president, through the Labor Department, also pursued a policy of affirmative action or racial preference in hiring by government contractors. Every president since World War Two had issued an executive order prohibiting discrimination by employers who did business with the federal government. (About half of the American workforce was employed by a company that conducted business with the federal government.) In 1961, President Kennedy added that contractors should not merely cease discriminating, but also should take "affirmative action" to seek out minority workers. The Johnson administration began to require contractors to adopt specific "goals and timetables" for increasing minority-group representation. The uproar over such "racial quotas" led to a movement in Congress to overturn these Labor Department policies, but President Nixon intervened to keep them going. Court challenges to government-contracting affirmative action also failed.[38]

Title VI of the Civil Rights Act prohibited segregation or discrimination in "any program or activity receiving federal financial aid." In 1972, Congress added sex discrimination to these prohibitions. It marked the beginning of serious strings being attached to federal grants-in-aid to the states.[39] The definition of "any program or activity" also invited administrative imagination. The Office of Civil Rights (OCR) in the Department of Health, Education and Welfare claimed that even if a college did not receive any direct federal aid, if it did not comply with OCR regulations then its students could not use federal financial aid to attend the school. Specifically, the OCR wanted these colleges to adopt race-conscious affirmative-action programs. It insisted on affirmative action even for colleges that had no history of racial discrimination—indeed, for colleges that had adopted nondiscrimination polices decades before most other institutions. In 1984, the Supreme Court accepted the OCR's interpretation of the act, but limited it to particular college programs that did not conform to the OCR rules. In 1987, Congress enacted the "Civil Rights Restoration Act" to overturn this decision; thus an entire college was ineligible for federal funds if any of its programs did not meet OCR regulations.

The Civil Rights Act provided the most dramatic and immediately controversial expansion of federal power in the Great Society. (The Voting Rights Act of 1965 added to this, with the federal government largely taking over the voting process in the southern states.) The Johnson administration also began new programs in health and education that, like Social Security, started small but became larger and more problematic in later years. Medicare, the program of health "insurance" for the elderly, began as a set of amendments to the Social Security Act. Liberals recognized that public opinion would not support a general program of "socialized medicine," so they focused on the elderly, a group they inaccurately identified as being in great danger of impoverishment due to health-care expenses. Medicare initially only provided hospitalization and physician payments for people age 65 and older, and the bill's sponsors engaged in a great deal of cost-concealment and misrepresentation. Part A (hospitalization) was funded by a payroll tax like that of Social Security, and Part B (physician services) was funded by beneficiary premiums. These funding systems gave the impression that these were contributor-funded insurance rather than redistributive "welfare" programs. Once its foot was in the door, however, the program could be expanded into a universal system of government-provided health care. As Medicare architect Wilbur Cohen put it, Medicare was "a small way of starting something big." An HEW official observed that "Those who wanted Medicare wanted something more. The AMA was right. This was to be the entering wedge for a universal plan."[40] As economist Charlotte Twight puts it, "all the familiar lies and misrepresentations honed so well in the passage of the 1935 Social Security Act were trotted out again."[41]

Medicaid began as a traditional grant-in-aid, with the federal government providing matching funds for states that established health insurance for the poor. It was a revival of the grant-in-aid system, which had been the most common means by which the federal government used the states to expand the welfare state. The states had been expanding their own welfare spending to pick up the slack in the period between the end of the New Deal and the start of the Great Society. Between 1948 and 1957, the federal share of non-defense public spending fell from 47 percent to 35 percent, and the states' share rose from 53 percent to 65 percent. State and local welfare spending rose 350 percent between 1960 and 1973. The federal workforce did not grow much after World War Two, but state employment more than tripled between 1950 and 1980.[42] By 1970, nearly one in five American workers worked for a government. Wilbur Cohen of the Department of Health, Education and Welfare also engineered the incremental expansion of health care regulation. One section of the Medicaid Act instructed the secretary to withhold payments unless the "state make a satisfactory showing that it is making efforts in the direction of broadening the scope of the care services made available."[43] The department also made extensive use of "waivers" to encourage states to innovate in such expansion. It was overshadowed by Medicare in 1965, but in time Medicaid would become the largest entitlement program after Social Security.

Federal involvement in health care immediately began to show signs of bureaucratization, especially evident in the alteration of the physician-patient relationship, which grew more impersonal. This was part of a long process by which the provision of health, education, and welfare moved from the family and community to the state and ultimately to the central government. Physicians formerly treated needy patients for a reduced fee, in accord with the view that medicine had important charitable dimensions. With the state paying the bills, providers sharply increased their rates—in Medicare's first year of operation, physician and hospital costs doubled their usual rate of increase. Health-care professionals formerly were not particularly highly paid but derived much compensation in terms of public esteem and gratitude. As the government became more involved, they were better paid monetarily but lost public respect.[44]

Another significant breakthrough of the Great Society was the Elementary and Secondary Education Act of 1965, also a grant-in-aid program. For decades, federal intervention in schooling had been inhibited by segregationist concerns of its racial effects, and by fears that religious schools would receive federal aid. The Civil Rights Act obviated the first problem, and the 1965 act permitted federal aid to needy students rather than to institutions, which would allow assistance to students in religious schools. Still the issue was controversial, and Congress drafted it like it did Medicare, with great secrecy and little debate. The amounts involved were very small (even today only about 11 percent of school spending comes from the federal treasury) but effective. The threat of losing federal aid is what finally got southern schools to desegregate, and congressmen who had opposed federal aid to secondary schools soon became attached to it.[45] It would be more than a decade before the establishment of a Department of Education and before the department began to attach significant strings to the funds. The 1965 act declared that the federal government could not "exercise any direction, supervision, or control over the curriculum, program of instruction, administration, or personnel, or over any instructional materials in any educational institution or school system."[46] Federal intervention would have a similar effect in education as in health care, producing bureaucratic impersonalization, and turning the teaching profession from an under-paid but highly esteemed profession into one that is highly paid but less-appreciated.[47]

The Department of Health, Education and Welfare, however, through its Office of Civil Rights, used Title VI (later amended to apply to discrimination based on sex and handicap) for more than desegregation. It began to press for the integration of school personnel, though the statute expressly did not apply to employment. It prohibited New York City from adopting teacher qualifications that were more stringent than the state's because such standards would screen out minorities. The office retreated from its effort to have homosexuality defined as a "handicap," although it did include drug addiction. The OCR was considered too meddlesome by conservatives and not effective enough by liberals, but its budgets and staffing continued to increase throughout the 1970s.[48]

The Intellectual Assault on Interest-Group Liberalism

Ironically, the greatest ever expansion of the federal bureaucracy took place at a time of cresting intellectual criticism of the New Deal state. In the late 1960s and early 1970s both left- and right-wing scholars lambasted the system of interest-group liberalism.

From the left, Cornell political scientist Theodore Lowi's 1969 book, *The End of Liberalism*, was probably the best-known of these analyses. Lowi described the New Deal state as "the second republic of the United States," succeeding the first, classically liberal or laissez-faire republic. Now both of the political parties had come to accept positive government, but they had no sense of the ends or purposes of positive government, no substantive deliberation about justice. The rule of law had been replaced by unrestrained logrolling. "Interest-group liberalism possesses the mentality of a world [of] universalized ticket-fixing," Lowi argued. The ethos of the new order was "Destroy privilege by universalizing it. Reduce conflict by yielding to it."[49] For many left-wing critics, the cynical political theory of interest-group liberalism prevented full-blown statism. They rejected it together with any system of limited government.[50] Its policies were "basically conservative, co-optive, demoralizing, and contrary to the very best sentiments and goals expressed by the liberals themselves."[51] Left-wing historian Gabriel Kolko made similar arguments about the origins of railroad and other regulation, depicting progressive reform as the "triumph of conservatism."[52]

On the libertarian right, scholars of the "public choice" or "law and economics" movements—associated with the economists of the Universities of Chicago and Virginia—applied economic theory to political behavior to explain the rise of 20th-century big government. They ridiculed the progressive idea that an independent, apolitical bureaucratic class would pursue the "public good." Rather, public individuals and groups behaved just like private individuals and groups. Legislators would promote policies that would maximize their chances of reelection, trading favors for votes. Bureaucrats would seek to maximize their powers and budgets. As Chicago economist George Stigler put it, the common condemnation of the Interstate Commerce Commission for being pro-railroad was "exactly as appropriate as a criticism of the Great Atlantic & Pacific Tea Company for selling groceries, or as a criticism of a politician for currying popular support."[53] Stigler did not hesitate to take on the Securities and Exchange Commission, the beau ideal of administrative statists, alleging that the SEC had "no important effect on the quality of new securities sold to the public," and that "Grave doubts exist whether if account is taken of the costs of regulation, the SEC has saved the purchasers of new issues one dollar." Rather than protecting small investors, the agency protected the "self-regulating cartel" of the New York Stock Exchange.[54] Stigler's colleague, Richard Posner (later a judge of the Sixth Circuit Court of Appeals), echoed this view in his analysis of the Federal Trade Commission. "By concentrating on trivial fraud cases they have created the illusion of tangible results, while minimizing controversy, acquiring litigation experience, and stimulating demand for lawyers experienced in FTC cases." Helping shield businesses from competition garnered political favor.[55] The libertarians (who tended to lean toward anarchism) agreed with the liberals (who were inclined toward socialism) that private groups had turned public power to their own benefit.

The academic critique of the bureaucratic state found a notable popularizer in Ralph Nader. A Harvard Law School graduate, Nader began his career as a "public advocate" by exposing the dangers posed to American drivers by the auto industry in his 1965 book, *Unsafe at Any Speed*. He then exposed General Motors' attempt to discredit him by using private detectives and honey traps (in which seduction is used to extract secrets). Nader attracted a following of young activists, called "Nader's Raiders," who compiled unflattering reports of a host of federal agencies, such as the "Interstate Commerce Omission" on the ICC and "The Chemical Feast" on the Food and Drug Administration. Nader and his followers represented a revival of muckraking journalism and the old progressive and New Deal idea of "public interest" regulation, but infused it with the ethos of the "New Left" and the "New Politics," which rejected the interest-group methods and economic preoccupations.

The New Social Regulation

The new liberalism of the 1960s thus produced a new kind of regulation, the "new social regulation," seen most prominently in the fields of environmental protection, workplace safety, public health, and consumer rights.[56] The new regulation did not cover a single industry, but nationwide, abstract subjects such as "the environment" or "the workplace." It was meant to be the opposite of the focused regulatory agencies that had been captured by those they were supposed to regulate. Rather than the broad delegations of the New Deal–era statutes, the new regulatory legislation included specific mandates that agencies had no choice but to meet—what has been called "command and control" legislation.[57] The old agencies had largely eschewed general rulemaking in favor of ad hoc, case-by-case adjudication. Congress now sought to encourage rulemaking. The new agencies would protect the large, diffuse, unorganized, and relatively powerless parties against the organized and concentrated interests that exploited and duped them. In economic terms, they dealt with "negative externalities" or "neighborhood effects." A single polluter suffered as much as any air-breather or water-drinker by his pollution, but reaped great benefits from the manufacturing process that caused the pollution. An employer did not suffer the consequences of his dangerous workplace; the costs were paid by the hapless worker or by society generally.

The new wave of administrative reform grew out of the "New Left" culture of the 1960s. The new reformers regarded the old, pluralist New Deal system as corrupt, and hoped to make government responsive to the public interest through the participation of ordinary citizens. The old pluralism rejected the idea of a public interest apart from a collection of private interests, and the libertarian critics of regulation also tended to reject the idea of a "public interest." The '60s reformers revived the idea of the public good and "participatory democracy" in a way that evoked the civic life of ancient Greece and Rome. The new liberals, however, like their progressive forebears, had an ambivalent attitude about democracy, and the new social regulation reduced rather than increased popular participation in government.[58] Thus, what superficially appeared to be an expansion of individual rights really was an extension of public obligation upon the individual. Many progressives had promoted free speech not because individuals had a right to express themselves, but because the government would benefit from such expression. Similarly, advocates of "public health" did not defend an individual right (more properly, entitlement) to health care, but a duty on the part of citizens to maintain their health to serve the state. It was a more-benign version of the progressive-era eugenics campaign. Critics pointed to public-health advocates who suggested that people be forbidden to reproduce without a license from the state, and noted that Nazi Germany had launched the first anti-smoking campaign.[59] There was a whiff of totalitarianism in the new liberalism.

The New Social Regulation was the work of a new class that desired to reshape not just the American economy but American society and culture. Progressivism and New Deal liberalism had largely limited themselves to economic stability; 1960s liberalism encompassed a wider range of "lifestyle" issues. Lyndon B. Johnson suggested this when he described the Great Society as a place of mental enrichment and leisure,

> where the city of man serves not only the needs of the body and the demands of commerce but the desire for beauty and the hunger for community. It is a place where man can renew contact with nature. It is a place which honors creation for its own sake and for what it adds to the understanding of the race. It is a place where men are more concerned with the quality of their goals than the quantity of their goods.[60]

The new regulatory class came out of the greatly expanded middle class of postwar America, and especially out of its burgeoning universities. Many had rebelled against the bureaucratization of the mega- or multi-versity, where students were treated as numbers.[61] They similarly protested the Vietnam War, which had been a product of the national-security bureaucracy.[62] (Ironically, the bureaucratic university kept them out of the armed services, the quintessential bureaucratic institutions, where they would be treated as serial numbers.) But many of them would end up leading such bureaucracies after graduating. This new class looked like what Hegel described as the "universal class" that accompanied a genuine state—an enlightened, technically trained cadre of experts who could see the public good above the sordid welter of interest-group politics.[63]

The Courts and the "New Property"

The federal courts were among the most important contributors to the new wave of regulation. Before the New Deal, the judiciary had been the jealous rival of the new bureaucracies. Even after the New Dealers had captured the courts, they did not promote them as instruments in the construction of the new state, and the judges were chary of engaging in liberal activism lest they be accused of imitating their conservative predecessors. Mid-century saw the "era of deference," as the judges let the agencies alone.[64] In the last third of the 20th century, the courts became active collaborators in regulation, the senior partners in the New American State. This was especially true of the Court of Appeals for the District of Columbia, the body that heard most cases involving regulatory agencies and increasingly a "junior Supreme Court." By the late 1960s, Johnson had packed it with liberal activists who had cut their teeth in the idealistic days of the New Deal and were now disillusioned at the torpor of the administrative state.[65] The old judiciary had tried to contain administrative action. The new judiciary tried to promote it, especially when a new generation of lawyers and judges arose who were no longer haunted by the specter of pre-New Deal conservative judicial activism.[66] The old "tax and spend" liberalism had run its course, and social reform would be continued by a new "mandate and sue" system. Federal courts became very close to the congressional subcommittees that oversaw regulatory agencies, transforming the "iron triangles" of committee, agency, and interest group into "iron rectangles."[67] Political scientist Stephen Skowronek described the late-19th-century American polity as a "state of courts and parties."[68] The late-20th-century polity would be a state of courts and agencies.

The Supreme Court had signaled its fundamental jurisprudential shift in 1938, in the little-noted footnote in the little-noted case of *United States v. Carolene Products*. Here the Court suggested that it would no longer give economic rights a high level of scrutiny. Business could take care of itself. Rather, the Court would apply more protection to non-economic rights (religion, free speech, and later reproductive and sexual freedom) and the rights of "discrete and insular minorities." This came to be called the "double standard" or "preferred freedoms" doctrine.[69] The old courts had been the guardians of individual rights; the new courts would guard non-economic rights and also promote the entitlements of the New Deal and Great Society. Environmentalism was an especially preferred freedom or entitlement. The new social regulation ushered in "a new era in administrative law," according to Judge David Bazelon of the District of Columbia Court of Appeals. "We are dealing here not with an airline's fares or a broadcaster's wattage, but all humanity's interest in life, health, and a harmonious relationship with the elements of nature."[70]

In 1964, Yale Law professor Charles Reich wrote an influential essay on "the new property," which fleshed out Franklin D. Roosevelt's "economic bill of rights" address. Government benefits had become a tremendous part of the overall economy. If these benefits were considered privileges that the government could limit or revoke, then non-economic individual rights such as free speech would be endangered. Publicly provided entitlements needed to be elevated to the status of rights. Echoing Dwight Waldo's utopian Administrative State two decades earlier, Reich concluded that "the highly organized, scientifically planned society of the future . . . promises the best life that men have ever known. In the place of the misery and injustice of the past there can be prosperity, leisure, knowledge, and rich opportunity open to all," but only if individuals' rights to government benefits were legally enforceable.[71]

Reich's "new property" argument was an updated version of the old progressive argument that all rights are actually privileges provided by the government. Its optimistic view of the future grew out of a grim, Hobbesian view of the past. This view was rooted in the progressives' rejection of the natural law and social contract theories of the Founders, which held that individual rights preceded the formation of government, and that governments were instituted to protect those antecedent natural rights. In this view, government is always the instrument of the dominant class, and it legitimizes by calling "property" what its class had taken from the weaker classes—thus yesterday's thefts become today's "rights." When those previously dispossessed classes take control of the government, it is only fitting that they exact reparations.[72]

The federal courts turned themselves into administrators of the new welfare state in a number of ways. They recognized a kind of "new property" theory by waiving the traditional distinction between "rights" and "privileges." In 1970, the Supreme Court held that a state had to provide a hearing before it cut off welfare benefits.[73] In a similar vein, Justice William O. Douglas, who had been one of the architects of the New Deal State, insisted that welfare recipients should be able to prevent caseworker visits required by law and continue to receive payments.[74] Although the Court later set limits on these types of new property principles—particularly after new appointments made by President Nixon—it certainly was evident that a new judicial attitude had been put in place. As Judge Bazelon put it in 1971, "we stand on the threshold of a new era in the long and fruitful collaboration of administrative agencies and reviewing courts."[75] But Bazelon still adhered to the old progressive stance of judicial deference to administrative agencies. The courts increasingly adopted the activist view of his colleague on the D.C. Circuit

Court, Harold Leventhal, that courts should take a "hard look" at agency action and not hesitate to compel them to fulfill their missions.[76]

Even before Congress began to write citizen-lawsuits into the New Social Regulation, the Court encouraged the intervention of the judiciary into administration by extending the doctrine of "standing"—extending the types of people who could bring suit. After compelling bureaucrats to be more open to appeals from entitlement recipients, the courts also gave those recipients more access to judicial review if they lost their case before the agency. Finally, the courts and Congress promoted suits by the new public-interest groups by paying the legal fees of their attorneys. As one academic observer noted, the federal courts had compelled the Department of Health, Education and Welfare to enforce the Civil Rights Act, the Department of Housing and Urban Development to remove lead paint from public housing, the Department of the Interior to protect Indians on trading posts, the Federal Housing Administration to comply with local building codes, and the Treasury Department to protect domestic milk producers from competition. "Judges thus began to assume the ultimate protection of the collective social interests which administrative schemes were designed to serve."[77]

A federal appeals court in 1965 granted standing to the Scenic Hudson Preservation Conference to challenge the Federal Power Commission's approval of a plan to build a hydroelectric power plant near Storm King Mountain on the Hudson River. The court recognized the "special interest in aesthetic, conservational, and recreational aspects" of the scenery.[78] In 1973, the Supreme Court accepted the claim of a group called Students Challenging Regulatory Agency Proceedings that it should have standing to challenge an ICC railroad rate increase, arguing that the rate increase would discourage recycling by generating more litter, and thus would diminish the group's enjoyment of the environment. Only Justice Byron White in dissent rejected the claim as being "remote, speculative, and insubstantial."[79]

The revival of judicial activism could be traced to the *Brown* decision, and could be seen as the Court extended *Brown* from desegregation to integration. The federal courts increasingly exercised direct control over schools to compel integration. Soon other state institutions, such as prisons and mental hospitals, came under federal court control after having violated the newly-defined rights of the 1960s. The Court prescribed a new set of procedures that local police forces had to apply in criminal prosecutions. One court provided a detailed code for the administration of a state hospital: no excessive medication, the right to physical exercise, no more than six patients per room, no room smaller than 100 square feet, 10 square feet per inmate in the dining room, 1 toilet for every 8 and 1 shower for every 15 inmates, and a room temperature between 68 and 83 degrees Fahrenheit.[80]

Nixon and the Crisis of the Imperial Presidency

The election of a Republican, Richard Nixon, in 1968 did not turn back the growth of federal power of the 1960s. In many ways Nixon extended Great Society liberalism. Whereas Republicans since Theodore Roosevelt had called for a congressionally centered federal government, Nixon was the first Republican president to embrace fully the progressive and New Deal model of presidential leadership. He was the principal promoter of affirmative action, for example, and the Environmental Protection Agency was his creation. Among the most impressive regulatory efforts of his administration was the Economic Stabilization Act of 1970, which allowed the president to set wages and prices to combat inflation. Such power raised serious constitutional problems earlier in the century even in wartime, yet it was now accepted with hardly any constitutional objection. A federal appellate court upheld it against an old-fashioned nondelegation challenge.[81]

Nixon had no serious objections to the ends and purposes of the liberal state, but he was determined to get the bureaucracy under presidential control. He believed that the career bureaucrats in the agencies opposed him.[82] He complained about the network of interest groups, congressional committees, and bureaucrats (the political scientists' "iron triangles") who regulated the society "regardless of changes in administrations."[83] Nixon revived the effort—undertaken by almost every president since FDR—to centralize the administrative state under presidential control. He set up another panel (the Ash Council) to diagnose the problem and recommend solutions. It followed the "unitary executive" position of the Brownlow Committee. Apart from turning the Bureau of the Budget into a stronger and more centralized Office of Management and Budget and the creation of a Domestic Council, Congress ignored the Ash Council recommendations. Nixon then turned toward unilateral executive reorganization, adopting a view of a "personalized" or "plebiscitary" presidency. He was especially aggressive in using the budgetary power and "impounding," or refusing to spend monies appropriated by Congress for programs that he did not favor. This effort threatened the "iron triangle" interest-group system, and its powerful congressional defenders responded.[84]

President Nixon was forced to resign after the Watergate scandal revelations. The criminal actions of that affair were certainly sufficient cause for his downfall, but they were augmented by many others. Many derived from Nixon's conduct of the Vietnam War and his belief that his domestic enemies composed a national security threat. War, which has provided the most significant occasions for the growth of the administrative state, now helped to preserve it from Nixon's attempt to take control of it. Nixon's personality, a long-hostile media, and his alienation from the Republican Party also contributed. Nixon was accused—with varying degrees of truth—of using agencies including the IRS and the FBI against political enemies, and of favoring political supporters by reining in the antitrust division of the Justice Department.[85] But the central political factor in his ruin appears to have been his challenge to the bureaucratic state.[86]

The illegitimate fourth branch seemed to benefit from the competition of the Constitution's three legitimate branches. The Madisonian structure of the Constitution—with its separation of powers and checks and balances—was designed to prevent the rise of a centralized bureaucratic state. Once that state was established, however, the same structure made it difficult to undo. In the next generation, this would be seen in the limits of the "deregulation" movement and the surge of a fourth wave of bureaucratic expansion.

CHAPTER 7

The Fourth Wave: From Partial Deregulation to Reregulation, 1975–2010

The 20th century ended with a remarkable peacetime rollback of administrative government, but the new millennium ushered in an even more impressive expansion of state power. In the aftermath of Nixon's effort to centralize control of the bureaucracy in the White House, Congress reasserted its influence over the fourth branch, to the point where fears of an "imperial presidency" gave way to those of an "imperial Congress." As the economic woes of the 1970s caused many to focus on the price of regulation, Congress cooperated in an unprecedented campaign to deregulate many of the nation's major industries.

The election of a markedly conservative president in 1980 suggested that the 1970s deregulation movement might turn into a wholesale dismantling of the 20th-century welfare state. The Reagan presidency, however, ended up doing more to strengthen the administrative state than to reduce its power. Reagan did more to make presidential control of the bureaucracy a reality than did all of his predecessors. His political failure to curtail the scale and scope of the administrative state showed how firmly the New Deal and especially Great Society had taken root.

The persistence of the modern liberal regime was seen in the two post-Reagan decades, in which two liberal Republican (Bushes) and a conservative Democratic (Clinton) executives presided over some contractions but more expansions of the welfare state. When the economy collapsed into the greatest depression since 1929, the stage was set for the fourth wave of modern liberalism to take the administrative state to the next level.

Congressional Government Redux

In the aftermath of the Watergate crisis of the "imperial presidency," Congress reasserted its powers in a variety of ways. Its 1973 War Powers Act attempted to impose a "legislative veto" on the power to declare war that it had effectively delegated to the president. The Independent Counsel Act tried to provide for an outside prosecutor to deal with cases where the Constitution's executive-branch law-enforcers were themselves suspected of violating the law. A less-noticed but more important innovation was the Budget Control Act of 1974. The act prohibited the "impoundment" of appropriations that Nixon had imposed, and established a Congressional Budget Office as a legislative counterpart to the White House's Office of Management and Budget. Above all, it adopted "baseline" budgeting, with automatic increases in spending based on inflation and population growth, which helped to lock in earlier bureaucratic expansions.

Congress had blocked Nixon's effort to establish a presidential administration or unitary executive, and in the course of doing so had further intruded itself into administrative affairs. The late 1970s harkened back to the Confederation period when Congress and the state legislatures tried to administer the government themselves. Woodrow Wilson had decried congressional government in the 1880s, and his critique had been carried on by progressive advocates of the centralized bureaucratic state.[1]

In the post-New Deal period, however, this critique was carried on by opponents of "Big Government." Congressmen, via their committees, subcommittees, and staff, did not legislate so much as they oversaw the implementation of either vague or excessively detailed statutes by the administrative agencies. They increasingly relied on the "legislative veto," which allowed executive agencies to make laws but allowed Congress to nullify them. Some acts provided for a veto by one house or both, with or without an opportunity of a presidential veto of the legislative veto.[2] This was, as one scholar put it, "a means by which Congress attempts to correct the maladministration bound to result from bad laws."[3] Through the budget process and committee "oversight" hearings, members of Congress attempted to fix bureaucratic problems for their constituents. Congress had taken on something of the role of "ombudsman" that many European countries had instituted to deal with bureaucratic government.[4] It appeared that an "imperial Congress" had replaced the "imperial presidency."[5] In the 20th century, conservative advocates of the Founders' Constitution usually warned that the president was trying to legislate. Now, like Woodrow Wilson did a century earlier, Congress was trying to execute the law.

Partial Deregulation

The most remarkable development of the late 1970s was the dismantling of major parts of the New Deal economic regulation of large industries—railroads, trucking, airlines, and telecommunications. The social science literature of the period emphasized the entrenched power of the "iron triangles," composed of congressional committees, industry lobbyists, and captured bureaucrats, that guarded these cartels. With benefits concentrated among a small number of interests, and costs diffused among the general population, these private interests were supposed to be all but immune to majoritarian politics. By the end of the decade, however, these industries were opened to competition at the expense of organized and concentrated insider-beneficiaries and to the benefit of diffuse consumer-outsiders.[6]

The economic malaise of the 1970s abetted the deregulation movement. This was the only decade other than the 1930s that Americans left poorer than when the decade began.[7] After World War II, Americans came to accept that Keynesian economists had figured out the business cycle and could provide full employment and stable prices by fiscal and monetary "fine tuning." This view was exploded by "stagflation"—the combination of high unemployment levels, stagnant consumer demand, and inflation. Economists challenging Keynesianism demonstrated that regulation contributed to stagflation. The "monetarists" explained that inept regulation of the money supply by the Federal Reserve was the chief cause of the economic chaos. Regulations acted like taxes (and it was convenient that Congress did not have to vote for them directly). Business could only pay these taxes by raising prices or reducing employment, the latter especially when productivity growth was low or negative. Regulation had long been promoted as a corrective to "market failure." Inflation was so clearly a "government failure," however, that deregulatory ideas gained credibility. Ronald Reagan in 1980 capitalized on this theme that government was the problem, not the solution.[8]

The most impressive aspect of the deregulation movement was the impact of ideas.[9] Academic economists had been decrying the inefficiency of the New Deal regulatory agencies for years, but there was no widespread popular complaint about these industries.[10] Now the public was paying the price of regulation. Organizations such as the Ford Foundation and the Brookings Institution helped fund the effort to translate academic ideas into public policy. Nader's organizations played the role of latter-day muckrakers, providing journalistic exposés of federal promotion of monopoly.[11]

Air transport had been an infant industry in the early 20th century, one that the federal government under Commerce Secretary Herbert Hoover tried to nurture by airmail delivery subsidies. Hoover's program of voluntary association—to manage but not eliminate competition—was made more coercive by the Civil Aeronautics Act of 1938. This act gave the Civil Aeronautics Board (CAB) the power to limit entry and control prices by the standard of "public interest, convenience, and necessity." The CAB granted licenses to approximately zero applicants for the next 40 years. Aviation was like banking—a safe business in which it was almost impossible to make great profits or to fail. The CAB did not allow airlines to compete by offering lower fares, so airlines offered many services to attract passengers. Air travel was a luxury for those who could afford it.[12] Reliable profits permitted the airlines to pay generous wages and benefits to their unionized workers, who comprised another politically influential beneficiary of this cartel system.[13]

Politicians such as Massachusetts Senator Ted Kennedy wanted to pick up on the "consumerism" movement of Ralph Nader, and he followed the counsel of Harvard law professor (now Supreme Court Justice) Stephen Breyer, and held hearings that exposed the abuses of the airline regulatory scheme. Regulated industries were shown to have treated customers callously and to have made illegal campaign contributions to the Nixon administration, a scandal which appeared to prompt the suicide of a CAB enforcement officer. Officials of the Teamsters union, whose members enjoyed premium wages and job security within the regulatory-cartel cocoon, were convicted of attempting to bribe a key senator in their effort to thwart deregulation.[14]

Advocates of deregulation were able to get Congress to act. Statutory reform ensured that deregulation would be permanent, not just the policy of one agency that could be reversed by a subsequent administration.[15] In the railroad industry, statutory reform began with the Railroad Revitalization and Regulatory Reform Act of 1975, strengthened by the Staggers Act of 1980, and led ultimately to the abolition of the Interstate Commerce Commission (replaced by the Surface Transportation Board) in 1996. Congress made airline deregulation permanent by statute in 1978, and the CAB was abolished in 1984. Trucks were deregulated by the Motor Carrier Act of 1980.

The deregulation campaign did shake up the regulated industries. The Interstate Commerce Commission (ICC) had been keeping the number of trucking firms artificially low and the number of railroads artificially high. The competition that deregulation produced caused the number of trucking firms to increase from 17,000 to 28,000 by 1983. The trend toward concentration in railroads led to 90 percent of national traffic being controlled by four systems.[16] In both cases, consumers benefited from the change in industrial structure. The unions in these industries took a significant hit; the unionization rate in trucking fell from 60 percent to 28 percent. (It was said that Ted Kennedy had done more to undermine the corrupt Teamsters Union by deregulation than his brother Robert had by prosecution when he had been attorney general.)

The benefits of deregulation were not undisputed. One analyst complained that "trends toward concentration, pricing and service discrimination, and deterioration of service and safety are now readily apparent."[17] Deregulation advocates, however, disputed the evidence for these claims—many of which were political—as to whether concentration was necessarily bad, and whether lower quality but more readily available service was not desirable.[18] Whether beneficial or harmful, deregulation clearly showed—contrary to progressive theory—that the administrators had been making political choices.

Other industries, such as telecommunications and banking, took longer to deregulate and were not as extensively deregulated, though they were subject to criticism similar to that of the transportation sector.[19] Former FCC chairman and law professor Glen Reynolds in 1978 added a measured and insightful critique of the New Deal regulatory regime. The record of the FCC belied most of the claims that "the administrative process" provided a superior way to deal with modern socioeconomic problems. The commission had been captured by broadcast companies. Its technical justification—that the limited radio wave spectrum required government control to prevent chaos—had been obviated by new media including cable television, but this only led the commission to protect broadcast media from cable competition. Instead of facilitating the development of new technology for the benefit of the public, the FCC thwarted it, providing "the classic example of a watchdog out of control," Robinson observed. (This resembled the ICC as railroad protector, when in 1935 it brought the new trucking competition under its regulatory umbrella rather than freeing railroads from it.) The problem was not just the administrative *process*, he emphasized, but the failure of government to consider the ends or purposes of regulation. "On the basis of experience, it is difficult to be entirely sanguine about the efficacy of regulation," he concluded. "Even where regulation seems grounded on reasonably sound principles, it has a mixed record of performance."[20]

The deregulation of the late 1970s was "partial" in that it did not extend far beyond the old New Deal economic agencies in transportation and their cartel-promoting system of entry controls and rate controls.

Liberals did not want wholesale deregulation that would threaten the new social regulation.[21] As Glen Robinson had observed, though even liberals were now complaining about "big government," they still wanted government to grow. "Big government," he concluded, was "that part of the government you don't like."[22] "Deregulation should be administered with a scalpel, not a scythe," Ralph Nader cautioned.[23] At the same time that the old agencies were curtailed, the "New Social" regulatory agencies flourished and Congress created new Departments of Energy and Education.[24]

Deregulation also was partial in that the deregulated industries continued to operate under a great deal of federal bureaucratic control. The Civil Aeronautics Board was abolished, but many of its regulatory functions were transferred to the Department of Transportation. An airline still answered to the SEC in its financing, to the NLRB (and state labor agencies) in bargaining with its unions, to the FAA on safety standards, to the antitrust division of the Justice Department, to the EPA with regard to its fuel and emissions, to the Labor Department as a government contractor, to the Equal Employment Opportunity Commission (EEOC) as an employer, and to many other agencies. An evaluation of truck deregulation claimed that residual regulations added between 20 percent and 40 percent to transportation costs. State motor carrier controls meant that it cost more to ship jeans from El Paso to Dallas than from Taiwan to Dallas. The ICC regulations made it cost more to ship dog food than livestock feed, peanuts in the shell cost more than shelled peanuts, and railroad ties cut lengthwise cost more than those cut crosswise.[25]

Jimmy Carter had won the presidency in 1976 running as an "outsider," and had overseen the first significant revision of the New Deal bureaucratic state. The election of Ronald Reagan in 1980 was even more of a challenge to administrative government, but the Reagan years would show the power and resilience, if not the legitimacy, that the new American state had acquired.

Reagan and the Limits of Deregulation

In 1980, Ronald Reagan won a landslide victory and Republicans won control of a house of Congress (the Senate) for the first time in 26 years, with an agenda of reducing the size and scope of the federal government in domestic policy, while increasing its commitment to national defense. The Party's platform announced that it "declares war on government overregulation." In his inaugural address, Reagan emphasized that "in this present crisis, government is not the *solution* to our problem; government *is* the problem," and decried the idea "that government by an elite group is superior to government for, by, and of the people." There was no part of the "Reagan Revolution," however, that accomplished less than its deregulatory arm. In many ways Reagan left the administrative state stronger than he found it.

The "war" mentality caused the Reagan team to attempt to run the deregulation campaign from the White House, and this was the principal reason for his failure to curtail the bureaucracy. Reagan, like Nixon (and, to a greater extent than usually seen, Eisenhower), had accepted the "imperial presidency" model historically associated with progressives and New Dealers. His most important steps to control the bureaucracy involved executive orders that required agencies to perform "cost-benefit analyses" of new rules and to clear them with the Office of Management and Budget, particularly its Office of Information and Regulatory Affairs (OIRA, which had been created under Carter by the 1980 Paperwork Reduction Act). He also established a Task Force on Regulatory Relief headed by his vice president, George H. W. Bush.

Though the executive orders exempted the "independent regulatory commissions," this was as close as any president came to fulfilling the "unitary executive" model advocated from presidential commissions from Brownlow to Ash.[26] It did not challenge *what* government did so much as *how* it did it.[27] The Reagan campaign confronted the administrative state principally on grounds of efficiency, not on more fundamental constitutional or libertarian grounds. Ironically, Reagan's efforts to control the administrative state strengthened it.[28] Although the new OMB oversight did make it more difficult to issue rules, it did not affect agencies' ability to impose standards by informal means—the threat of lawsuits especially.[29]

In fact, Reagan did not make deregulation a top priority.[30] The metaphorical war on the bureaucratic state took a backseat to the cold war with the Soviet Empire. Increasing defense spending—like cutting taxes— was less threatening to the established, congressional-bureaucratic-interest group state. Indeed, increased defense spending traditionally had been an important source of that state—what President Eisenhower had called the "military-industrial complex" in his 1961 Farewell Address. War has been the principal engine of centralized bureaucratic state-building throughout human history, and was clearly visible in the growth of American government in the 20th century.[31] War had nurtured the bureaucratic state; now it preserved it from the conservative attack of the 1980s. Reagan's priority was to defeat the Soviets, thus regulatory reform had to wait.[32] Tax cuts also did not threaten the congressional-bureaucratic-interest group *ménage à trois*; both political parties were able to kick down the road the consequences of deficit spending. To some critics, it seemed that Reagan was pursuing a program of regulatory *relief*—immunities for politically favored insiders—rather than thoroughgoing regulatory *reform*, and thus imitated the worst features of the administrative state.[33]

Reagan and his advisers also underestimated the level of popular support for—and corporate accommodation to—the new federal regulation, especially of environmentalism, which showed many signs of becoming a new religious movement.[34] The "new social regulation" agencies had grown rapidly and acquired great influence. By 1980 the EPA had more employees than the ICC, SEC, FTC, and Federal Power Commission combined. It supervised 40,000 sources of air pollution, 68,000 sources of water pollution, 650,000 generators of hazardous waste, 27,000 dumps, 79,000 public water systems, and hundreds of millions of mobile pollution sources. Businesses spent nearly $200 billion a year complying with EPA regulations—nearly 3 percent of the GDP.[35] The conservatives also underestimated the power that the new "public interest" groups had acquired on Capitol Hill—indeed, their attacks strengthened groups including the Sierra Club and the Natural Resources Defense Council, whose apocalyptic interpretation of Reagan policies, abetted by the media, increased fundraising and membership.[36]

Much of the new regulatory system had become accepted and internalized by the business community. Major corporations that already had complied with new regulations did not want relief for their noncompliant competitors. Like railroad owners in the 19th century, some businessmen preferred one federal policy to 50 state regulatory standards.[37] Reagan could easily ("with the stroke of a pen" was the phrase) have abolished affirmative action in government contracting, a system that had been established by earlier executive orders. By 1980, however, big business had come to terms with race-based personnel practices, and preferred an orderly and predictable system of racial quotas to the uncertainty of lawsuits over merit-based hiring, especially after the Supreme Court had insulated them from "reverse discrimination" suits by whites in the 1979 *Weber* case.[38] Nixon had saved affirmative action from congressional reform; the Reagan White House bowed to big business' wish to leave well enough alone.[39]

Many administration agenda-setters were pragmatic businessmen or lawyers who prided themselves on their ability to negotiate and compromise, and believed that they should make government more efficient rather than limit its power.[40] Additionally, the social or cultural conservatives in the Reagan coalition were willing to make use of new federal regulations for their own agendas. Instead of abolishing the Department of Education, they tried to promote "outcome-based education," focusing on results rather than inputs.[41] In the conservatives' view, the National Endowment for the Humanities could be used to fund conservative rather than liberal scholarship and writing. Also, efforts to limit federal spending under earlier entitlement programs could lead to more regulation, as when the administration proposed the first price controls under Medicare.[42]

The administration also relied on budget cuts and personnel changes to alter bureaucratic behavior. "Personnel is policy" is a modern version of Alexander Pope's adage, "for forms of government let fools contest/ that which is best administered is best," which Publius repudiated as a "political heresy" in *Federalist* 68. The Nixon administration likewise had a sense that the chief problem of administrative control was an entrenched corps of ideological opponents in the career civil service.[43] David Stockman warned about the "McGovernite no-growth activists" whom Carter had installed in the new agencies.[44] The career bureaucrats in many agencies offered little resistance to the new political appointees.[45] The administration did win real cuts in the budgets and personnel of the bureaucracy. But the budget and personnel cuts were temporary, and the choice of leaders was decidedly mixed.

A former ICC head called the Reagan appointees to that agency "zealots, evangelicals, and crusaders." They reminded some of the New Dealers, "boys with their hair ablaze."[46] James Watt at the Interior Department and especially Anne Gorsuch Burford as Environmental Protection Administrator were notoriously poor choices.[47] They did not offer an intellectually respectable alternative to liberal environmental, consumer, and health regulations; they appeared openly contemptuous of their agencies, and eager to demoralize and sabotage them. Career bureaucrats responded in kind, leaking embarrassing documents to the press.[48] Liberal interest groups and their congressional and media allies capitalized on Watt's and Burford's numerous gaffes, such as when Watt announced that liberal critics should be impressed that he had put together a coal-leasing panel with "a black, a woman, two Jews, and a cripple."[49] Environmentalists in Congress accused Burford of mishandling the "Superfund" toxic-waste cleanup program to the point of holding her in contempt of Congress. Both appointees resigned in 1983.

Congress again showed that it was capable of defending its prerogatives in the shaping of regulatory policy. In 1984, it ignored the administration's budgetary recommendations and increased funding for the

EPA. The chairman of the House Energy and Commerce Committee required the agencies that it reviewed to provide him with their correspondence with the OMB; another committee chairman considered cutting off OIRA funding.[50] In the midst of these partisan fights, liberal "public interest" groups used these episodes to increase membership and fundraising. Although they hated him, James Watt did the environmentalists more good than harm. He was called "the Fort Knox of the environmental movement."[51] The administration induced the Social Security Administration to enforce tighter controls on the disability program that Congress had enacted in 1980, and benefits were revoked for about one million recipients. Congress responded with new rules that made it easier to get benefits.[52]

Last but not least, the federal courts impeded Reagan's deregulatory efforts. In the 1960s and '70s, the courts had dropped their deferential attitude toward the bureaucrats and adopted the position of senior partner in the administrative state, using liberal judicial activism to prod sluggish agencies to act.[53] This posture comported with the movement of the judiciary from protecting individual rights to assisting in the provision of entitlements.[54] This attitude continued in the 1980s. Initially, the deregulators faced a judiciary that was hostile to their agenda, especially in the DC Circuit Court of Appeals, which heard most cases concerning administrative rules. In 1980, it was dominated by liberals such as J. Skelly Wright, Abner Mikva, and Ruth Bader Ginsburg. The attitude persisted even after Reagan had "packed" the courts with his own appointees. Even conservative judges were reluctant to part with the power that their liberal predecessors had acquired.[55] Ironically, this was in keeping with the Founders' idea that the Constitution would limit government by making ambition in one branch counter ambition in another, and connect the interest of the man to the constitutional rights of his office.[56]

In 1980, the Supreme Court hinted that it might take a more stringent view of congressional and agency power. The Occupational Safety and Health Administration (OSHA) had prohibited any worker exposure to benzene, a carcinogenic chemical. The Court overturned the rule, however, saying that the agency had failed to make a factual determination based on "substantial evidence." The justices were closely divided on the moot question of whether the agency could or must weigh costs and benefits in making such a determination. Justice Rehnquist went so far as to say that Congress could not delegate that power to OSHA. The statute's language, he said, was "completely precatory, admonishing the Secretary to adopt the most protective standard he can, but excusing him from that duty if he cannot."[57] Law professor Antonin Scalia— whom Reagan would appoint to the DC Circuit in 1982 and to the Supreme Court in 1986—was making a similar argument for a revival of the non-delegation principle.[58]

The next year, though, the Benzene case dissenters prevailed and held that Congress did not intend OSHA to weigh costs and benefits when it issued rules restricting worker exposure to cotton dust in textile mills.[59] Two years later, in what one scholar called the Reagan administration's "deregulatory Waterloo," the Court overturned the National Highway Traffic Safety Administration's repeal of its "passive restraint" (automatic seatbelt or airbag) rules for automakers. The Court rejected the administration's argument that deregulation should be held to an easier procedural standard than regulation. The Court found the agency's reversal on passive restraints "arbitrary and capricious."[60]

The Supreme Court further impeded the deregulatory effort. In the 1984 *Chevron* case it adopted a very permissive standard in regulatory review in a case involving a more pro-environmental rule by a post-Burford EPA. Far from scrutinizing unconstitutional delegations, the Court would assume that if Congress had enacted a vague statute, it intended to give the bureaucrats a great deal of legislative power. This position came to be called "*Chevron* deference," and it came to be celebrated by Justice Scalia after he joined the Court. Scalia hoped that this judicial deference would prompt Congress to enact clearer legislation. If it knew that the bureaucrats would get the benefit of the doubt when interpreting vague acts, he surmised, then Congress would draft the acts more carefully. An advocate of judicial self-restraint, Scalia believed that such deference would compel Congress to enact clearer statutes, making the difficult policy choices rather than shunting them onto the bureaucrats. This renewed deferential position was more apparent than real, however, and Scalia lived to see the Court distance itself from and finally repudiate it.[61] The Supreme Court has never found a coherent standard for review of administrative agencies. That is an impossible task in the American constitutional system.[62] Fitting the fourth branch into the three-branch system of the Constitution was like trying to square the circle—or, more accurately, designing a four-sided triangle.

The courts, especially the DC Circuit, also were selectively deferential, indulgent in cases involving the old economic regulation and remaining activist in matters of the new social regulation. The Court would maintain its power to decide when to defer and when not to act, as one scholar describes it, as the "high commission of the administrative state."[63] In 1907, New York Governor Charles Evans Hughes said, "We live under a Constitution, but the Constitution is what the judges say it is."[64] A century later he might have said that the Constitution is what the judges let the administrators say it is. Administrative law started out as a marginal subset of constitutional law, but has come to consume constitutional law.

The limitations of the "Reagan Revolution" were nowhere more apparent than in its deregulation campaign. It reinforces the view that the Reagan administration did not present a challenge to the fundamental premises of 20th-century liberalism, and had more in common with the caretaker role seen in the Eisenhower administration.[65] Above all, the administration's concentration of regulatory oversight in the White House made it possible for later Democratic administrations to increase regulatory power.[66] The Reagan deregulatory failure might have helped provide the legitimacy that many progressives admitted that the regulatory state lacked.[67]

From Bush to Bush

For two decades after Reagan left office, the bureaucratic state that had survived his presidency remained largely intact. There were notable expansions and some contractions of administrative programs in this period of ideological flux and divisions. Between the unusually conservative President Reagan and the unusually liberal President Obama were the two relatively liberal Republican presidents Bush and the relatively conservative Democratic President Clinton. This was also a period of unprecedentedly divided government, with regular turnover in party control of the presidency, the House, and the Senate. The nine election cycles between 1986 and 2002 saw seven of the eight possible permutations, lacking only the combination of a Democratic president and the House with a Republican Senate.

President George H. W. Bush represented the eastern, liberal, "establishment" or "country-club" wing of the Republican Party, and the principal rival to Ronald Reagan in the 1980 campaign. Reagan made him his running mate to unite the party, as Eisenhower had similarly adopted Nixon to placate the Republican right wing.[68] Bush tacitly accepted the liberal view of Reagan as a heartless laissez-faire Social Darwinist when he made "a kinder, gentler America" his campaign theme. Bush attacked his opponent, Michael Dukakis, for his poor environmental record in Massachusetts. Dukakis was running from the "liberal" label and did not make regulation an issue. He did emphasize an old progressive ideal, however, when he claimed that the election was about "competence, not ideology."[69]

Bush oversaw several important extensions of liberal regulatory policy. He signed the Civil Rights Act of 1991, which restored the "disparate impact" definition of racial discrimination established by the EEOC when the Supreme Court began to return to the original intent of the Civil Rights Act of 1964. The Americans with Disabilities Act added another protected class to the labor-force regulatory apparatus. The Clean Air Act amendments were a model of detailed "command and control" congressional direction. But Bush got no credit from liberals, and conservatives denounced him as "the reregulation president." Though he shifted gears in the second half of his term, and announced a moratorium on new regulations in his 1992 State of the Union address, he failed to win reelection.[70]

Bill Clinton defeated Bush as a "New Democrat," having been part of the Democratic Leadership Council, which tried to get the party to shed its liberal image. Once elected, however, he pursued more liberal policies, especially his proposal to nationalize the health-care system (overseen by his wife Hillary). The public response to this, and other policies, produced the first Republican takeover of both houses of Congress in 40 years. The president responded by declaring in his 1995 State of the Union address that "the era of big government is over." In conjunction with Congress he presided over the first-ever curtailment of an entitlement program, Aid to Families with Dependent Children, in the 1996 "welfare reform act." But this reform was really a shell game, shifting recipients from AFDC to the Social Security disability program.[71]

Other deregulation acts actually did not deregulate. The Telecommunications Act of 1996 shifted from protecting monopoly to promoting new companies to enter the industry. This was really another campaign of "regulated competition" of the sort that informed the Federal Trade Commission Act of 1914, designed more to promote small business than to enhance consumer welfare. It was characteristic of the partial deregulation of the 1970s, with both benefits and costly distortions.[72] It produced overinvestment in the telecom sector, and a bubble that burst in 2000.[73] A 1999 banking reform act ended the New Deal–era Glass-Steagall Act's separation of commercial and investment banking, but left finance as the most regulated industry in the country after health care.[74] The welfare-reform act coincided with an explosion of Social Security disability claims—and this was no coincidence, as the states welcomed the opportunity to shift their welfare recipients into a completely federal program.[75] And the "Goals 2000" education act marked the first significant intervention by the federal government into matters of pedagogy and curriculum, trends that would be continued in the next Bush administration.[76]

President George W. Bush combined the executive-centered administrative strategy of Reagan with the more liberal ideological orientation of his father. H. W. Bush's "kinder, gentler America" became G. W. Bush's "compassionate conservatism." Rather than dismantling federal programs, W. tried to open them up to religious organizations in his "faith-based initiative," an effort to show that the welfare state could be used for conservative ends.[77]

George W's belief that a more-liberal Republican Party could be a majority party appeared to be vindicated by the 2002 elections, which put Republicans in control of the presidency and Congress for the first time in 50 years.[78] The administration made no effort to enact legislative alterations to the New Deal/Great Society state that Reagan had been unable to achieve. Congress added to it with the No Child Left Behind education act and the addition of a prescription-drug entitlement to the Medicare program. The budget for regulatory agencies increased by 65 percent in the Bush years, and he won praise from environmentalists and from Law Professor Cass Sunstein, perhaps the leading advocate of the administrative state who would go on to become chief of regulation in the Obama administration.[79] Republican congressmen showed themselves to be as addicted to the entitlement state as the Democrats they had displaced. As one liberal critic wryly observed, they ran for office complaining that Washington was a cesspool; but once they arrived they discovered it was a hot tub.[80]

Even if the Bush administration had had any inclination to reform the bureaucratic state, it probably would have been overwhelmed by national-defense priorities after the September 11 attacks, much as Reagan placed the Cold War ahead of deregulation. Indeed, the administration created the Department of Homeland Security, the most extensive reorganization of the federal bureaucracy since the creation of the Department of Defense in 1952. The new department absorbed the Immigration and Naturalization Service, the Federal Emergency Management Agency, the Coast Guard, and the Secret Service, and encompassed nearly a quarter of a million employees.[81] Congress also passed the Aviation and Transportation Safety Act, creating the Transportation Safety Administration. The intrusive security procedures at American airports brought home to millions of Americans what a bureaucratic state is like, and certainly made the idea of air transport as a "deregulated" industry sound ironic.

Obama and the Fourth Wave of the Administrative State

The 9/11 terror attacks defined the beginning of the Bush administration and probably accounted for its electoral successes in 2002 and 2004.

When the war in Iraq went badly, it cost the Republicans control of Congress in 2006.[82] Finally, the financial crisis of 2008 gave the Democrats control of both Congress and the presidency. This produced the greatest expansion of the administrative state since the Great Society. Most of President Obama's policies had precedents in earlier administrations, however, as much—and often even more—Republican as well as Democratic.[83]

This fourth wave of the administrative state depended in large part on an interpretation—a "narrative"—of the financial crash as the result of "market failure" and deregulation.[84] Democrats claimed that the crisis was the product of Bush-administration deregulation—a charge that honest leftists recognized was a "fairy tale"; but the fairy tale was widely propagated by the media.[85] Journalists and participants still are in the first stages of composing this "first draft of history," but later drafts are more likely to record that the crash was the result of government failure and "partial deregulation" which, as was done so often in the past, were used as a pretext for further regulation, in what journalist M. Stanton Evans calls "the phenomenon of self-generating interventions."[86] As Publius put it, "One legislative interference is but the first link of a long chain of repetitions, every subsequent interference being naturally produced by the effects of the preceding."[87]

It was above all the federal government's effort to increase homeownership that produced the housing "asset bubble" that burst in 2008.[88] Advocates of the administrative state usually lament how far behind Europe the United States has been in building a welfare state, but in housing policy the United States was way ahead. Though federal programs to promote home ownership can be traced to the 1863 Homestead Act and the first (1913) income tax law's provision for the deductibility of mortgage interest payments, it became widespread in the New Deal. Of central importance was the creation of the Federal National Mortgage Association (Fannie Mae) to purchase private-bank mortgages. After 1968, Fannie Mae was an ostensibly private corporation but it enjoyed crucially important public privileges—exemption from state and local taxation, exemption from SEC rules, and a $2 billion line of credit from the U.S. Treasury. These produced the *impression* that its liabilities were guaranteed by the federal government, and allowed it to borrow on better terms than its competitors.[89] Fannie (and its smaller competitor, Freddie Mac, founded in 1970) actually was an immensely profitable corporation that used its profits to pay its officers lavishly, to corrupt Congress, and to avoid serious regulation. Indeed, the entire banking industry, the most thoroughly regulated industry in the country, was a classic illustration of "regulatory capture."[90] The monetary policy of the federal government—the Treasury Department and the Federal Reserve—had caused high inflation that ruined the savings-and-loan industry in the 1980s, after another "partial deregulation." Fannie and Freddie filled the S&L void and dominated the residential mortgage market in the United States.

"Government-sponsored entities" like Fannie Mae were an integral part of the Clinton administration's plan to increase homeownership through the financial and housing regulatory system. Congress told Fannie that 30 percent of its business should be in loans to low- and moderate-income borrowers; this mandate reached 56 percent in 2008. Fannie Mae purchased and guaranteed billions of dollars of "subprime" mortgages, which Wall Street firms bundled into securities and sold to investors. These dubious bonds were given the highest ratings by the only three firms (Moody's, Standard & Poor, and Fitch) which were anointed by the SEC.

The system began to unravel in 2006 with federal interest-rate changes. The following year the "toxic assets" began to be downgraded and subprime companies began to go bankrupt. In March of 2008, the Federal Reserve took extraordinary steps to arrange the takeover of the Bear Stearns investment bank by J. P. Morgan-Chase, which fed the perception that the federal bureaucrats would keep the system going. The collapse became precipitous in September 2008, however, on the eve of the presidential election, when the authorities allowed the bankruptcy of the Lehman Brothers investment bank. The bureaucrats' capricious response added to the panic, as they saved some firms and let others go under. The Federal Reserve and the U.S. Treasury, the agencies least bound by legislative restrictions, pushed the boundaries of established law and engaged in what was called "regulation by deal."[91]

The Treasury and the Federal Reserve implored Congress to provide a fund for further relief or "bailouts." The legislation proposed by Treasury Secretary Paulson was concise (about 3 pages and 850 words) and audacious. It would have given him $700 billion to purchase assets of financial institutions. "The Secretary is authorized to take such actions as the Secretary deems necessary to carry out" the act, and his decisions would be "non-reviewable and committed to agency discretion, and may not be reviewed by any court of law or any administrative agency." When the House of Representatives rejected these pleas it caused further market panic; the House reversed itself and accepted the Troubled Asset Relief Program (TARP), although it provided for judicial review and added 400 pages of benefits for favored constituencies. The TARP Act delegated extraordinary power to the Treasury to decide which assets were "troubled." Indeed, the Treasury did not purchase troubled assets at all, but instead used the TARP money to purchase shares of the big banks. Treasury and bank regulators pressured healthy banks to accept TARP funds that they didn't need so as not to stigmatize those banks that did need them. The Obama administration used TARP funds to bail out General Motors and Chrysler, even though Congress had considered and rejected a program to relieve the ailing auto industry. The auto bailout also circumvented regular bankruptcy law to rescue the United Auto Workers pension funds at the expense of GM and Chrysler bondholders. Most scholars agreed that the auto bailout was beyond the constitutional pale, but it was defended on pragmatic grounds.[92]

The TARP bailout could be excused as a bipartisan, panic-induced, temporary measure. More worrisome were the measures enacted by the 111th Congress elected with Barak Obama in 2008. The most important of these was the "Patient Protection and Affordable Care Act," commonly called "Obamacare" even though the president left its drafting to his congressional allies. Without statutory change, the Reagan administration's White House-led "deregulation" proved ephemeral and even counterproductive. President Obama's reregulation might be more permanent for being congressionally led. The president did not need to concern himself with the details of the act, because any unclear mandates could be massaged by bureaucrats at the U.S. Department of Health and Human Services (HHS) and the IRS, abetted by a Supreme Court full of administrative lawyers.

The ACA was a hodgepodge of special-interest bargains, especially because the congressional Democrats had to enact it without a single Republican vote. It was far from the sweeping, single-payer "socialized medicine" system favored by the Left. It imposed an "individual mandate"—a requirement that every American purchase health insurance.[93] An immense host of health-care interest groups—insurers, hospitals, pharmaceutical companies, unions—swarmed the Capitol, cutting deals with the legislators, knowing that "if you're not at the table, you're on the menu." The health-care industry spent a quarter of a billion dollars lobbying in 2012, more than the banking, insurance, and real estate industries combined.[94]

The ACA invited the states to expand their Medicaid programs by promising to cover almost all of the additional cost, and by threatening to cut off all Medicaid matching funds if a state did not. Mostly it looked like another tremendous delegation of legislative authority to the Department of Health and Human Services and other bureaucracies. It established an "Independent Payments Advisory Board" to control Medicare spending. The board's cuts were to be law unless Congress enacted greater ones. In an audacious effort to control future legislatures, the 111th Congress declared that no law could repeal the board before January 2017, and no changes could take effect until after 2020.[95]

Obamacare was an awesome gambit. Health care represented 15% of the American economy, half of which was already paid for by the federal and state governments directly, and much of the remainder through tax incentives. Like its predecessors, Social Security and Medicare, the ACA looked like a planned partial step toward a full nationalization of health care. It represented a fundamental transformation of the American people's sense of their relationship to their government, a point of no return toward a complete welfare state. It certainly augurs a further step in the relationship between individual patients and their health-care providers. Its cost-containment provisions led opponents to envision "death panels" of bureaucrats who determined who lived and died. Additionally, "public health" theorists did say that the time had come for physicians to regard their principal loyalty to the state rather than to the patient. The movement toward an individual "right" to health care had the potential to turn into a citizen's public obligation to stay healthy. If government could require individuals to purchase health insurance, critics asked, why could it not also compel them to eat their vegetables and exercise?[96] As law professor Philip Hamburger recently observed, for a long time the administrative state has directly affected only big business, but now it will be felt by ordinary Americans.[97]

The other major piece of Obama administration legislation, the Wall Street Reform and Consumer Protection (Dodd-Frank) Act, showed many of the worst pathologies of the modern bureaucratic state. It was a startling illustration of the "phenomenon of self-generating interventions." The Federal Reserve, whose monetary policy had contributed to the 2008 collapse just as it had in 1929, was given even more regulatory power.[98] The act established a Financial Security Oversight Council that can designate institutions as "systemically important" and extend regulation to them. Though the act was intended to preclude future bailouts, it seemed more likely to promote them by designating institutions as "too big to fail." The act's compliance costs, like earlier banking acts, further concentrated the banking system.[99] The act also created the Consumer Financial Protection Bureau, with power to prohibit and punish "abusive" lending practices, a term without any legal definition.[100] The Bureau draws its budget from the Federal Reserve, and is insulated from both presidential control and judicial review.

The fourth wave of modern liberal legislation broke very rapidly, as the Democrats lost control of the House of Representatives in 2010.

President Obama, however, showed that presidential administration could continue with just the Senate, or without Congress at all. "We're not just going to wait for legislation," he said. "I've got a pen and I've got a phone—and I can use that pen to sign executive orders and take executive actions that move the ball forward[101] Obama was prepared to fashion what his Solicitor General, Elena Kagan, whom he would later appoint to the Supreme Court, called "presidential administration."[102] He chose Cass Sunstein, the leading advocate of the administrative state in the legal academy, to head the OIRA—the so-called "czar of regulation."

President Obama adopted many novel methods to make law without Congress. When Republicans held up the appointment of controversial nominees to the National Labor Relations Board, the President decided that Senate adjournments of a few days enabled him to make "recess" appointments without Senate confirmation. (The Supreme Court overturned this interpretation.[103]) The administration also toyed with the idea that section 4 of the Fourteenth Amendment ("The validity of the public debt . . . shall not be questioned") enabled the U.S. Treasury to borrow money without congressional approval. The president, however, decided that this was not "a winning argument." He got the FCC and EPA to issue new rules to regulate the internet and impose "clean energy" rules. Senate majority leader Harry Reid altered Senate rules to allow the president to "pack" the District of Columbia Court of Appeals, the court that would interpret the new regulations.

Perhaps the most notable innovation in the Obama era was the amped-up use of "waivers" to regulate.[104] In the New Deal regulatory system, Congress would delegate broad discretionary powers to bureaucrats. The "new social regulation" of the post–Great Society period more often contained numerous and specific directives to limit agency discretion (the "command and control" model). The administration would then grant exemptions to regulated parties, especially states that implemented federal programs. Sometimes Congress explicitly gives the administration the power to grant waivers, on the theory that if Congress can delegate the power to make law, then it can delegate the power to unmake it.[105]

The use of waivers as a tool of presidential administration could be traced to the Reagan era, but the Obama administration went further, waiving where Congress had not granted permission.[106] The Bush administration's No Child Left Behind Act, for example, imposed standards that states had to meet to receive federal funds. The Obama administration wanted to replace NCLB with its own ("Common Core") educational standards, but Congress refused to enact them.[107] Thus Education Secretary Arne Duncan offered to waive NCLB requirements only if a state adopted the administration's new ones.[108] The implementation of the ACA (Obamacare) compelled the administration to waive many of its requirements the implementation of which would have been politically embarrassing. The administration told states that they did not have to comply with the work requirements of the 1996 welfare reform law. In immigration enforcement, the administration can be said to have waived all of the immigration laws under the guise of "prosecutorial discretion."[109] It acted similarly when it ceased to prosecute low-level offenders against federal drug laws, and refused to defend the Defense of Marriage Act.[110]

Congressional opponents of President Obama's administrative gambits were divided. The ultimate congressional "power of the purse" to cut off funds for the administration was widely perceived to have backfired in 1995 when President Clinton faced down Republicans and vetoed their budgets. (A similar, briefer shutdown came off badly in 2013.) The public held Congress rather than the president responsible, and contributed to Clinton's reelection in 1996. There was a similar response to such confrontations in the Obama years. So Republicans resorted to the courts, challenging the president's novel uses of executive power.

The Supreme Court, however, showed that it was a loyal part of the new administrative state, engaging in some of the most impressive interpretive contortions in its history. The first significant challenge to the ACA, the *Sibelius* case in 2012, was a true *tour de force*. The ACA depended on the "universal mandate," the requirement that everyone purchase health insurance. Failure to have insurance would result in a "regulatory penalty," not a "tax," although it was enforced by the IRS. The act also assumed that the states would expand their Medicare programs because the federal government offered generous matching funds ("teaser rates," the Consumer Financial Protection Bureau might hold) and severe penalties—the cutoff of all Medicaid matching funds—if a state did not. The Court held that the "individual mandate" requirement to purchase health insurance was not valid as an exercise of the commerce power, but that it was a legitimate exercise of the taxing power—despite the fact that the act referred to the mandate's enforcement not as a tax but as a regulatory penalty, and its sponsors repeatedly averred that it was not a tax—even as they made the Internal Revenue Service the enforcer of the mandate. Then the Court held, for the first time, that there were limits on Congress' "spending" power—that it could not tell the states that they must establish insurance "exchanges" or lose all of their federal matching funds.[111]

Consequently, 36 states did not establish state insurance exchanges. Thus the Internal Revenue Service decided that subsides due to people who enrolled in exchanges established "by the states" could get federal subsidies through *federal* exchanges in those states that did not play ball.[112] When this IRS interpretation was brought to the Court, the majority again rescued the ACA, effectively rewriting a law that congressional Democrats were no longer in a position to fix. In this case, the Court continued its postwar "double standard" or "preferred freedoms" jurisprudence, acting vigorously when non-economic or minority rights were concerned (as in the same term's homosexual-marriage decision), while letting Congress regulate economic matters—not only permitting it, but helping it to do so. The Supreme Court—perhaps the most powerful institution in the old constitutional system—has thrown its weight behind the administrative state of the new system.

CONCLUSION

The Way Out

It is a decidedly grim picture that I have painted of the loss of constitutional government and the rise of a bureaucratic state. Some might ask, "What can we do about it?" A historian, however, only can tell us how we got here, not how we get out. If you're lost and ask a historian for directions, expect to hear "I wouldn't start from here." But I will offer here what I think the history that I have presented suggests to other citizens and statesmen who share my desire to restore constitutional government.

The academic is apt to give pride of place to ideas, so let's give first place to the erosion of fidelity to the Founders' constitutional ideas, and the rise of modern, European views of government. It usually is said that their respective fall and rise was the *product* of social and economic change, but that is not necessarily true. In the period of the American Revolution, "things" had been changing since the Glorious Revolution, but the American Founders *returned* to the principles of the Glorious Revolution. Similarly, socioeconomic reality changed between the American Revolution and the Civil War, but Lincoln and the Republicans persuaded the American people to *return* to the principles of the Founding. The late-19th-century progressives chose not to return to our founding principles, but to adopt modern, continental European theories of government. This is not to endorse a Hegelian "germ theory" or to see "a German intellectual under every bed,"[1] but the Prussian-German influence is undeniable. Educating to refamiliarize ourselves with our founding principles will not be enough to get back, but we certainly cannot get back without it.

The central intellectual difference between the Founders and the progressives concerns the question of the purpose of government. The

Founders assumed that governments are formed to protect our natural rights, and thus should be limited or constitutional. Progressives believe that government should provide entitlements, so that they cannot be limited. Unlimited or "big" government is necessarily bureaucratic. Prior to these theories about the nature of government are conflicting theories about the nature of man. The Founders believed man to be limited, imperfect, fallen (the terms most often connected to human nature in the *Federalist* are folly, depravity, wickedness, and the like). Progressives deny that there is any such thing as "human nature" and believe that man and society are perfectible, that we can bring about heaven on earth. At its simplest, the rise of the administrative state can be seen as the byproduct of the declension of Calvinism, the accompaniment of the evolution of liberal Protestantism. Along with an intellectual revival of the Founders' enlightened rationalism, a religious revival would help.

Of nearly equal importance was the translation of foreign or military influences into domestic politics. America was blessed by more than a century of "free security," in which politicians could not easily dress unconstitutional domestic schemes in the guise of national security necessity, or "reasons of state." This began to change with the Spanish-American War and the arguments for American imperialism, received a bigger but temporary boost with World War One, and a much larger and longer one with World War Two and its extenuation by the Cold War. Scholars who claim that America before the progressive era had a hidden or forgotten administrative state almost always use foreign or military affairs as examples—and these are almost all illustrations of the evils of bureaucracy. Bureaucracy might be necessary in war and foreign affairs, but the federal government's dealings with Indians and Chinese alien immigrants should show the danger of turning that foreign necessity into a domestic virtue. At their worst, progressives seem to want to turn us all into Indians and Chinese aliens, to have elite experts with arbitrary power regulate every aspect of our lives. Obviously we can no longer return to the relative isolation and free security of the 19th century, but we ought to give more consideration to domestic constitutional consequences of our foreign-policy choices.

A constitutional revival must begin with the people, and popular government depends on political parties. The progressives knew what they were doing when they replaced the 19th-century party system with an executive-bureaucratic state. It is arguable that since the New Deal the United States has been a one-party state, with no alternative to modern liberalism, only temporary pauses in its advance. In 1940, FDR called for a reorganization of the parties along ideological lines so that we would have a liberal and a conservative party. The Democrats have become a liberal party, but the Republicans have not become a coherent conservative party. We still lack a party committed to dismantling the administrative state and restoring limited, constitutional government.

Reform must begin with—and certainly cannot succeed without—Congress. The Founders intended and expected the legislature—as the branch closest to the people—to be the predominant branch. And it *is*. It is aptly called "the keystone of the Washington establishment," but it is scandalously irresponsible, handing over lawmaking power to the bureaucrats and then interfering in administration for the interests of their constituents. Scholars have discussed the "nondelegation" problem at great length, particularly as a judicial tool to control Congress. But nondelegation—legislative responsibility—must come from Congress itself. It must return to the idea of enumerated powers. It must be made responsible by the discipline of a constitutional party system.

It is especially important for reformers to keep their eye on the *substantive* ball, on the question of *what it is* that the federal government does. Discussion of the problem of the administrative state tends to veer off into arcane *procedural* questions, about abuses in *how* the administrative state acts. One proposal, the Regulations from the Executive in Need of Scrutiny (REINS) Act, would require congressional approval for a significant regulation to become effective. This sounds attractive but would actually make things worse by giving legitimacy to unconstitutional regulation. The real problem is not so much that Congress delegates legislative power, but that it delegates legislative powers that the Constitution does not give it.

The president appears to have gained the most from the rise of the administrative state. This makes sense, because "administration" traditionally was an equivalent term for "executive." The innumerable tasks that the federal government has given to the agencies to perform, however, make the presidency into an office virtually impossible to fulfill. Since the 1980s, the White House has gone a long way toward establishing a "unitary executive," but this has hardly improved the record of the government. Indeed, it contains the potential for tyranny in a well-organized and effective bureaucratic machine in the hands of one man. There is no reason to expect the executive to lead the effort to rein in what is largely the expansion of the executive branch of government. Presidential reform should follow rather than lead legislative reform.

Even more than the president, the federal judiciary has grown in power along with the bureaucracy. This is perhaps the most surprising part of this history, as the courts were the jealous rivals of the new "quasi-judicial" agencies. They found a way to make room for bureaucracy, however, and to reserve for themselves review of their acts through "administrative law." For the most part, especially with regard to economic regulation, the courts defer to the agencies but are able to weigh in on what they consider important questions. It would only aggravate the problem of the "imperial judiciary" to ask the courts to lead the campaign to restrain bureaucracy.

The states also have been abettors of the administrative state, which does much of its work through subsidies to individual states. State politicians should reacquaint themselves with their constitutional responsibilities, and stop sacrificing the constitutional health of the republic for short-term political gain. Here, again, it is incumbent upon citizens of the states to hold their elected delegates responsible.

Finally, some are likely to call for constitutional amendments as the way to fix the problems of the administrative state. The overwhelming majorities required for constitutional amendments (two-thirds of Congress and three-quarters of the states), however, make this daunting and to a large degree unnecessary. By the time that such majorities could be assembled, it would be already possible to deal with the problem politically, by ordinary majorities. What is most needed is for political actors to abide by the terms of the original Constitution.

Ultimately, the people are sovereign, and need to retake control of their government—the principals must hold their agents accountable. As defenders of the administrative state still admit, that state lacks legitimacy. The American people have not consented to it. It has arisen in fits and starts, largely amidst wars and emergencies or deep in the bowels of subcommittee hearing rooms. As Publius noted in the first *Federalist* paper, the American people were the first people in history to be able to establish a government "from reflection and choice," and not to "depend for their political constitutions on accident and force." The people need to reflect and choose—to think and vote—and I hope that this history will help them to do so.

Notes

Preface

1. Charles Kesler, *I Am the Change: Barack Obama and the Crisis of Liberalism* (New York, 2012).

2. Gary Lawson, "Burying the Constitution Under a TARP," *Harvard Journal of Law and Public Policy* 33 (2010), 55–72.

3. David Skolnick, "Lawmakers from Region Rip Obama over Delphi," *Youngstown Vindicator*, July 11, 2012.

4. Its income comes from fees charged to Federal Reserve System member banks.

5. C. Boyden Gray and John Shu, "The Dodd-Frank Wall Street Reform and Consumer Protection Act of 2010: Is It Constitutional?" *Engage* 11 (2010); C. Boyden Gray and Jim R. Purcell, "Why Dodd-Frank Is Unconstitutional," *Wall St. Journal*, June 21, 2012.

6. Eric Zimmermann, "Pelosi to Reporter: 'Are You Serious?'" *The Hill*, Oct. 23, 2009; "Pelosi: People Won't Appreciate Reform Until It Passes," *Politico*, March 9, 2010.

7. Philip Klein, "The Empress of Obamacare," *American Spectator*, June 2010.

8. Ian Simpson, "Personal Trainers Sweat as Washington, DC Readies New Rules," *Business Insider*, September 12, 2015.

9. "Contrary to White House Denials, Emails Show Jonathan Gruber Was 'Integral' to Obamacare," *Forbes*, June 21, 2015.

10. Maeve P. Carey, "Counting Regulations: An Overview of Rulemaking, Types of Federal Regulations, and Pages in the *Federal Register*," Congressional Research Service, July 14, 2015.

11. "Happy New Regulatory Year," *Wall St. Journal*, January 1, 2016.

12. In 2007, yes, Congress passed the Virginia Graeme Baker Pool and Spa Safety Act, "to prevent the tragic and hidden hazard of drain entrapments and eviscerations in pools and spas." Under the law, all public pools and spas must

have drain covers compliant with ANSI/ASME A112.19.8 performance standard—or the successor standard ANSI/APSP-16 2011—installed; and when there is a single main drain other than an unblockable drain, pools and spas must have a second anti-entrapment system installed.

13. Robert A. Rogowsky, "Sub Rosa Regulation: The Iceberg Beneath the Surface," in *Regulation in the Reagan Era: Politics, Bureaucracy and the Public Interest*, ed. Roger E. Meiners and Bruce Yandle (New York, 1989); David McIntosh and William J. Haun, "The Separation of Powers in an Administrative State," in *Liberty's Nemesis: The Unchecked Expansion of the State*, ed. Dean Reuter and John Yoo (New York, 2016), 246.

14. May 3, 2013 Press Conference; Cleta Mitchell, "Scandal at the IRS," in *Liberty's Nemesis*, 255.

15. Gauthan Nagesh and Brody Mullin, "Net Neutrality: White House Thwarted FCC Chief," *Wall St. Journal*, Feb. 4, 2015; Harold Furchgott-Roth, "Executive Interference with a Supposedly Independent Agency: The Federal Communications Commission," in *Liberty's Nemesis*, 117.

16. *Washington Post*, December 14, 2013.

17. Quoted in Daniel R. Ernst, *Tocqueville's Nightmare: The Administrative State Emerges in America, 1900–1940* (Oxford, 2014), 98.

18. Gary Lawson, "The Rise and Rise of the Administrative State," *Harvard Law Review* 107 (1994), 1248. *See also* Joshua D. Wright, "The FTC, Unfair Methods of Competition, and Abuse of Prosecutorial Discretion," in *Liberty's Nemesis*, 357.

19. Theodore J. Lowi, *End of Liberalism: The Second Republic of the United States*, 40th anniversary ed. (New York, 2009).

20. "The Clean Power Plan Is Unconstitutional," *Wall Street Journal*, December 23, 2014, A13.

21. Philip Hamburger, *Is Administrative Law Unlawful?* (Chicago, 2013).

22. James O. Freedman, *Crisis and Legitimacy: The Administrative Process and American Government* (Cambridge, 1978); Cass R. Sunstein, *After the Rights Revolution: Reconceiving the Regulatory State* (Cambridge, 1990).

23. For the "lost history" interpretation, see Jerry L. Mashaw, *Creating the Administrative Constitution: The Lost One Hundred Years of American Administrative Law* (Yale, 2012); William J. Novak, "The Legal Origins of the Modern American State," in *Looking Back at Law's Century*, ed. Austin Sarat, Bryant Garth, and Robert A. Kagan (Cornell, 2002), 273.

24. Mike Konczal, "Hail to the Pencil Pusher," *Boston Review*, September 21, 2015; John A. Rohr, "The Administrative State and Constitutional Principle," in *A Centennial History of the American Administrative State*, ed. Ralph C. Chandler (New York, 1987).

25. See *To Promote the General Welfare: The Case for Big Government*, ed. Steven Conn (Oxford, 2012).

26. These are both fine scholarly works, but are recondite even to scholars.

27. Richard A. Brisbin Jr., *Administrative Law Review* 44 (1992), 107–29.

28. 2 Maccabees 2: 31–33.

29. Ibid.

Chapter 1

1. "Arbitrary Government Described," 1644, in *Life and Letters*, ed. Robert C. Winthrop (Boston, 1869), 445; A. E. Dick Howard, *The Road from Runnymede: Magna Carta and Constitutionalism in America* (Virginia, 1968), 35–48. Nathanael Hawthorne exaggerated this point in *The Scarlet Letter. See* Laura Hanft Korobkin, "The Scarlet Letter of the Law: Hawthorne and Criminal Justice," *Novel* 30 (1997), 193–217.

2. "Dr. Bonham's Case (1610)," in *The Selected Writings and Speeches of Sir Edward Coke*, ed. Steve Sheppard, 3 vols. (Indianapolis, 2003), I: 275.

3. Aristotle, *Politics* IV: 14; M. J. C. Vile, *Constitutionalism and the Separation of Powers*, 2d ed. (Indianapolis, 1998), 16–24.

4. David C. Flatto, "The King and I: The Separation of Powers in Early Hebraic Political Theory," *Yale Journal of Law and the Humanities* 20 (2008), 61.

5. 2 Chron. 19: 11, 26: 19.

6. Mark 12: 17.

7. G. E. Aylmer, *The Struggle for the Constitution: England in the Seventeenth Century* (London, 1963), 44.

8. John Locke, *Second Treatise of Civil Government,* II: 9 (1689).

9. Locke, *Second Treatise of Civil Government,* XIV: 159 (1689).

10. Locke, *Second Treatise of Civil Government,* II: 7 (1689).

11. Locke, *Second Treatise of Civil Government,* II: 12 (1689).

12. Montesquieu, *De l'Espirit des Lois*, XI: 6.

13. William Blackstone, *Commentaries* I: 149, 259 (1975).

14. Donald S. Lutz, "The Relative Importance of European Writers on Late Eighteenth Century American Political Thought," *American Political Science Review* 189 (1984), 189–97.

15. Pauline Maier, "The Origins and Influence of Early American Local Self-Government," in *Dilemmas of Scale in America's Federal Democracy*, ed. Martha Derthick (Cambridge, 1999).

16. Lois Green Carr, "The Foundations of Social Order: Local Government in Colonial Maryland," in *Town and County: Essays on the Structure of Local Government in the American Colonies*, ed. Bruce C. Daniels (Wesleyan, 1978), 74. *See also* Ann Woolhandler, "Judicial Review of Administrative Action—A Revisionist History," *Administrative Law Review* 43 (1991), 197.

17. Edward L. Metzler, "The Growth and Development of Administrative Law," *Marquette Law Review* 19 (1935), 209.

18. See the classic treatment by A. V. Dicey, *Introduction to the Study of the Law of the Constitution* (Indianapolis, 1982 [1885]), 110; Frank J. Goodnow, *The Principles of the Administrative Law of the United States* (New York, 1905), 396; Michael Les Benedict, "Law and Regulation in the Gilded Age and

Progressive Era," in *Law as Culture and Culture as Law: Essays in Honor of John Philip Reid* (Wisconsin, 2000), 241.

19. Albert Alschuler and Andrew D. Deiss, "A Brief History of the Criminal Jury in the United States," *University of Chicago Law Review* 61 (1994), 925; Edwin C. Surrency, "The Courts in the American Colonies," *American Journal of Legal History* 11 (1967), 253–76; Hendrik Hartog, "The Public Law of a County Court: Judicial Government in Eighteenth Century Massachusetts," *American Journal of Legal History* 20 (1976), 282–329; Stanley Katz, "The Politics of Law in Colonial America: Controversies over Chancery Courts and Equity Law in the Eighteenth Century," *Perspectives in American History* 5 (1971), 485–518.

20. Michael Nelson, "A Short, Ironic History of American Bureaucracy," *Journal of Politics* 44 (1982), 750.

21. James A. Henretta, "Magistrates, Common Law Lawyers, and Legislators: The Three Legal Systems of British America," in *The Cambridge History of Law in America*, 3 vols. (Cambridge, 2006), I: 578.

22. Gordon S. Wood, *The Radicalism of the American Revolution* (New York, 1992), 276.

23. John Phillip Reid, *Constitutional History of the American Revolution: The Authority of Rights* (Wisconsin, 1986), 181.

24. M. J. C. Vile, *Constitutionalism and the Separation of Powers* 2d ed. (Indianapolis, 1986), 120.

25. George Anastaplo, "The Declaration of Independence," *St. Louis University Law Journal* 9 (1965), 390.

26. Wesley F. Craven, *Colonies in Transition, 1660–1713* (New York, 1968), 284.

27. Wood, *The Creation of the American Republic, 1776–1789* (North Carolina, 1969), 118, 428.

28. George Washington Letter to Alexander Hamilton, September 1, 1796.

29. Charles Royster, *A Revolutionary People at War: The Continental Army and American Character, 1775–1783* (North Carolina, 1980); Richard B. Morris, *Forging the Union, 1781–1789* (New York, 1987), 53.

30. Jack N. Rakove, *The Beginnings of National Politics: An Interpretive History of the Continental Congress* (New York, 1979), 175, 383.

31. John Adams Wettergreen, "Bureaucratizing the American Government," in *The Imperial Congress: Crisis in the Separation of Powers*, ed. Gordon S. Jones and John A. Marini (New York, 1988); "Constitutional Problems of American Bureaucracy, Beginning with *INS v. Chada*," *Political Communication* 9 (1992), 93–110; "The Regulatory Revolution and the New Bureaucratic State," Heritage Lecture 153 (1988).

32. Jennings B. Sanders, *Evolution of the Executive Departments of the Continental Congress, 1774–1789* (North Carolina, 1935), 4.

33. Lloyd M. Short, *The Development of National Administrative Organization in the United States* (Johns Hopkins, 1923), 35–75.

34. *The Federalist* 38. A similar point is made in *The Federalist* 16 and *The Federalist* 22.

35. Willi Paul Adams, *The First American Constitutions: Republican Ideology and the Making of State Constitutions in the Revolutionary Era* (North Carolina, 1980), 100.

36. Gordon S. Wood, *Creation of the American Republic* (North Carolina, 1969), 127–61.

37. Query XIII, 120–21.

38. Thomas Jefferson Letter to James Madison, March 15, 1789.

39. John Winslow, *The Trial of the Rhode Island Judges: An Episode Touching Currency and Constitutional Law* (Brooklyn, 1887).

40. Alexander Hamilton Letter to James Duane, September 3, 1780.

41. Joseph Story, *Commentaries on the Constitution of the United States* (1833), 1410.

42. John Adams Wettergreen, "Bureaucratizing the American Government" (1988); "Constitutional Problems of American Bureaucracy," *Political Communication* 9(2): 93–110 (March, 1992); "The Regulatory Revolution and the New Bureaucratic State" (April 2, 1988).

43. Except when popular conventions might propose or ratify constitutional amendments; however, these conventions only could be called by Congress or the states.

44. *The Federalist* 22.

45. Arnold I. Burns and Stephen J. Markman, "Understanding Separation of Powers," *Pace Law Review* 7 (1987), 580; Willi Paul Adams, *The First American Constitutions: Republican Ideology and the Making of State Constitutions in the Revolutionary Era* (North Carolina, 1980), 275.

46. Joel Hood, *Before There Were Mouseholes: Resurrecting the Non-Delegation Doctrine* (2014), 22.

47. "Parliamentary Government in America," *Fortnightly Review* 32 (1879), 516.

48. *The Federalist* 76 (emphasis added).

49. Joseph Postell, "'The People Surrender Nothing': The Social Compact Foundation of the Nondelegation Doctrine, forthcoming, *Missouri Law Review*.

50. The literature on the "unitary executive" is enormous. *See* Lawrence Lessig and Cass Sunstein, "The President and the Administration," *Columbia Law Review* 94 (1994), 1–123.

51. "The Study of Administration," *Political Science Quarterly* 2 (1887), 198.

52. *The Records of the Federal Convention of 1787,* ed. Max Farrand, 4 vols. (Yale, 1966), II: 328–29, 335, 367.

53. Seth Barrett Tillman, "The Puzzle of Hamilton's Federalist No. 77," *Harvard Journal of Law and Public Policy* 33 (2010), 149.

54. Saikrishna B. Prakash, "Hail to the Chief Administrator: The Framers and the President's Administrative Powers," *Yale Law Journal* 102 (1993), 1016.

55. Alfred H. Kelly, Winfred A. Harbison, and Herman Belz, *The American Constitution: Its Origins and Development*, 7th ed. (New York, 1991), 115.

56. Publius suggests in *Federalist* 40 that the movement from the Articles of Confederation to the Constitution—an "amendment" of the Articles that wiped them out—was equivalent to a revolution.

57. See especially Michael S. Greve, *The Upside-Down Constitution* (Harvard, 2012).

58. Jack N. Rakove, *Beginnings of National Politics* (New York, 1988), 183, 381.

Chapter 2

1. *Federalist* 76.

2. Saikrishna Prakash, "New Light on the Decision of 1789," *Cornell Law Review* 91 (2006), 1021–1076; Steven G. Calebresi and Christopher S. Yoo, "The Unitary Executive During the First Half-Century," *Case Western Reserve Law Review* 47 (1997), 1451–1561; Lawrence Lessig and Cass Sunstein, "The President and the Administration," *Columbia Law Review* 94 (1994), 1–123.

3. *Annals of Congress*, 2d Cong., 1st Sess. (1791), 238.

4. David P. Currie, *The Constitution in Congress: The Federalist Period, 1789–1801* (Chicago, 1997), 149.

5. Paul P. van Riper, "The American Administrative State: Wilson and the Founders—An Unorthodox View," *Public Administration Review* 43 (1983), 477–90.

6. *Federalist* 62, 71.

7. Lynton K. Caldwell, *The Administrative Theories of Hamilton and Jefferson: Their Contribution to Thought on Public Administration* (New York, 1944), 31.

8. Douglas A. Irwin, "The Aftermath of Hamilton's 'Report on Manufactures,'" *Journal of Economic History* 64 (2004), 800.

9. Richard H. Timberlake, *Monetary Policy in the United States: An Intellectual and Institutional History* (Chicago, 1993), 28; Richard Sylla et al., "Alexander Hamilton, Central Banker: Crisis Management During the United States Financial Panic of 1792," *Business History Review* 83 (2009), 61–86; Scott C. Miller, "Financial Speculation and America's First Financial Crisis," *Financial History* 108 (2013), 28–31.

10. Contra Jerry L. Mashaw, *Creating the Administrative Constitution: The Lost One Hundred Years of American Administrative Law* (Yale, 2012), 47. Compare Elizabeth Tandy Shermer, "Banking on Government," in *To Promote the General Welfare: The Case for Big Government*, ed. Steven Conn (Oxford, 2012), 70.

11. Leonard D. White, *The Federalists: A Study in Administrative History* (New York, 1948), 326, 353; Eugene R. Sheridan, "Thomas Jefferson and the Giles Resolutions," *William & Mary Quarterly* 49 (1992), 589–608.

12. White, *The Federalists*, 441.

13. To James Madison, Oct. 1, 1792, in *The Papers of James Madison*, ed. Robert A. Rutland and Thomas A. Mason, 17 vols. (Virginia and Chicago, 1962-91), XIV: 375.

14. Charles E. Merriam and Frank P. Bourgin, "Jefferson as a Planner of National Resources," *Ethics* 53 (1943), 284–92. Bourgin's 1944 dissertation was finally published as *The Myth of Laissez-Faire in the New Republic* in 1988.

15. Richard Mannix, "Gallatin, Jefferson and the Embargo of 1808," *Diplomatic History* 3 (1979), 151.

16. Leonard D. White, *The Jeffersonians: A Study in Administrative History, 1801–29* (New York, 1951), 423–73.

17. Mannix, "Gallatin," 167.

18. A federal district court overturned these in *United States v. Hoxie*, 26 F. 397 (1808).

19. Alfred H. Kelly, Winfred A. Harbison, and Herman Belz, *The American Constitution: Its Origins and Development*, 7th ed. (New York, 1991), 146. But see Arthur Scherr, "Thomas Jefferson's Nationalist Vision of New England and the War of 1812," *Historian* 69 (2007), 1–35.

20. Douglas L. Jones, "'The Caprice of Juries': The Enforcement of the Jeffersonian Embargo in Massachusetts," *American Journal of Legal History* 24 (1980), 319.

21. Caldwell, *Administrative Theories*, 147.

22. *Gilchrist v. Collector*, 10 F. 355 (1808), 357; Oliver Schroeder, Jr., "The Life and Work of Justice William Johnson, Jr.," *University of Pennsylvania Law Review* 95 (1946), 179–85; Charles Warren, *The Supreme Court in United States History*, 3 vols. (Boston, 1922), I: 324–41. Congress amended the act to give the president the disputed power, and the Supreme Court later ruled that federal judges could not issue mandamus in such cases.

23. *Aurora v. United States*, 11 U.S. 382 (1813), 388.

24. David Schoenbrod, *Power Without Responsibility: How Congress Abuses the People Through Delegation* (Yale, 1993), 31.

25. Five years later, the Court held that state bank notes were altogether unconstitutional, violating the Article I, section 10, prohibition of state "bills of credit." Seven years subsequently, the Court reversed that decision (*Craig v. Missouri*, 29 U.S. 410 (1830); *Briscoe v. Bank of Kentucky*, 26 U.S. 357 (1837)).

26. *Wayman v. Southard*, 25 U.S. 1 (1825), 43–46.

27. Gary Lawson, "Delegation and Original Meaning," *Virginia Law Review* 88 (2002), 358. See Andrew J. Ziaja, "Hot Oil and Hot Air: The Development of the Nondelegation Doctrine through the New Deal: A History, 1813–1944," *Hastings Constitutional Law Quarterly* 35 (2008), 931.

28. Message to Congress, Dec. 6, 1825.

29. White, *The Jeffersonians*, 92, 352, 384–392; Carl R. Fish, *The Civil Service and the Patronage* (New York, 1905), 186.

30. "First Annual Message," 8 Dec. 1829, in *A Compilation of the Messages and Papers of the Presidents*, ed. James D. Richardson, 11 vols. (New York, 1911), II: 1012.

31. In contrast to Michael Nelson's argument that the spoils system promoted bureaucracy ("A Short, Ironic History of American National Bureaucracy," *Journal of Politics* 44 [1982], 747–78), see John, *Spreading the News*, 105, 256; Leonard D. White, *The Jacksonians: A Study in Administrative History: 1829–1861* (New York, 1954), 319, 343; James Q. Wilson, "The Rise of the Bureaucratic State," *Public Interest* 41 (1975); Richard R. John, "In Retrospect: Leonard D. White and the Invention of Administrative History," *Reviews in American History* 24 (1996), 348.

32. The Senate was in recess, so Taney served temporarily. When the Senate reconvened it rejected the appointment. When Jackson later appointed Taney to the Supreme Court, the Senate also rejected him for that office. Once the Democrats won control of the Senate, it confirmed Taney's appointment as Chief Justice.

33. *Kendall* v. *Stokes*, 37 U.S. 524 (1838), 610. Stokes won a personal suit against Kendall for $11,000. This was the traditional way of keeping bureaucrats under control. But the Supreme Court overturned the judgment, because Kendall could not be held liable for ministerial acts. Then Congress reimbursed Kendall for his legal expenses in defending himself—the traditional way of immunizing bureaucrats. Carl B. Swisher, *The Taney Period, 1836–1864* (New York, 1974), 158–68.

34. Jerry L. Mashaw, "The American Model of Federal Administrative Law: Remembering the First Hundred Years," *George Washington Law Review* 78 (2010), 984.

35. J. E. D. Shipp, *Giant Days, or the Life and Times of William H. Crawford* (Americus, GA, 1909), 105–06.

36. G. A. Kelly, "Hegel's America," *Philosophy and Public Affairs* 2 (1972), 3–36.

37. Alexis de Tocqueville, *Democracy in America*, ed. Eduardo Nolla, trans. James T. Schleifer (Indianapolis, 2010), 254.

38. Ibid., 427.

39. Ibid., 895, 475.

40. Ibid., 1248. For similar observations, see Paul Rahe, *Soft Despotism, Democracy's Drift: Montesquieu, Rousseau, Tocqueville and the Modern Prospect* (Yale, 2009); Amanda Claybaugh, "Bureaucracy in America: De Forest's Paperwork," *Studies in American Fiction* 37 (2010), 203–23.

41. Henry James Sumner Maine, *Ancient Law* (New York, 1931 [1861]), ch. 5. *See also* Lawrence Friedman, *A History of American Law* (New York, 1973), 275; Grant Gilmore, *The Death of Contract* (Ohio State, 1974).

42. Tocqueville noted that democratic societies are prone to perfectionism, but did not see evangelical religion as the source—*Democracy in America*, 759.

43. Sydney Ahlstrom, *A Religious History of the American People* (Yale, 1972), 470–76.

44. As opposed to the more traditional "premillennialist" view that Christ would come and bring about that 1,000-year period.

45. Address at Springfield, Feb. 22, 1842, Basler I: 241.

46. David Tyack, Thomas James, and Aaron Benavot, *Law and the Shaping of Public Education, 1785–1954* (Wisconsin, 1987), 44–53.

47. Matt Miller, "First, Kill All the School Boards: A Modest Proposal to Fix the Schools," *Atlantic* (Jan./Feb. 2008), 92; John Taylor Gatto, *The Underground History of American Education: A Schoolteacher's Intimate Investigation into the Problem of American Schooling* (Sydney, 2000).

48. Philip Hamburger, *Is Administrative Law Unlawful?* (Chicago, 2013), 118, 515.

49. David P. Currie, *The Constitution in Congress: Democrats and Whigs, 1829–1861* (Chicago, 2005), 124.

50. White, *The Jacksonians*, 442, 458; Mashaw, *Creating the Administrative State*, 188–208; Robert L. Rabin, "Federal Regulation in Historical Perspective," *Stanford Law Review* 38 (1986), 1196. Tocqueville noted that the Americans' democratic belief in progress led them to build shoddy steamboats, because they believed that rapid technological innovation would quickly make them obsolete (*Democracy in America*, 762).

51. William J. Novak, "The Myth of the 'Weak' American State," *American Historical Review* 113 (2008), 752–72.

52. Brian Balogh, *A Government Out of Sight: The Mystery of National Authority in Nineteenth Century America* (Cambridge, 2009).

53. Stephen J. Rockwell, *Indian Affairs and the Administrative State in the Nineteenth Century* (Cambridge, 2010); Jeff Pasley, "Midget on Horseback: American Indians and the History of the American State," *Common-Place* 9 (2008).

54. William W. Freehling, *Prelude to Civil War: The Nullification Controversy in South Carolina, 1816–1836* (New York, 1965), 255–57.

55. 1 Stat. 302 (1789), sec. 3.

56. 9 Stat. 462 (1850), secs. 3, 5, 6; Charles A. Lindquist, "The Origins and Development of the United States Commissioner System," *American Journal of Legal History* 14 (1970), 1–16.

57. 9 Stat. 462 (1850), sec. 5.

58. Gantham Rao, "The Federal *Posse Comitatus* Doctrine: Slavery, Compulsion, and Statecraft in Mid-Nineteenth Century America," *Law and History Review* 26 (2008), 29.

59. Speech at Bloomington, April 10, 1860, in *Collected Works of Abraham Lincoln*, IV: 41.

60. Philip S. Paludan, "The American Civil War Considered as a Crisis in Law and Order," *American Historical Review* 77 (1972), 1013.

61. This is discussed in more detail in Paul D. Moreno and Jonathan O'Neill, "'The Legitimate Object of Government': Constitutional Problems of Civil-War Era Republican Policy," in *Constitutionalism in the Approach and Aftermath*

of the Civil War (New York, 2013); and Paul D. Moreno, *The American State from the Civil War to the New Deal: The Twilight of Constitutionalism and the Triumph of Progressivism* (New York, 2013), 7–22.

62. 12 Stat. 665 (1863). The following year, Congress amended the act, allowing the president to remove the comptroller "upon reasons to be communicated by him to the Senate," but not requiring the Senate's consent. 13 Stat. 99 (1864).

63. Herbert Croly, *The Promise of American Life* (New York, 1909), 364.

64. John Wilson Million, "The Debate on the National Bank Act of 1863," *Journal of Political Economy* 2 (1894), 274.

65. Amanda Claybaugh, "Bureaucracy in America: De Forest's Paperwork," *Studies in American Fiction* 37(2) (Fall 2010), 203–23; James L. Huston, "An Alternative to the Tragic Era: Applying the Virtues of Bureaucracy to the Reconstruction Dilemma, *Civil War History* 51 (2005), 403–15.

66. Robert Harrison, "New Representations of a 'Misrepresented Bureau': Reflections of Recent Scholarship on the Freedmen's Bureau," *American Nineteenth-Century History* 8 (2007), 205–29; Robert C. Lieberman, "The Freedmen's Bureau and the Politics of Institutional Structure," *Social Science History* 18 (1994), 428.

67. Oz Frankel, *States of Inquiry: Social Investigations and Print Culture in Nineteenth-Century Britain and the United States* (Johns Hopkins, 2006), 207–09; James D. Schmidt, *Free to Work: Labor Law, Emancipation and Reconstruction, 1815–1880* (Georgia, 1998), 6.

68. Adam Fairclough, "Congressional Reconstruction: A Catastrophic Failure," *Journal of the Historical Society* 12 (2012), 271–82; Heather Cox Richardson, "A Marshall Plan for the South? The Failure of Republican and Democratic Ideology During Reconstruction," *Civil War History* 51 (2005), 378–87; William G. Shade, "'Revolutions May Go Backwards': The American Civil War and the Problem of Political Development," *Social Science Quarterly* 55 (1974), 767.

69. Rockwell, *Indian Affairs and the Administrative State in the Nineteenth Century*; James L. Huston, "An Alternative," 413; Bethany Berger, "Birthright Citizenship on Trial: *Elk* v. *Wilkins* and *United States v. Wong Kim Ark*," *Cardozo Law Review* 37 (2016).

70. Jeff Pasley, "Midget on Horseback."

71. Eric Foner, *Reconstruction, 1863–77: America's Unfinished Revolution* (New York, 1988), 153.

72. Claybaugh, "Bureaucracy in America."

Chapter 3

1. Leonard D. White, *The Republican Era, 1869–1901: An Administrative History* (New York, 1958), 234.

2. Ibid., 242.

3. Elizabeth Sanders, *Roots of Reform: Farmers, Workers, and the American State, 1877–1917* (Chicago, 1999), 391–94.

4. Ibid., vii, 2. For similar assessments, see Harold Melvin Hyman, *A More Perfect Union: The Impact of the Civil War and Reconstruction on the Constitution* (New York, 1973), 380, 546; Phillip Shaw Paludan, *A Covenant with Death: Constitution, Law, and Equality in the Civil War Era* (Illinois, 1975), 54, 233, 275; Morton Keller, *Affairs of State: Public Life in Late Nineteenth-Century America* (Evergreen, CO, 1977), 6; William G. Shade, "'Revolutions May Go Backwards': The American Civil War and the Problem of Political Development," *Social Science Quarterly* 55 (1974), 767; R. Hal Williams, "The Politics of the Gilded Age," in *American Political History: Essays on the State of the Discipline*, eds. John F. Marszalek and Wilson D. Miscamble (Notre Dame, 1997), 117.

5. Ari Hoogenboom, "The Pendleton Act and the Civil Service," *American Historical Review* 64 (1959), 311–12.

6. Stephen Skowronek, *Building a New American State: The Expansion of National Administrative Capacities, 1877–1920* (Cambridge, 1982), 52.

7. William James Hull Hoffer, *To Enlarge the Machinery of Government: Congressional Debates and the Growth of the American State, 1858–1891* (Johns Hopkins, 2007), 114.

8. William J. Novak, "The Legal Origins of the Modern American State," in *Looking Back at Law's Century*, ed. Austin Sarat et al. (Cornell, 2002), 266.

9. Journal entry, December 28, 1889, *Papers of Woodrow Wilson* V: 55; Scot J. Zentner, "Liberalism and Executive Power: Woodrow Wilson and the American Founders," *Polity* 26 (1994), 595.

10. C. Edward Merriam, *A History of American Political Theories* (New York, 1920 [1903]), 307–22.

11. Woodrow Wilson, *Congressional Government: A Study in American Politics* (New York, 1956 [1885]), 34.

12. Ibid., 38–39.

13. Ibid., 49.

14. Ibid., 134.

15. Woodrow Wilson. "The Study of Administration," *Political Science Quarterly* 2 (1887), 202. It is notable that in the 1880s Wilson used the foreign term "bureaux," sometimes italicized, as the plural of "bureau." The word was still foreign.

16. A. V. Dicey, *Introduction to the Study of the Law of the Constitution* (Indianapolis, 1982 [1885]).

17. Ibid., 219–20.

18. Ibid., 216, 202, 209–11.

19. *Marbury v. Madison*, 5 U.S. 137 (1803).

20. Ari Hoogenboom, *Outlawing the Spoils: A History of the Civil Service Reform Movement, 1865–1883* (Westport, CT, 1961), 91.

21. Lionel Murphy, "The First Civil Service Commission 1871–75," *Public Personnel Review* 3, nos. 1, 3, 4 (1941) 213.

22. Deil S. Wright, "A Century of the Intergovernmental Administrative State," in *A Centennial History of the American Administrative State*, ed. Ralph C. Chandler (New York, 1987), 231.

23. Paul P. Van Riper, "The American Administrative State: Wilson and the Founders," in *A Centennial History of the American Administrative State*, 3, ibid.; Arthur S. Link, "Woodrow Wilson and the Study of Administration," *Proceedings of the American Philosophical Society* 112 (1968), 431–33.

24. Frank J. Goodnow, *Politics and Administration* (New Brunswick, 2003 [1900]).

25. *Federalist* 41; Leonard R. Sorenson, *Madison on the "General Welfare": His Consistent Constitutional Vision* (Lanham, MD, 1995).

26. John A. Rohr, Introduction to *Politics and Administration*, xvi–xix.

27. Ronald Pestritto, *Woodrow Wilson and the Roots of Modern Liberalism* (Lanham, MD, 2006), 230.

28. James E. Fleming, "The Role of Government in a Free Society: The Conception of Lester Frank Ward," *Social Forces* 24 (1946), 257–66; Lester Frank Ward, *Dynamic Sociology or Applied Social Science*, 2 vols. (New York, 1883), II: 252.

29. Jurgen Herbst, *The German Historical School in American Scholarship: A Study in the Transfer of Culture* (Cornell, 1965).

30. Richard W. Van Alstyne, "Woodrow Wilson and the Idea of the Nation State," *International Affairs* 37 (1961), 299; Edward L. Meltzer, "The Growth and Development of Administrative Law," *Marquette Law Review* 19 (1935), 209; Paul Carrington, "Law and the Wisconsin Idea," *Journal of Legal Education* 47 (1997), 316; Herbst, *The German Historical School*, 176.

31. *The Wisconsin Idea* (1912), quoted in LaVern J. Rippley, "Charles McCarthy and Frederic C. Howe: Their Imperial German Sources for the Wisconsin Idea," *Monatshefte* 80 (1988), 71.

32. Ibid., 75.

33. Cara L. Burnidge, "The Business of Church and State: Social Christianity in Woodrow Wilson's White House," *Church History* 82 (2013), 659–66; Richard J. Stillman II, *Creating the American State: The Moral Reformers and Modern Administrative World They Made* (Alabama, 1998).

34. Gary Scott Smith, *Faith and the Presidency: From George Washington to George W. Bush* (New York, 2006), 163–73; Burnidge, "The Business of Church and State"; Gregory S. Butler, "Visions of a Nation Transformed: Modernity and Ideology in Wilson's Political Thought," *Journal of Church and State* 39 (1997), 37–51.

35. Walter Rauschenbusch, *Christianizing the Social Order* (New York, 1912), 120, 116, 44, 41.

36. Henry F. May, *Protestant Churches and Industrial America* (New York, 1949), 231.

37. Rauschenbusch, *Christianizing the Social Order*, 109.

38. J. David Hoeveler, Jr., "The University and the Social Gospel: The Intellectual Origins of the 'Wisconsin Idea,'" *Wisconsin Magazine of History 59* (1976), 282–98.

39. Richard T. Ely, "Socialism in America," *North American Review 355* (1886), 519; Michael Salman, *The Embarrassment of Slavery: Controversies over Bondage and Nationalism in the American Colonial Philippines* (California, 2001), 52; Wilson quote at note 9 above.

40. Ely, "Socialism in America," 521.

41. Richard T. Ely, *Social Aspects of Christianity and Other Essays* (Boston, 1889), 124.

42. Ibid., 15, 37.

43. *Social Aspects of Christianity*, 17; Herbst, *German Historical School*, 95.

44. Hoeveler, "The University and the Social Gospel," 289.

45. Paul D. Moreno, *The American State from the Civil War to the New Deal: The Twilight of Constitutionalism and the Triumph of Progressivism* (Cambridge, 2013), 122–24.

46. *Wabash, St. Louis and Pacific Ry. v. Illinois*, 118 U.S. 557 (1886).

47. 24 Stat. 379 (1887).

48. Ari Hoogenboom and Olive Hoogenboom, *A History of the Interstate Commerce Commission: From Panacea to Palliative* (New York, 1976), 31–40, argue that the commission was relatively effective in curtailing rate discrimination until the Court crippled it.

49. John A. Rohr, *To Run a Constitution: The Legitimacy of the Administrative State* (Kansas, 1986), 95. *See also* Steven G. Calabresi and Christopher S. Yoo, "The Unitary Executive During the Second Half-Century," *Harvard Journal of Law and Public Policy* 26 (2003), 798.

50. Hoffer, *To Enlarge the Machinery of Government*, 162; Skowronek, *Building a New American State*, 146.

51. Quoted in Marver H. Bernstein, *Regulating Business by Independent Commission* (Princeton, 1955), 365.

52. Hoogenboom & Hoogenboom, *History of the Interstate Commerce Commission*, 33; Gabriel Kolko, *Railroads and Regulation, 1877–1916* (Princeton, 1965). For a similar state-level argument, see Bruce W. Dearstyne, "Regulation in the Progressive Era: The New York Public Service Commission," *New York History* 58 (1977), 330–47; Alan Jones, "Thomas M. Cooley and the Interstate Commerce Commission: Continuity and Change in the Doctrine of Equal Rights," *Political Science Quarterly* 81 (1966), 612.

53. James W. Ely, Jr., "The Troubled Beginning of the Interstate Commerce Commission," *Marquette Law Review* 95 (2012), 1131–34.

54. *Kentucky & Indiana Bridge Co. v. Louisville & Nashville Ry.*, 2 ICC 351 (C.C.K.Y., 1889).

55. Charles A. Prouty, "Court Review of the Orders of the Interstate Commerce Commission," *Yale Law Journal* 18 (1909), 297.

56. *I.C.C. v. Cincinnati, New Orleans & Texas Pacific Ry.*, 167 U.S. 479 (1897), 494.

57. *Brown v. Walker*, 161 U.S. 591 (1896).

58. Skowronek, *Building a New American State*, 158.

59. George W. Hilton, "The Consistency of the Interstate Commerce Act," *Journal of Law and Economics* 9 (1966), 87–113; Hoogenboom, *The Interstate Commerce Commission*, 35; *United States v. Trans-Missouri Freight*, 166 U.S. 290 (1897); *United States v. Joint Traffic Association*, 171 U.S. 505 (1898); Gerald Berk, *Alternative Tracks: The Constitution of American Industrial Order, 1865–1917* (Johns Hopkins, 1994), 110.

60. Thomas W. Merrill, "Article III, Adjudication, and the Origins of the Appellate Model of Administrative Law," *Columbia Law Review* 111 (2011), 939–1003.

61. James C. Scott, *Seeing Like a State: How Certain Schemes to Improve the Human Condition Have Failed* (Yale, 1998).

62. William A. Niskasen, Jr., *Bureaucracy and Representative Government* (Chicago, 1971), 4.

63. Charles Freeman, *Egypt, Greece, and Rome: Civilizations of the Ancient Mediterranean* (Oxford, 1996), compares the Egyptian and Mandarin systems.

64. 2 Kings 24; Luke 2.

65. Edward C. Lunt, "History of the U.S. Census," *Publications of the American Statistical Association* 1 (1888), 63–93; Carroll D. Wright, "The History and Growth of the U.S. Census," S. Doc. 194, 56th Cong., 1st Sess. (Washington, DC, 1900). Some strict constructionist conservatives objected to this expansion of the limited language of the census clause. William F. Rickenbacker was fined $100 and spent a day in jail for refusing to fill out the 1960 census long form. Daniel Kelly, *James Burnham and the Struggle for the World: A Life* (Wilmington, DE, 2002), 275.

66. Oz Frankel, *States of Inquiry: Social Investigations and Print Culture in Nineteenth-Century Britain and the United States* (Johns Hopkins, 2006), 1, 207–09.

67. Eliza Wing-Yee Lee, "Political Science, Public Administration, and the Rise of the American Administrative State," *Public Administration Review* 55 (1995), 542.

68. *Chicago, Milwaukee & St. Paul Ry. v. Minnesota*, 134 U.S. 418 (1890); *Chicago, Burlington & Quincy Ry. v. Chicago*, 166 U.S. 226 (1897).

69. Henry Wollman, "The Bane of Friendly Receiverships," *North American Review* 158 (1894), 250–51; Jones, "Thomas M. Cooley," 611; James W. Ely, Jr., *Railroads and American Law* (Kansas, 2001), 177; Berk, *Alternative Tracks*, 47–58.

70. William H. Dunbar, "Government by Injunction," *Economic Studies* 3 (1898), 5–43; Goodnow, *Politics and Administration*, 102; Hardgrove, "Judicial Review of Actions of Administrative Bodies," 28.

71. Gabriel J. Chin, "Regulating Race: Asian Exclusion and the Administrative State," *Harvard Civil Rights–Civil Liberties Law Review* 37 (2002), 1–64; Sandi Zellmer, "The Devil, the Details, and the Dawn of the Twenty-First Century Administrative State: Beyond the New Deal," *Arizona State Law Journal* 32 (2000), 1031.

72. *Fong Yue Ting v. United States*, 149 U.S. 698 (1893), 743.

73. Adam McKeown, "Ritualization of Regulation: The Enforcement of Chinese Exclusion in the United States and China," *American Historical Review* 108 (2003), 383.

74. Lucy Sawyer, "Captives of Law: Judicial Enforcement of the Chinese Exclusion Laws, 1891–1905," *Journal of American History* 76 (1989), 91–117.

75. *United States v. Ju Toy*, 198 U.S. 253 (1905), 268.

76. Chin, "Regulating Race," 24.

77. Roscoe Pound, "Executive Justice," *American Law Register* 46 (1907), 142.

78. Bruce Wyman, *The Principles of the Administrative Law Governing the Relations of Public Officers* (Clark, NJ, 2014 [1903]).

79. Prouty, "Court Review," 302.

80. "The Growth of Administrative Law in America," *Harvard Law Review* 31 (1918), 644–46.

81. Earl Maltz, "The Federal Government and the Problem of Chinese Rights in the Era of the Fourteenth Amendment," *Harvard Journal of Law and Public Policy* 17 (1994), 223–52.

82. *Yick Wo v. Hopkins*, 118 U.S. 356 (1886), 366, 373.

83. Dan Kaylor, "Orders that Wouldn't Wash: Historical Background of *Yick Wo v. Hopkins*," *Lincoln Law Review* 11 (1980), 205–10.

84. 26 Stat. 567 (1890), 612.

85. 29 Stat. 604 (1897).

86. *Field v. Clark*, 143 U.S. 649 (1892), 683, 692.

87. Ibid. The Court unanimously upheld the Tea Inspection Act in 1897 in *Buttfield v. Stranahan*, 192 U.S. 470.

88. Edward Whitney, "The Reciprocity Acts of 1890—Are They Constitutional?" *American Law Register and Review* 40 (1892), 177, 185.

89. Frank J. Goodnow, *The Principles of the Administrative Law of the United States* (New York, 1905), 337.

90. Woodrow Wilson, "The Ideals of America," *Atlantic Monthly* (1902); Wilson, *Congressional Government: A Study in American Politics* (New York, 1956 [1885])—from the 1900 preface to the 15th edition; John W. Burgess, *Recent Changes in American Constitutional Theory* (Columbia, 1923).

91. William E. Forbath, "Politics, State-Building, and the Courts, 1870–1920," in *The Cambridge History of Law in America*, ed. Michael Grossberg and Christopher Tomlins, 3 vols. (New York, 2011), II: 690; William E. Leuchtenburg, "Progressivism and Imperialism: The Progressive Movement and American

Foreign Policy, 1898–1916," *Mississippi Valley Historical Review* 39 (1952), 483–504.

92. McKeown, "Ritualization of Regulation," 378.

93. July 4, 1821.

94. Christopher C. Burkett, "Remaking the World: Progressivism and American Foreign Policy," Heritage Foundation (2013).

95. *Congressional Record*, 55th Cong., 3rd Sess. (January 9, 1899), 493–503.

96. Albert Beveridge, "The March of the Flag," September 16, 1898; *Congressional Record*, 56th Cong., 1st Sess. (January 9, 1900), 704–12.

97. Ibid.

98. "Platform of the American Anti-Imperialist League," in *Speeches, Correspondence, and Political Papers of Carl Schurz,* ed. Frederic Bancroft, 6 vols. (New York, 1913), VI: 77.

99. Rebecca Edwards, *New Spirits: Americans in the Gilded Age, 1865–1905* (New York, 2006), 263.

100. E. L. Godkin, "The Eclipse of Liberalism," *Nation*, August 9, 1900.

101. Ibid.

102. Ibid.

103. Thomas A. Bailey, "Was the Presidential Election of 1900 a Mandate on Imperialism?" *Mississippi Valley Historical Review* 24 (1937), 43–52.

104. Quoted in Philip S. Jessup, *Elihu Root* (New York, 1938), 354.

105. *Downes v. Bidwell*, 182 U.S. 244 (1901), 379; Christina Duffy Burnett, "United States: American Expansion and Territorial Deannexation," *University of Chicago Law Review* 72 (2005), 797–879; Eric Sheppard, "The Great Dissenter's Greatest Dissents: The First Justice Harlan, the 'Color Blind' Constitution and the Meaning of His Dissents in the *Insular Cases* for the War on Terror," *American Journal of Legal History* 48 (2006), 119–46; Krishanti Vignarajah, "The Political Roots of Judicial Legitimacy: Explaining the Enduring Validity of the Insular Cases," *University of Chicago Law Review* 77 (2010), 781–845.

Chapter 4

1. *Northern Securities v. United States*, 193 U.S. 197 (1904).

2. Don L. Hofsommer, "Hill's Dream Realized," *Pacific Northwest Quarterly* 79 (1988), 138–46.

3. Robert H. Wiebe, "The House of Morgan and the Executive, 1905–13," *American Historical Review* 65 (1959), 45, 55.

4. *The Letters of Theodore Roosevelt*, ed. Elting Morison, 8 vols. (Harvard, 1951–54), VII: 630.

5. As the Supreme Court put it in the "rule of reason" cases in 1911, good combinations provided benefits to consumers via economies of scale or other economic efficiencies.

6. Nicola Giocoli, "When Law and Economics Was a Dangerous Subject: The Controversy over Railroad Before the Hepburn Act" (2015); Nicola Giocoli,

"The (Rail) Road to *Lochner*: Reproduction Cost and the Gilded Age Controversy over Rate Regulation" (2015); Herbert Hovenkamp, "Regulatory Conflict in the Gilded Age: Federalism and the Railroad Problem," *Yale Law Journal* 97 (1988), 1052.

7. Thomas W. Merrill, "Article III, Adjudication, and the Origins of the Appellate Model of Administrative Law," *Columbia Law Review* 111 (2011), 939–1003.

8. Ari Hoogenboom and Olive Hoogenboom, *A History of the Interstate Commerce Commission: From Panacea to Palliative* (New York, 1976), 57; Samuel P. Huntington, "The Marasmus of the Interstate Commerce Commission: The Commission, the Railroads, and the Public Interest," *Yale Law Journal* 61 (1952), 482; Albro Martin, "The Troubled Subject of Railroad Regulation in the Gilded Age—A Reappraisal," *Journal of American History* 61 (1974), 361; *Enterprise Denied: Origins of the Decline of American Railroads, 1897–1917* (New York, 1971).

9. John Braeman, "The Square Deal in Action: A Case Study in the Growth of a 'National Police Power,'" in *Change and Continuity in Twentieth-Century America*, ed. John Braeman et al. (Ohio State, 1964).

10. Donna J. Wood, "The Strategic Uses of Public Policy: Business Support for the 1906 Pure Food and Drugs Act," *Business History Review* 59 (1985), 403–42; Ilyse D. Barkan, "Industry Invites Regulation: The Passage of the Pure Food and Drugs Act of 1906," *American Journal of Public Health* 75 (1985), 18–26.

11. Randall G. Holcombe, "Crony Capitalism: By-Product of Big Government," *Independent Review* 17 (2013), 541–59.

12. Daniel P. Carpenter, *The Forging of Bureaucratic Autonomy: Reputations, Networks, and Policy Innovation in the Executive Agencies, 1862–1928* (Princeton, 2001).

13. To Albert Shaw, May 26, 1906, quoted in Logan E. Sawyer III, "Constitutional Principle, Partisan Calculation, and the Beveridge Child Labor Bill," *Law and History Review* 31 (2013), 330.

14. The act originally was administered by the USDA's Bureau of Chemistry. It became the FDA in 1930.

15. Marc T. Law, "How Do Regulators Regulate? Enforcement of the Pure Food and Drugs Act, 1907–1938," *Journal of Law, Economics, and Organization* 22 (2006), 472.

16. Ibid.

17. Law, "How Do Regulators Regulate? 464; Barkan, "Industry Invites Regulation," 22.

18. John W. Burgess, *Recent Changes in American Constitutional Theory* (Columbia, 1923); George Madden Martin, "American Women and Paternalism," *Atlantic Monthly,* June 1924, 744–53; "The American Woman and Representative Government," *Atlantic Monthly,* March 1925, 363–71.

19. Jonathan Laurie, *William Howard Taft: The Travails of a Progressive Conservative* (Cambridge, 2012).

20. Donald F. Anderson, *William Howard Taft: A Conservative's Conception of the Presidency* (Cornell, 1968), 95, 289–95. For Taft's views on executive power, see his book, *Our Chief Magistrate and His Powers* (New York, 1916) and his opinion in *Myers v. United States*, 272 U.S. 52 (1926).

21. Charles F. Wilkinson, "The Forest Service: A Call for a Return to First Principles," *Public Land and Resources Law Review* 5 (1984), 7; James C. Scott, *Seeing Like a State: How Certain Schemes to Improve the Human Condition Have Failed* (Yale, 1998), 11.

22. Carpenter, *The Forging of Bureaucratic Autonomy*, 205; David H. Getches, "Managing the Public Lands: The Authority of the Executive to Withdraw Lands," *Natural Resources Journal* 22 (1982), 284–86.

23. Henry F. Pringle, *The Life and Times of William Howard Taft: A Biography*, 2 vols. (New York, 1939), I: 480; II: 758.

24. James L. Penick, Jr., "The Age of the Bureaucrat: Another View of the Ballinger-Pinchot Controversy," *Forest History* 7 (1963), 15–21.

25. Donald J. Pisani, "The Many Faces of Conservation: Natural Resources and the American State, 1900–1940," in *Taking Stock: American Government in the Twentieth Century*, ed. Morton Keller and R. Shep Melnick (Cambridge, 1999), 136–141.

26. Pringle, *Life and Times*, I: 471.

27. Ironically, this embarrassing antedating—a typical bureaucratic snafu (abetted by Taft's habitual laziness)—aided the progressive bureaucratic empire builders. The Pinchot-Ballinger affair was an important step in the collapse of the Taft administration. Brandeis became an even greater progressive hero, to whom Woodrow Wilson would turn in shaping his administrative state.

28. Assuming that all of the justices whom President Taft had replaced had voted for Grimaud in the first case, one justice (Harlan, Holmes, Day, McKenna, or White) in the second case must have switched his vote from Grimaud to the government.

29. *United States v. Grimaud*, 220 U.S. 506 (1911); Logan Sawyer, "Grazing, *Grimaud*, and Gifford Pinchot: How the Forest Service Overcame the Classical Nondelegation Doctrine to Establish Administrative Crimes," *Journal of Law and Politics* 24 (2008), 171–208.

30. *I.C.C. v. Illinois Central RR*, 215 U.S. 452 (1910). Only Justice Brewer dissented, without opinion.

31. James Wallace Bryan, "The Railroad Bill and the Court of Commerce," *American Political Science Review* 4 (1910), 547.

32. Noga Morag-Levine, "Common Law, Civil Law, and the Administrative State: From Coke to *Lochner*," *Constitutional Commentary* 24 (2007), 660; Robert E. Cushman, *The Independent Regulatory Commissions* (New York, 1972 [1941]), 426–39; Bogdan Iancu, *Legislative Delegation: The Erosion of Normative Limits in Modern Constitutionalism* (New York, 2012), 152, 218; William C. Chase, *The American Law School and the Rise of Administrative Government* (Wisconsin, 1982), 134.

33. Speech Before the Elmira Chamber of Commerce, May 3, 1907, in *Addresses of Charles Evans Hughes*, 2d ed. (New York, 1916), 179–92.

34. Edward A. Purcell, "Understanding *Curtiss-Wright*," *Law and History Review* 31 (2013), 668.

35. Glen O. Robinson, "The Federal Communications Commission: An Essay on Regulatory Watchdogs," *Virginia Law Review* 64 (1978), 176.

36. George E. Dix, "The Death of the Commerce Court: A Study in Institutional Weakness," *American Journal of Legal History* 8 (1964), 238–60; Cushman, *The Independent Regulatory Commissions*, 723; Hoogenboom and Hoogenboom, *The Interstate Commerce Commission*, 67.

37. Frank J. Goodnow, *Politics and Administration* (New Brunswick, NJ, 2003 [1900]), xxxi, 192–97.

38. "Address of the Temporary Chairman," *Official Report of the Proceedings of the Fifteenth Republican National Convention* (New York, 1912), 88.

39. Stephen Skowronek, *Building a New American State: The Expansion of National Administrative Capacities, 1877–1920* (Cambridge, 1982), 24.

40. "The Government and Business," March 14, 1908, in *The Papers of Woodrow* Wilson, ed. Arthur S. Link, 69 vols. (Princeton, 1966–1994), XVIII: 36.

41. "An Address to the New York Press Club," September 9, 1912, in *The Papers of Woodrow* Wilson, XXV: 124; "Labor Day Address," September 2, 1912, ibid., XXV: 78.

42. *Philip Dru, Administrator: A Story of Tomorrow* (New York, 1920 [1912]). The author of the book was not indicated. Many readers assume that it was Theodore Roosevelt.

43. Godfrey Hodgson, *Woodrow Wilson's Right Hand: The Life of Colonel Edward M. House* (Yale, 2006), 7, 48–52; Robert S. Rifkind, "The Colonel's Dream of Power," *American Heritage* 10 (1959), 61.

44. Frank Burdick, "Woodrow Wilson and the Underwood Tariff," *Mid-America* 50 (1968), 272–90; Joshua Bernhardt, *The Tariff Commission: Its History, Activities and Organization* (New York, 1922).

45. 26 Stat. 209 (1890).

46. *United States v. Trans-Missouri Freight.* This decision's impact was limited by the Court's earlier ruling that the act extended only to activity that was genuinely interstate and commercial—railroads especially. It did not apply to production or to commerce within a state. Scott C. James, "Prelude to Progressivism: Party Decay, Populism, and the Doctrine of a 'Free and Unrestrained Competition' in American Antitrust Policy, 1890–1897," *Studies in American Political Development* 13 (1999), 288–333.

47. Neil W. Averitt, "The Meaning of 'Unfair Methods of Competition' in Section Five of the Federal Trade Commission Act," *Boston College Law Review* 21 (1980), 227–300; George Rublee, "The Original Plan and Early History of the Federal Trade Commission," *Proceedings of the Academy of Political Science of the City of New York* 11 (1926), 667; Gerald Berk, *Louis D. Brandeis and the Making of Regulated Competition, 1900–1932* (Cambridge, 2009).

48. James, "Prelude to Progressivism."

49. 38 Stat. 717 (1914).

50. Cushman, *Independent Regulatory Commissions*, 200.

51. Allan H. Meltzer, *A History of the Federal Reserve: Volume I, 1913–1951* (Chicago, 2003), 1–3, 65–73.

52. James Parthenos, "The Federal Reserve Act of 1913 in the Stream of U.S. Monetary History," *Economic Review* (July/August 1988), 27.

53. The price level was flat from the Civil War until 1913. It increased twelvefold in the century after the establishment of the Fed.

54. David M. Wright, "Is the Amended Federal Reserve Act Unconstitutional?" *Virginia Law Review* 23 (1937), 629–53; Milton Friedman and Anna Jacobson Schwartz, *A Monetary History of the United States, 1867–1960* (Princeton, 1963), 193.

55. Norbert Michel, "Dodd-Frank's Expansion of Fed Power: A Historical Perspective," *Cato Journal* 34 (2014), 557–67.

56. Christopher Howard, *The Hidden Welfare State: Tax Expenditures and Social Policy in the United States* (Princeton, 1997); Brian Balogh, *A Government Out of Sight: The Mystery of National Authority in Nineteenth-Century America* (Cambridge, 2009).

57. In 1895, the Supreme Court had declared an income tax to be a direct tax, which had to be apportioned among the states according to population. This would have defeated the purpose of southerners and westerners to shift the burden of taxation onto the urban, industrial states.

58. Theodore Roosevelt, "A Premium on Race Suicide," *Outlook*, September 27, 1913, 163.

59. Herbert Croly, *The Promise of American Life* (New York, 1909), 243.

60. John Teaford, *The Rise of the States: Evolution of American State Government* (Johns Hopkins, 2002); Martha Derthick, "How Many Communities? The Evolution of American Federalism," in *Dilemmas of Scale in America's Federal Democracy*, ed. Martha Derthick (Cambridge, 1999); James A. Maxwell, *The Fiscal Impact of Federalism in the United States* (New York, 1946), 187; Balogh, *Government Out of Sight*, 325.

61. U.S. Department of Transportation, *America's Highways, 1776–1976: A History of the Federal-Aid Program* (Washington, 1976), 83.

62. Balogh, *Government Out of Sight*, 391.

63. Pierre Purseigle, "The First World War and the Transformations of the State," *International Affairs* 90 (2014), 249–64; Robert Higgs, "War and Leviathan in Twentieth Century America," *Society* (1996), 57–63.

64. William R. Doezema, "Railroad Management and the Interplay of Federal and State Regulation, 1885–1916," *Business History Review* 50 (1976), 153–78; William R. Childs, "State Regulators and Pragmatic Federalism in the United States, 1888–1945," *Business History Review* 75 (2001), 720.

65. Nancy Bristow, *Making Men Moral: Social Engineering During the Great War* (New York, 1996).

66. Cushman, *The Independent Regulatory Commissions*, 241.

67. *United States v. L. Cohen Grocery*, 255 U.S. 81 (1921).

68. William E. Leuchtenburg, *The F.D.R. Years: On Roosevelt and His Legacy* (Oxford, 1995), 40; N. E. H. Hull, *Roscoe Pound and Karl Llewellyn: Searching for an American Jurisprudence* (Chicago, 1997), 120.

69. Peri E. Arnold, *Making the Managerial Presidency: Comprehensive Reorganization Planning, 1905–1980* (Princeton, 1986), 33–47; Skowronek, *Building a New American State*, 204–09.

70. Ronald C. Moe, *Administrative Renewal: Reorganizing Commissions in the Twentieth Century* (Lanham, MD, 2003), 192.

71. James L. McCaffery, "The Development of Public Budgeting in the United States," in *A Centennial History of the American Administrative State*, ed. Ralph C. Chandler (New York, 1987), 365.

72. Not to be confused with his twin brother, Westel Woodbury Willoughby, another important progressive academic.

73. Lewis L. Gould, *The Modern American Presidency* (Kansas, 2003), 39; Roy T. Meyers and Irene S. Rubin, "The Executive Budget in the Federal Government: The First Century and Beyond," *Public Administration Review* 72 (2011), 334–44; W. F. Willoughby, "National Financing—The Old Way and the New," *Congressional Digest* (Nov. 1922), 41.

74. Arnold, *Making the Managerial Presidency*, 55.

75. Cushman, *The Independent Regulatory Commissions*, 299.

76. Reuel Schiller, "Free Speech and Expertise: Administrative Censorship and the Birth of the Modern First Amendment," *Virginia Law Review* 86 (2000), 45–46.

77. David A. Moss and Michael R. Fein, "Radio Regulation Revisited: Coase, the FCC, and the Public Interest," *Journal of Policy History* 15 (2003), 389–416.

78. Ruth O'Brien, *Workers' Paradox: The Republican Origins of New Deal Labor Policy, 1886–1935* (North Carolina, 1998).

79. G. Edward White, "The Emergence and Development of a Law of Torts," *St. Thomas Law Journal* 11 (2015), 43; Price V. M. Fishback and Shawn Everett Kantor, "The Adoption of Workers' Compensation in the United States, 1900–1930," *Journal of Law and Economics* 41 (1998), 316.

80. Paul A. Carter, "Prohibition and Democracy: The Noble Experiment Reassessed," *Wisconsin Magazine of History* 56 (1973), 201.

81. Teaford, *Rise of the States*, 102.

82. David M. P. Freund, *Colored Property: State Policy and White Racial Politics in Suburban America* (Chicago, 2007), 46.

83. William E. Forbath, "Politics, State-Building, and the Courts, 1870–1920," in *The Cambridge History of Law in America*, ed. Michael Grossberg and Christopher Tomlins, 3 vols. (New York, 2011), II: 688; Ely, *Outlines of Economics*, rev. ed. (New York, 1908), 63, quoting economist Francis A. Walker.

84. John G. West, "Darwin's Public Policy: Nineteenth-Century Science and the Rise of the American Welfare State," in *The Progressive Revolution in*

Political and Social Science, ed. John Marini and Ken Masugi (Lanham, MD, 2008), 266–74.

85. Victoria Nourse, "*Buck v. Bell*: A Constitutional Tragedy from a Lost World," *Pepperdine Law Review* 39 (2011), 101–18. As the old joke put it, the plural of *anecdote* is *data*.

86. Paul A. Lombardo, "Three Generations, No Imbeciles: New Light on *Buck v. Bell*," *New York University Law Review* 60 (1985), 30–62; Alfred L. Brophy and Elizabeth Troutman, "The Eugenics Movement in North Carolina" (2015) describes similarly summary procedures in that state.

87. Ibid.

88. Reuel Schiller, "The Era of Deference: Courts, Expertise, and the Emergence of New Deal Administrative Law," *Michigan Law Review* 106 (2007), 434.

89. *F.T.C. v. Gratz*, 253 U.S. 421 (1920).

90. *Federal Radio Commission (F.R.C.) v. General Electric*, 281 U.S. 464 (1930).

91. *J. W. Hampton v. United States*, 276 U.S. 394 (1928), 409.

92. *Euclid v. Ambler Realty*, 272 U.S. 365 (1926).

93. *Massachusetts v. Mellon*, 262 U.S. 447 (1923), 488.

94. Mancur Olson, *The Logic of Collective Action: Public Goods and the Theory of Groups* (Cambridge, 1965).

95. *Myers v. United States*, 272 U.S. 52 (1926).

96. J. David Alvis et al., *The Contested Removal Power* (Kansas, 2013).

97. Nicholas Henry, "The Emergence of Public Administration as a Field of Study," in *A Centennial History of the American Administrative State*; Ralph F. Fuchs, "Concepts and Policies in Anglo-American Administrative Law Theory," *Yale Law Journal* 47 (1938), 538.

98. John Dickinson, *Administrative Justice and the Supremacy of Law* (Cambridge, 1927). See Freund's review of Frankfurter's administrative law casebook in *Harvard Law Review* 46 (1932), 167–71.

99. William C. Chase, *The American Law School and the Rise of Administrative Government* (Wisconsin, 1982); Daniel R. Ernst, *Tocqueville's Nightmare: The Administrative State Emerges in America, 1900–1940* (Oxford, 2014); Martin Shapiro, *The Supreme Court and Administrative Agencies* (New York, 1968), 105.

100. John M. Gaus, "The New Problem of Administration," *Minnesota Law Review* 8 (1924).

101. James M. Beck, *Our Wonderland of Bureaucracy: A Study of the Growth of Bureaucracy in the Federal Government and Its Destructive Effect upon the Constitution* (New York, 1932), 75, 85, 167, 191, 225–26.

102. Charles and William Beard, "The Case for Bureaucracy," *Scribner's*, April 1933, reprinted in *Public Administration Review* 46 (1986), 107–12. It is notable that the Beards used the 1904 disaster of the *General Slocum*—a steamboat wreck in New York's East River which killed more than 1,000 passengers,

mostly women and children—as an example of the need for bureaucracy. A presidential commission held the U.S. Steamboat Inspection Service (USSIS) largely responsible for the calamity. The USSIS often is held to be the most significant example of the overlooked 19th-century administrative state. Lloyd M. Short, *Steamboat Inspection Service: Its History, Activity, and Organization* (New York, 1922), 18; Jerry L. Mashaw, *Creating the Administrative Constitution: The Lost One Hundred Years of American Administrative Law* (Yale, 2012), 188–208.

103. Ibid.

104. Address, San Francisco, September 23, 1932.

Chapter 5

1. Address, San Francisco, September 23, 1932.

2. Murray N. Rothbard, *America's Greatest Depression*, 5th ed. (Auburn, AL, 2000); Gary M. Anderson, William F. Shughart II, and Robert D. Tollison, "A Public Choice Theory of the Great Contraction," *Public Choice* 59 (1988), 3–23; Milton Friedman and Anna Jacobson Schwartz, *The Great Contraction, 1929–1933* (Princeton, 1965).

3. 73 Stat. 195 (1933). The "hundred days" extended from FDR's inauguration in March 1933 until the adjournment of his first Congress in June. The phrase derived from the period in which Emperor Napoleon I escaped from his exile in Elba to try to restore his dictatorship, which finally was defeated at the Battle of Waterloo. It was redolent of the Progressives' campaign to lure Theodore Roosevelt out of retirement in 1912, urging him to come "back from Elba."

4. Daniel J. Gifford, "The New Deal Regulatory Model: A History of Criticisms and Refinements," *University of Minnesota Law Review* 68 (1983), 299–332.

5. Colin Gordon, *New Deals: Business, Labor, and Politics in America, 1920–1935* (Cambridge, 1994), 175; "The Business of Burlesque, A.D. 1935," *Fortune* (Feb. 1935), 140.

6. David A. Horowitz, "Senator Borah's Crusade to Save Small Businessmen from the New Deal," *Historian* 55 (1993), 702.

7. Earlier cases *implicitly* dealt with the delegation principle. The Court had held that the World War One Lever Act had established an unconstitutionally vague standard for price controls. *United States v. L. Cohen Grocery*, 255 U.S. 81 (1921).

8. *Panama Refining Co. v. Ryan*, 293 U.S. 388 (1935), 415.

9. John Locke, *Second Treatise of Civil Government*, II, 9 (1689).

10. *Landmark Briefs and Arguments of the Supreme Court of the United States*, ed. Philip B. Kurland and Gerhard Casper (Arlington, VA, 1975), 837.

11. *Schechter v. United States*, 295 U.S. 495 (1935), 537, 541, 553.

12. Ibid.

13. Ibid.

14. Robert E. Cushman, *The Independent Regulatory Commissions* (New York, 1974 [1941]), 376; James Morlath, "Individual Rights Versus a Seat at the Table: The Guffey Act as an Alternative Model to the Wagner Act," *Georgetown Journal on Poverty Law and Policy* 21 (2013), 123; Lewis L. Lorwin and Arthur Wubnig, *Labor Relations Boards: The Regulation of Collective Bargaining Under the National Industrial Recovery Act* (Washington, 1935), 35.

15. *Carter v. Carter Coal*, 298 U.S. 238 (1936), 310; Andrew J. Ziaja, "Hot Oil and Hot Air: The Development of the Nondelegation Doctrine through the New Deal, a History, 1813–1944," *Hastings Constitutional Law Quarterly* 35 (2008), 921–64.

16. *Jones v. Securities and Exchange Commission*, 298 U.S. 1 (1936), 21; Mark Tushnet, "Administrative Law in the 1930s: The Supreme Court's Accommodation of Progressive Legal Theory," *Duke Law Journal* 60 (2011), 1608.

17. *Jones v. SEC*, 24–28. Jones ultimately was indicted for mail fraud and acquitted.

18. Ibid., 32–33.

19. James M. Landis, *The Administrative Process* (Yale, 1938), 15.

20. Abe Fortas, "The Securities Act and Corporate Reorganizations," *Law and Contemporary Problems* 4 (1937), 239.

21. Ellis Hawley, *The New Deal and the Problem of Monopoly: A Study in Economic Ambivalence* (Princeton, 1966), 272; Marc Allen Eisner, "Discovering Patterns in Regulatory History: Continuity, Change, and Regulatory Regimes," *Journal of Policy History* 6 (1994), 172.

22. It was only partially successful, as no more than one-third of American workers were union members when organized labor was at its strongest, in the decade following World War II.

23. 49 Stat. 449 (1935).

24. Kevin J. McMahon, *Reconsidering Roosevelt on Race: How the Presidency Paved the Road to* Brown (Chicago, 2004), 53–54; Irving Bernstein, *Turbulent Years: A History of the American Worker, 1933–1941* (Boston, 1970), 341.

25. Andrew Jackson similarly overplayed his hand when he faced down the South Carolina nullifiers a century earlier. Richard E. Ellis, *The Union at Risk: Jacksonian Democracy, States' Rights and the Nullification Crisis* (Oxford, 1987), 74–101.

26. *National Labor Relations Board v. Jones & Laughlin Steel Corp.*, 301 U.S. 1 (1937). This was the leading case of five decisions upholding the Wagner Act, often referred to as "the Labor Board cases."

27. A symposium, "The Debate over the Constitutional Revolution of 1937," *American Historical Review* 110 (2005), 1046–1115, covers much of the literature. *See also* Daniel E. Ho and Kevin M. Quinn, "Did a Switch in Time Save Nine?" *Journal of Legal Analysis* 2 (2010), 69–113.

28. Daniel R. Ernst, *Tocqueville's Nightmare: The Administrative State Emerges in America, 1900–1940* (Oxford, 2014), 68.

29. *National Labor Relations Board v. Friedman-Harry Marks Clothing Co.*, 301 U.S. 58 (1937), 93.

30. Harvey Pinney, "Administrative Discretion and the National Labor Relations Board," *Social Forces* 18 (1939), 275–80; Bernard H. Fitzpatrick, "The Employer Must Guess What the Labor Act Means," *America* (July 1940), 400.

31. The British had privileged unions decades earlier. A. V. Dicey noted this as a major undermining of the rule of law. The Trades Disputes Act of 1906 simply "legalized wrongdoing." *Introduction to the Study of the Law of the Constitution* (Indianapolis, 1982 [1885]), lviii (introduction to the 8th edition of 1915).

32. Cushman, *The Independent Regulatory Commissions*, 362.

33. *Humphrey's Executor v. United States*, 295 U.S. 602 (1935), 624.

34. J. David Alvis, Jeremy D. Bailey, and F. Flagg Taylor IV, *The Contested Removal Power, 1789–2010* (Kansas, 2013), 163; Daniel A. Crane, "Debunking Humphrey's Executor," University of Michigan Law School Working Paper (2015).

35. President's Committee on Administrative Management, *Report* (Washington, DC, 1937); Marver H. Bernstein, "Independent Regulatory Agencies: A Perspective on Their Reform," *Annals of the American Academy of Political and Social Science* 400 (1972), 15. Robert Cushman did the research on the independent regulatory commissions for the Brownlow Committee, which he turned into *The Independent Regulatory Commissions* (New York, 1972 [1941]).

36. Richard Polenberg, *Reorganizing Roosevelt's Government: The Controversy over Executive Reorganization, 1936–39* (Harvard, 1969); Barry D. Karl, *Executive Reorganization and Reform in the New Deal: The Genesis of Administrative Management, 1900–1939* (Chicago, 1963).

37. Peri E. Arnold, "The Brownlow Committee, Regulation, and the Presidency: Seventy Years Later," *Public Administration Review* 67 (2007), 1030–40. It was not clear whether the Humphrey case really limited the President's *removal* power at all. Humphrey's estate had gotten his back pay, but Humphrey was not (and could not be) reinstated. Commissioners might be entitled to their salaries, but not to their jobs. Crane, "Debunking Humphrey's Executor."

38. Nicholas S. Zeppos, "The Legal Profession and the Development of Administrative Law," *Chicago-Kent Law Review* 72 (1997) 1119–57.

39. Roscoe Pound, "Liberty of Contract," *Yale Law Journal* 18 (1909), 454–87.

40. "Executive Justice," *American Law Register* 46 (1907), 137–46; Joseph Postell, "The Anti-New Deal Progressive: Roscoe Pound's Alternative Administrative State," *Review of Politics* 74 (2012), 53–85.

41. N. E. H. Hull, *Roscoe Pound and Karl Llewellyn: Searching for an American Jurisprudence* (Chicago, 1997); David Wigdor, *Roscoe Pound, Philosopher of Law* (Westport, CT, 1974).

42. These terms reflect modern rather than classical usage. In the ancient, Aristotelean sense, "politics" was the art of doing justice, of deliberation about the right and the good, of bringing human action into accord with Reason or Nature. In the modern era, "politics" became mere will. The progressives recognized nothing higher than politics; "administration" was the science or technique of achieving whatever the people willed.

43. See Chapter 3, herein.

44. Luther Gulick, "Politics, Administration and the New Deal, " *Annals of the American Academy of Political and Social Science* 169 (1933), 55–66; John A. Rohr, Introduction to Frank J. Goodnow, *Politics and Administration* (New Brunswick, 2003 [1900]), xix; Louis B. Schwartz, "Legal Restriction of Competition in the Regulated Industries: An Abdication of Judicial Responsibility," *Harvard Law Review* 67 (1954), 473; Robert W. Gordon, "Willis's American Counterparts: The Legal Realists' Defense of Administration," *University of Toronto Law Journal* 55 (2005), 424.

45. "Report of the Special Committee on Administrative Law," *Annual Report of the American Bar Association* 63 (1938), 331–62.

46. Ibid.

47. Ibid.

48. *Final Report of the Attorney General's Committee on Administrative Procedure* (Washington, DC, 1941), especially 203–04.

49. Benjamin Cardozo, *The Nature of the Judicial Process* (Yale, 1921).

50. James M. Landis, *The Administrative Process* (Yale, 1938), 10–12, 375, 5; James O. Freedman, *Crisis and Legitimacy: The Administrative Process and American Government* (Cambridge, 1978), 172.

51. Landis, *The Administrative Process*, 5.

52. Alan Brinkley, *The End of Reform: The New Deal in Depression and War* (New York, 1995); Brian Waddell, *The War Against the New Deal: World War II and American Democracy* (Northern Illinois, 2001).

53. Melvin I. Urofsky, *Big Steel and the Wilson Administration: A Study in Business-Government Relations* (Ohio State, 1969); Brinkley, *The End of Reform*.

54. Steve Fraser, "The Good War and the Workers," *American Prospect*, September 20, 2009.

55. Harvey C. Mansfield, "Federal Executive Reorganization: Fifty Years of Experience," *Public Administration Review* 29 (1969), 343.

56. Ironically, the genius was the libertarian economist Milton Friedman.

57. Brinkley, *The End of Reform*, 147.

58. Lawrence Sullivan, *Bureaucracy Runs Amuck* (Indianapolis, 1944), 171; Andrew H. Bartels, "The Office of Price Administration and the Legacy of the New Deal, 1939–1946," *Public Historian* 5 (1983), 5–29.

59. You catch a glimpse of George Bailey (Jimmy Stewart) helping run the OPA as he fights "the Battle of Bedford Falls" in *It's a Wonderful Life*.

60. Meg Jacobs, "'How About Some Meat?': The Office of Price Administration, Consumption Politics, and State Building from the Bottom Up, 1941–1946," *Journal of American History* 84 (1997), 925.

61. Reuel Schiller, "Enlarging the Administrative Polity: Administrative Law and the Changing Definitions of Pluralism," *Vanderbilt Law Review* 53 (2000), 1398, 1404.

62. Howard E. McCurdy, "How Novelists View Public Administration," in *A Centennial History of the American Administrative State*, ed. Ralph C. Chandler (New York, 1987).

63. Martin Krygier, "Weber, Lenin and the Reality of Socialism," in *Bureaucracy: The Career of a Concept*, ed. Eugene Kamenka and Martin Krygier (New York, 1979), 89–101; Daniel Kelly, *James Burnham and the Struggle for the World: A Life* (Wilmington, DE, 2002).

64. See also Herman Finer's response to Hayek, *The Road to Reaction* (Boston, 1945).

65. Franklin Delano Roosevelt, State of the Union Address, January 11, 1944.

66. Cass Sunstein, *The Second Bill of Rights: FDR's Unfinished Revolution and Why We Need It More than Ever* (New York, 2004), 203.

67. Dwight Waldo, *The Administrative State: A Study of the Political Theory of American Public Administration* (New York, 1948), 66–80. Somehow Waldo imagined that a regime devoted to hedonistic gratification could inspire the public-spiritedness of the ancient *polis*. See also his "Politics and Administration: On Thinking About a Complex Relationship," in *A Centennial History of the American Administrative State*, 90.

68. Ibid.

69. 60 Stat. 237 (1946).

70. James E. Brazier, "An Anti-New Deal Legacy: The Administrative Procedure Act," *Journal of Policy History* 8 (1996), 206–26; Mendelson, "Mr. Justice Frankfurter," 448.

71. "The Federal Administrative Procedure Act: Codification or Reform?" *Yale Law Journal* 56 (1947), 670–705; Postell, "The Anti-New Deal Progressive," 80. The wishful thinking by the ABA recalls that of the American Federation of Labor with regard to the labor provisions of the Clayton Antitrust Act.

72. McNollgast, "The Political Origins of the Administrative Procedure Act," *Journal of Law and Economic Organization* 15 (1999), 180–217.

73. George B. Shepard, "Fierce Compromise: The Administrative Procedure Act Emerges from New Deal Politics," *Northwestern University Law Review* 90 (1996), 1557–1683; Joanna L. Grisinger, *The Unwieldy American State: Administrative Politics since the New Deal* (Cambridge, 2012), 11.

74. Schiller, "Enlarging the Administrative Polity," 1399; "The Era of Deference," 429; M. J. C. Vile, *Constitutionalism and the Separation of Powers*, 2nd ed. (Indianapolis, 1998 [1967]), 303.

75. John Kenneth Galbraith, *American Capitalism: The Concept of Countervailing Power* (New York, 1952).

76. Ignoring what Madison called "the permanent and aggregate interests of the community" in *Federalist* 10, Charles Beard began this misattribution in his *Economic Interpretation of the Constitution* of 1913.

Chapter 6

1. Robert L. Rabin, "Federal Regulation in Historical Perspective," *Stanford Law Review* 38 (1986), 1295.

2. Andrew J. Dunbar, *The Truman Scandals and the Politics of Morality* (Missouri, 1984), 10.

3. "Harry S Truman, Domestic Affairs," http://millercenter.org/president /biography/truman-domestic-affairs (accessed August 11, 2016).

4. Jeffrey Frank, *Ike and Dick: Portrait of a Strange Political Marriage* (New York, 2013), 184.

5. Edwin O'Connor, *The Last Hurrah* (Boston, 1956), 374–75.

6. *American National Biography,* ed. John A. Garrity and Marc C. Carnes, 24 vols. (Oxford, 1999).

7. Joanna L. Grisinger, *The Unwieldy State: Administrative Politics Since the New Deal* (Cambridge, 2012), 158.

8. Michael E. Parrish, "The Great Depression, the New Deal, and the American Legal Order," *Washington Law Review* 59 (1984), 748; Nicholas R. Parrillo, "Leviathan and Interpretive Revolution: The Administrative State, the Judiciary, and the Rise of Legislative History, 1890–1950," *Yale Law Journal* 123 (2013), 266; Jon Meacham, "Is Little Rock Corrupting Washington? C'Mon," *Washington Monthly* (May 1994).

9. As Hoover had been a largely apolitical engineer before the 1920s, Eisenhower was an apolitical soldier before the 1950s. Democrats considered both of them as potential candidates, although Eisenhower was more instinctively conservative than the progressive Hoover. Their ideological orientations crisscrossed, with Hoover becoming more conservative and Eisenhower more · liberal.

10. President Eisenhower to Edgar N. Eisenhower, November 8, 1954.

11. David L. Stebenne, *Modern Republicanism: Arthur Larson and the Eisenhower Years* (Indianapolis, 2006).

12. Richard E. Neustadt, *Presidential Power and the Modern Presidents: The Politics of Leadership from Roosevelt to Reagan* (New York, 1991), 10.

13. Alonzo L. Hamby, *Liberalism and Its Challengers: FDR to Bush*, 2d ed. (Oxford, 1992), 100; Peri E. Arnold, *Making the Managerial Presidency: Comprehensive Reorganization Planning, 1905–80* (Princeton, 1986), 160; Charles E. Neu, "The Rise of the National Security Bureaucracy," in *The New American State: Bureaucracies and Policies Since World War Two*, ed. Louis Galambos (Baltimore, 1987), 88.

14. Edward Berkowitz, *America's Welfare State: From Roosevelt to Reagan* (Johns Hopkins, 1991), 14.

15. Memorandum on Conference with FDR, Summer 1941.

16. Berkowitz, *America's Welfare State*, 60–64; Carolyn L. Weaver, "The Social Security Bureaucracy in Triumph and Crisis," in *The New American State*; Willian N. Eskridge Jr. and John Ferejohn, *A Republic of Statutes: The New American Constitutionalism* (Yale, 2010), 167.

17. Cynthia R. Farina, "Due Process at Rashomon Gate: The Stories of *Matthews v. Eldridge*," in *Administrative Law Stories*, ed. Peter L. Strauss (New York, 2006), 235.

18. Marver Bernstein, *Regulating Business by Independent Commission* (Princeton, 1955), 74–102; Marc Allen Eisner, "Discovering Patterns in Regulatory History: Continuity, Change, and Regulatory Regimes," *Journal of Policy History* 6 (1994), 175.

19. Samuel P. Huntington, "The Marasmus of the ICC: The Commission, the Railroads, and the Public Interest," *Yale Law Journal* 61 (1952), 467.

20. Louis B. Schwartz, "Legal Restriction of Competition in the Regulated Industries: An Abdication of Judicial Responsibility," *Harvard Law Review* 67 (1954), 436–75.

21. Louis L. Jaffe, "The Effective Limits of the Administrative Process: A Reevaluation," *Harvard Law Review* 67 (1954), 1134; David H. Rosenbloom, "Retrofitting the Administrative State to the Constitution: Congress and the Judiciary's Twentieth Century Progress," *Public Administration Review* 60 (2000), 39–46.

22. Bernard Schwartz, "The Administrative Agency in Historical Perspective," *Indiana Law Journal* 36 (1961), 263; Bernard Schwartz, *The Professor and the Commissions* (New York, 1959).

23. Patrick Parsons, *Blue Skies: A History of Cable Television* (Philadelphia, 2008), 143; Glen O. Robinson, "The Federal Communications Commission: An Essay on Regulatory Watchdogs," *Virginia Law Review* 64 (1978), 169–262.

24. John R. Walter, "The 3-6-3 Rule: An Urban Legend?" *Economic Quarterly* 92 (2006), 51–78.

25. Ira Stoll, *JFK: Conservative* (New York, 2013).

26. Commencement address, Yale University, June 11, 1962.

27. Justin O'Brien, *The Triumph, Tragedy and Lost Legacy of James M. Landis: A Life on Fire* (Oxford, 2014), 136–39. Ironically, one of the scions of Landis' patron, Ted Kennedy, would be instrumental in abolishing the Civil Aeronautics Board in the 1970s.

28. James Landis, *Report on Regulatory Agencies to the President-Elect*, December 21, 1960.

29. Ibid.

30. Carl McFarland, "Landis' Report: The Voice of One Crying in the Wilderness," *Virginia Law Review* 47 (1961), 392, 416.

31. Stoll, *JFK*.

32. Hamby, *Liberalism and Its Challengers*, 239.

33. David Vogel, "The 'New' Social Regulation in Historical and Comparative Perspective," in *Regulation in Perspective: Historical Essays*, ed. Thomas K. McCraw (Harvard, 1981), 172.

34. *Griggs v. Duke Power Co.*, 401 U.S. 424 (1971). The Court deferred to the EEOC's interpretation of the statute, but might well have adopted the disparate impact theory itself, without it being proffered by the agency.

35. Hugh Davis Graham, "The Great Society's Civil Rights Legacy," in *The Great Society and the High Tide of Liberalism*, ed. Sidney Milkis and Jerome M. Mileur (Massachusetts, 2005), 376.

36. Alfred W. Blumrosen, "The Law Transmission System and the Southern Jurisprudence of Employment Discrimination," *Industrial Relations Law Journal* 6 (1984), 313–52; Paul D. Moreno, *From Direct Action to Affirmative Action: Fair Employment Law and Policy in America, 1933–1972* (Louisiana State, 1997), 237.

37. Eskridge and Ferejohn, *A Republic of Statutes.*

38. Herman Belz, *Equality Transformed: A Quarter-Century of Affirmative Action* (New Brunswick, NJ, 1991), 18–41.

39. Hugh Davis Graham, "Since 1964: The Paradox of American Civil Rights Regulation," in *Taking Stock: American Government in the Twentieth Century*, ed. Morton Keller and R. Shep Melnick (Cambridge, 1999), 194.

40. Theodore R. Marmor, *The Politics of Medicare*, 2d ed. (New York, 1999), 17, 152; Robert B. Helms, "The Origins of Medicare," *World and I* 14 (1999); Edward Berkowitz, "Medicare: The Great Society's Enduring National Health Insurance Program," in *The Great Society and the High Tide of Liberalism*, 322.

41. Charlotte Twight, "Medicare's Origin: The Economics and Politics of Dependency," *Cato Journal* 16 (1997), 309–38.

42. John Teaford, *The Rise of the States: Evolution of American State Government* (Johns Hopkins, 2002); Carolyn L. Weaver, "The Social Security Bureaucracy in Triumph and Crisis," in *The New American State*; Paul P. Van Riper, "The American Administrative State: Wilson and the Founders—An Unorthodox View," *Public Administration Review* 43 (1983).

43. Judith D. Moore and David G. Smith, "Legislating Medicaid: Considering Medicaid and Its Origins," *Health Care Financing Review* 27 (2005), 44–51.

44. Marmor, *Politics of Medicare*, 83–89, 163; Nicholas Bagley, "Medicine as a Public Calling," *Michigan Law Review* 114 (2015); Philip K. Howard, *The Rule of Nobody: Saving America from Dead Laws and Broken Government* (New York, 2014), 17.

45. Gareth Davies, "Toward Big-Government Conservatism: Conservatism and Federal Aid to Education in the 1970s," *Journal of Contemporary History* 43 (2008), 621–35.

46. Patrick McGuinn and Frederick Hess, "Freedom from Ignorance? The Great Society and the Evolution of the Elementary and Secondary Education

Act of 1965," in *The Great Society and the High Tide of Liberalism*, 302; David Brooks, *How We Got Here: The Seventies—The Decade that Brought You Modern Life (for Better or Worse)*, 139. The unionization of teaching had more of an immediate effect than the ESEA. For a similar effect in welfare, see William H. Simon, "Legality, Bureaucracy, and Class in the Welfare System," *Yale Law Journal* 92 (1983), 1198–1269.

47. Jeremy Rabkin, "Office for Civil Rights," in *The Politics of Regulation*, ed. J. Q. Wilson (New York, 1980).

48. Ibid.

49. Theodore J. Lowi, *The End of Liberalism: The Second Republic of the United States*, 40th anniversary ed. (New York, 2009), 297.

50. Herman Belz, "New Left Reverberations in the Academy: The Antipluralist Critique of Constitutionalism," *Review of Politics* 36 (1974), 265–83; William L. Morrow, "The Pluralist Legacy in American Public Administration," in *A Centennial History of the American Administrative State*, ed. Ralph C. Chandler (New York, 1987).

51. Lowi, *The End of Liberalism*, 225.

52. Gabriel Kolko, *The Triumph of Conservatism: A Reinterpretation of American History, 1900–1916* (New York, 1963)

53. George J. Stigler, "The Theory of Regulation," *Bell Journal of Economics and Management Science* 2 (1971), 17. See the critical review of Thomas K. McCraw, "Regulation, Chicago Style," *Reviews in American History* 4 (1976), 297–303.

54. George Stigler, "Public Regulation of the Securities Markets," *Journal of Business* 37 (1964), 117–42.

55. Richard A. Posner, "The Federal Trade Commission," *University of Chicago Law Review* 37 (1969), 87.

56. Vogel, "The 'New' Social Regulation," 155–85; William Lilley III and James C. Miller III, "The New 'Social Regulation,'" *Public Interest* 47 (1977), 49.

57. Richard A. Harris and Sidney M. Milkis, *The Politics of Regulatory Change: A Tale of Two Agencies*, 2nd ed. (Oxford, 1996), 7; Alfred Marcus, "Environmental Protection Agency," in *The Politics of Regulation*.

58. Sidney M. Milkis, "Remaking Government Institutions in the 1970s: Participatory Democracy and the Triumph of Administrative Politics," *Journal of Policy History* 10 (1998), 53.

59. Prina Lahav, "Holmes and Brandeis: Libertarian and Republican Justifications for Free Speech," *Journal of Law and Politics* 4 (1988), 451–82; Pierre Lemieux, "The Dangers of 'Public Health,'" *Regulation* (Fall 2013), 30–35.

60. May 22, 1964.

61. Gary L. Wansley et al., "The Pubic Administration and the Governing Process: Refocusing the American Dialogue," in *A Centennial History of the American Administrative State*, 303.

62. Leslie H. Gelb and Richard K. Betts, *The Irony of Vietnam: The System Worked* (Washington, DC, 1979); R. W. Komer, *Bureaucracy at War: US Performance in the Vietnam Conflict* (Boulder, CO, 1986); Paul Joseph, "The Politics of 'Good' and 'Bad' Information: The National Security-Bureaucracy and the Vietnam War," *Politics and Society* 7 (1977), 105–26.

63. Paul H. Weaver, "Regulation, Social Policy, and Class Conflict," *Public Interest* 50 (1978), 56; Daniel Kelly, *James Burnham and the Struggle for the World: A Life* (Wilmington, DE, 2002), 95; David Vogel, "The Public-Interest Movement and the American Reform Tradition," *Political Science Quarterly* 95 (1981), 626; Sidney M. Milkis, "Remaking Government Institutions in the 1970s: Participatory Democracy and the Triumph of Administrative Politics," *Journal of Policy History* 10 (1998), 51–74; Hamburger, *Is Administrative Law Unlawful?* (Chicago, 2014), 502.

64. Reuel Schiller, "The Era of Deference: Courts, Expertise, and the Emergence of New Deal Administrative Law," *Michigan Law Review* 106 (2007), 399–441; Richard B. Stewart, "Administrative Law in the Twenty-First Century," *New York University Law Review* 78 (2003), 439, 443.

65. Gary Lawson, ed., *Federal Administrative Law*, 5th ed. (St. Paul, MN, 2009), 253; Thomas W. Merrill, "Capture Theory and the Courts, 1967–1983," *Chicago-Kent Law Review* 72 (1997), 1051.

66. Richard B. Stewart, "The Reformation of American Administrative Law," *Harvard Law Review* 88 (1975), 1682; David H. Rosenbloom, "Retrofitting the Administrative State to the Constitution: Congress and the Judiciary's Twentieth-Century Progress," *Public Administration Review* 60 (2000), 44; Steven M. Teles, *The Rise of the Conservative Legal Movement: The Battle for Control of the Law* (Princeton, 2008), 43.

67. R. Shep Melnick, "From Tax and Spend to Mandate and Sue: Liberalism after the Great Society," in *The Great Society and the High Tide of Liberalism*; "Risky Business," 170; "The Politics of Partnership," *Public Administration Review* 45 (1985), 658; Hugh Davis Graham, *The Civil Rights Era*, 470.

68. Stephen Skowronek, *Building a New American State: The Expansion of National Administrative Capacities, 1877–1920* (Cambridge, 1982), 24.

69. 304 U.S. 144 (1938); David H. Rosenbloom, "The Judicial Response to the Rise of the Administrative State," *American Review of Public Administration* 15 (1981), 29–51.

70. *International Harvester v. Ruckelshaus*, 478 F.2d 615 (1973) 651.

71. Charles A. Reich, "The New Property," *Yale Law Journal* 73 (1964), 786.

72. William J. Novak, "The Myth of the 'Weak' American State," *American Historical Review* 113 (2008), 770.

73. *Goldberg v. Kelly*, 397 U.S. 254 (1970).

74. *Wyman v. James*, 400 U.S. 309 (1971).

75. Rosenbloom, "The Judicial Response to the Rise of the American Administrative State."

76. Ronald J. Krotoszynski, Jr., "'History Belongs to the Winners': The Bazelon-Leventhal Debate and the Continuing Relevance of the Process/Substance Dichotomy in Judicial Review of Administrative Action," *Administrative Law Review* 58 (2006), 995–1015; Gillian E. Metzger, "The Story of *Vermont Yankee*: A Cautionary Tale of Judicial Review and Nuclear Waste," in *Administrative Law Stories,* ed. Peter L. Strauss (New York, 2006), 126; R. Shep Melnick, "The Politics of Partnership," 653–60.

77. Stewart, "Reformation of American Administrative Law," 1755; Robert L. Rabin, "Federal Regulation in Historical Perspective," *Stanford Law Review* 38 (1986), 1309; Teles, *Rise of the Conservative Legal Movement*, 52.

78. *Scenic Hudson Preservation Conference v. Federal Power Commission,* 354 F.2d 608 (1965).

79. *United States v. SCRAP*, 412 U.S. 669 (1973).

80. Rosenbloom, "The Judicial Response," 41.

81. Alfred H. Kelly, Winfred A. Harbison, and Herman Belz, *The American Constitution: Its Origins and Development*, 7th ed. (New York, 1991), 653; *Amalgamated Meat Cutters v. Connally*, 337 F. Supp. 737 (1971).

82. The FBI would not do his bidding in illegal domestic spying, so he set up a parallel espionage corps in the White House. One disgruntled FBI careerist, Mark Felt, was the "Deep Throat" source that did so much to expose Watergate. Keith Olson, *Watergate: The Presidential Scandal that Shook America* (Kansas, 2003), 7.

83. *RN: The Memoirs of Richard Nixon* (New York, 1990), 352.

84. Ronald C. Moe, *Administrative Renewal: Reorganizing Commissions in the Twentieth Century* (Lanham, MD, 2003), 93–95; Kelly, Harbison, and Belz, *The American Constitution*, 660–67.

85. Suzanne Weaver, "Antitrust Division of the Department of Justice," in J. Q. Wilson (ed.), *The Politics of Regulation* (New York, 1980), 145.

86. Richard P. Nathan, *The Plot that Failed: Nixon and the Administrative Presidency* (New York, 1975); Kelly, Harbison, and Belz, *The American Constitution*, 674–76, 713.

Chapter 7

1. James MacGregor Burns, *Congress on Trial: The Legislative Process and the Administrative State* (New York, 1949).

2. The Supreme Court held the legislative veto unconstitutional in 1986, but Congress has continued to enact them.

3. John Adams Wettergreen, "Constitutional Problems of American Bureaucracy, Beginning with *INS v. Chada*," *Political Communication* 9 (1992), 93–110.

4. Morris P. Fiorina, *Congress: Keystone of the Washington Establishment*, 2nd ed. (Yale, 1989), 44; William West and Joseph Cooper, "The Congressional Veto and Administrative Lawmaking," *Political Science Quarterly* 98 (1983),

285–304; Charles Frankel, "Bureaucracy and the New Europe," *Daedalus* 93 (1964), 471–92.

5. *The Imperial Congress: Crisis in the Separation of Powers*, ed. Gordon S. Jones and John A. Marini (New York, 1988).

6. Martha Derthick and Paul J. Quirk, *The Politics of Deregulation* (Brookings Institution Press, 1985), the authors downplay the economic theory of regulation; *cf.* Joseph D. Kearney and Thomas W. Merrill, "The Great Transformation of Regulated Industries Law," *Columbia Law Review* 98 (1998), 1394.

7. David Frum, *How We Got Here: The 70s—The Decade that Brought You Modern Life (For Better or Worse)* (New York, 2000), 291.

8. *The Oxford Handbook of American Bureaucracy*, ed. Robert F. Durant (2010), 18.

9. James Q. Wilson, *The Politics of Regulation* (Basic Books, 1980), 393; Derthick and Quirk, *The Politics of Deregulation*; Thomas F. Walton and James Langenfeld, "Regulation Under Reagan—The Right Way and the Wrong Way," in *Regulation in the Reagan Era: Politics, Bureaucracy, and the Public Interest*, ed. Roger E. Meiners and Bruce Yandle (New York, 1989), 61. A similar transformation took place in antitrust law in this period.

10. Bradley Behrman, "Civil Aeronautics Board," in Wilson, *The Politics of Regulation*, 96.

11. Derthick and Quirk, *The Politics of Deregulation*, 36–42.

12. Thomas K. McCraw, *Prophets of Regulation: Charles Francis Adams, Louis D. Brandeis, James M. Landis, Alfred E. Kahn* (Harvard, 1984), 260; Anthony Downer Crain, "Ford, Carter, and Deregulation in the 1970s," *Journal of Telecommunications and High Technology Law* 5 (2007), 413–47.

13. George W. Douglas and Peter Metrinko, "Civil Aeronautics Board Sunset: Surprise at the Department of Transportation?" in *Regulation in the Reagan Era: Politics, Bureaucracy and the Public Interest*, 188.

14. Derthick and Quirk, *Politics of Deregulation*; Crain, "Ford, Carter, and Deregulation," 421, 435; Thomas Gale Moore, "The Beneficiaries of Trucking Regulation," *Journal of Law and Economics* 21 (1978), 327.

15. John Howard Brown, "Jimmy Carter, Alfred Kahn, and Airline Deregulation," *Independent Review* 19 (2014), 85–99; Joseph D. Kearney and Thomas W. Merrill, "The Great Transformation of Regulated Industries Law."

16. Mina Kimes, "Railroads: Cartel or Free Market Success Story?" *CNN Money*, September 13, 2011. It is probable that this would have occurred much sooner had the railroads never been regulated.

17. Paul S. Dempsey "The Empirical Results of Deregulation: A Decade Later, and the Band Played On," *Transportation Law Journal* 17 (1988), 92.

18. Douglas W. Caves, Lauritis R. Christensen, and Joseph A. Swanson, "The Staggers Act, 30 Years Later," *Regulation* (Winter 2011), 28; Donald V. Harper and James C. Johnson, "The Potential Consequences of Deregulation of Transportation Revisited," *Land Economics* 63 (1987), 137–46; Thomas Gale

Moore, "Unfinished Business in Motor Carrier Deregulation," *Regulation* 7 (1991), 49–57.

19. The biggest step in telecom deregulation was the dissolution of the AT&T monopoly, which came about by an old-fashioned Justice Department antitrust suit. Derthick and Quirk, *Politics of Deregulation*, 137.

20. Glen O. Robinson, "The Federal Communications Commission: An Essay on Regulatory Watchdogs," *Virginia Law Review* 64 (1978), 169–262.

21. Matthew A. Creson and Francis E. Rourke, "By Way of Conclusion: American Bureaucracy Since World War Two," in *The New American State: Bureaucracies and Policies since World War Two*, ed. Louis Galambos (Johns Hopkins, 1987), 168.

22. Robinson, "The Federal Communications Commission," 170.

23. Mark Green and Ralph Nader, "Economic Regulation vs. Competition: Uncle Sam the Monopoly Man," *Yale Law Journal* 82 (1973), 871–89.

24. Matthew A. Creson and Francis E. Rourke, "By Way of Conclusion: American Bureaucracy Since World War Two," in *The New American State*, 168.

25. George C. Greanis and Duane Windsor, "Is Judicial Restraint Possible in an Administrative State?" *Judicature* 64 (1981), 405; Moore, "Unfinished Business in Motor Carrier Deregulation"; Benjamin J. Allen, "Nature and Implications of the 'Partial Deregulation' of the Railroad Industry in the United States," *International Journal of Transportation Economics* 10 (1983), 373–84; Douglas and Metrinko, "Civil Aeronautics Board Sunset"; Martin Shapiro, *Who Guards the Guardians? Judicial Control of Administration* (Georgia, 1988), 96.

26. Toby S. Edelman, "Reagan's Attempt to Control the Federal Administrative Process Is Unconstitutional," *Clearinghouse Review* 15 (1981), 646–48; Morton Rosenberg, "Congress' Prerogative over Agency Decisions: The Rise and Demise of the Reagan Administration's Theory of the Unitary Executive," *George Washington Law Review* 57 (1989), 627–702.

27. Murray L. Weidenbaum, "Regulatory Reform Under the Reagan Administration," in *The Reagan Regulatory Strategy*, ed. George C. Eads and Michael Fix (Washington, DC, 1984), 15.

28. Richard A. Harris and Sidney M. Milkis, *The Politics of Regulatory Change: A Tale of Two Agencies* (Oxford 1989), 5, 16.

29. Robert A. Rogowsky, "Sub Rosa Regulation: The Iceberg Beneath the Surface," in *Regulation and the Reagan Era: Politics, Bureaucracy and the Public Interest*, ed. Roger E Meiners and Bruce Yandle (New York, 1989), 218.

30. Robert Maranto, "The Administrative Strategies of Republican Presidents from Eisenhower to Reagan," *Presidential Studies Quarterly* 12 (1993), 686–88.

31. Robert Higgs, *Crisis and Leviathan: Critical Episodes in the Growth of American Government* (Oxford, 1987).

32. Similarly, any chance that Nixon's second term might curtail the bureaucratic state was undone by his illegal activities that he justified using national security concerns.

33. Weidenbaum, "Regulatory Reform Under the Reagan Administration," 17–19.

34. Harris and Milkis, *The Politics of Regulatory Change*, 64. It is notable that Alexis de Tocqueville, who envisioned the inclination of democracies to the "soft despotism" of the bureaucratic state, also noted their tendency to the religious pantheism evident in environmentalism. *Democracy in America*, ed. Eduardo Nolla, trans. James T. Schleifer (Indianapolis, 2012), 757.

35. R. Shep Melnik, "Regulation," in *The Oxford Companion to American Law*, ed. Kermit Hall (Oxford, 2002); "Risky Business: Government and the Environment After Earth Day," in *Taking Stock: American Government in the Twentieth Century*, ed. Morton Keller and R. Shep Melnik (Cambridge, 1999), 159.

36. Michael S. Greve, "Why 'Defunding the Left' Failed," *Public Interest* 89 (1987), 91–106.

37. Harris and Milkis, *The Politics of Regulatory Change*, 258; John Adams Wettergreen, "The Regulatory Revolution" (The Heritage Foundation, 1988), 4; Mark Green, "The Gang that Can't Deregulate," *New Republic*, March 21, 1983, 14–17; Roger E. Meiners and Bruce Yandle, "Regulatory Lessons from the Reagan Era: An Introduction," in *Regulation in the Reagan Era*, 7.

38. *United Steelworkers v. Weber*, 443 U.S. 193 (1979).

39. Herman Belz, *Equality Transformed: A Quarter Century of Affirmative Action* (New Brunswick, NJ, 1991), 195–209; Barry D. Friedman, *Regulation in the Reagan-Bush Era: The Emergence of Presidential Influence* (Johns Hopkins, 1995), 173; Steven M. Teles, *The Rise of the Conservative Legal Movement: The Battle for Control of the Law* (Princeton, 2008), 59, 88, 228; R. Shep Melnik, "Risky Business," 176; Hugh Davis Graham, "Since 1964: The Paradox of American Civil Rights Regulation," in *Taking Stock*, 205, 208.

40. Maranto, "Administrative Strategies," 687–89.

41. Jonathan Zimmerman, "Uncle Sam at the Blackboard: The Federal Government and American Education," in *To Promote the General Welfare: The Case for Big Government*, ed. Steven Conn (Oxford, 2012).

42. Theodore R. Marmor, *The Politics of Medicare*, 2d ed. (New York, 1999), 108. Marmor calls these price controls "a new regulatory regime," precisely what Harris and Milkis argue that Reagan had *failed* to achieve—*The Politics of Regulatory Change*, 275.

43. Richard P. Nathan, *The Plot that Failed: Nixon and the Administrative Presidency* (New York, 1975), 82; Harris and Milkis, *Politics of Regulatory Change*, 366.

44. David A. Stockman, "How to Avoid an Economic Dunkirk," *Challenge* 24, No. 1 (March/April 1981), 17–21.

45. Marissa Martino Golden, *What Motivates Bureaucrats? Politics and Administration During the Reagan Years* (New York, 2000).

46. Paul S. Dempsey, "The Rise and Fall of the ICC: The Tortuous Path from Regulation to Deregulation of America's Infrastructure," *Marquette Law Review* 95 (2012), 1180.

47. Thomas O. McGarity, "Regulatory Reform in the Reagan Era," *Maryland Law Review* 45 (1986), 261; Thomas F. Walton and James Langenfeld, "Regulation Under Reagan—The Right Way and the Wrong Way," in *Regulation in the Reagan Era*, 41.

48. David C. Vladeck, "Delay, Unreasonable Intervention: The Battle to Force Regulation of Ethylene Oxide," in *Administrative Law Stories,* ed. Peter L. Straus (New York, 2006), 201; Weidenbaum, "Regulatory Reform Under the Reagan Administration," 39; Golden, *What Motivates Bureaucrats?* 135.

49. Steven R. Weisman, "Watt Quits Post," *New York Times*, Oct. 10, 1983.

50. Harris and Milkis, *The Politics of Regulatory Change,* 112; Robert E. Litan, "Regulatory Policy in the Second Reagan Term," *Brookings Review* (Spring 1985), 21–27.

51. Greve, "Why 'Defunding the Left' Failed," 99; Samuel P. Hays, "The Politics of Environmental Administration," in *The New American State,* 37.

52. Jordan Weissmann, "Disability Insurance: America's $124 Billion Secret Welfare Program," *Atlantic*, March 25, 2013; Chana Joffe-Walt, "Unfit for Work: The Startling Rise of Disability in America," NPR Planet Money broadcast, http://apps.npr.org/unfit-for-work/ (accessed December 20, 2015).

53. Richard B. Stewart, "Administrative Law in the Twenty-First Century," *New York University Law Review* 78 (2003), 439–43.

54. Harris and Milkis, *The Politics of Regulatory Change*, 43. The New Deal Court, in *United States v. Carolene Products* (1938), signaled that it would no longer protect "property" rights as much as it did "personal" rights, especially those of "discrete and insular minorities."

55. Reuel E. Schiller, "An Unexpected Antagonist: Courts, Deregulation, and Conservative Judicial Ideology, 1980–1984," in *Making Legal History: Essays in Honor of William E. Nelson*, ed. Daniel J. Hulsebosch and R. B. Bernstein (New York, 2013), 264–292. For a contrary view, see Friedman, *Regulation in the Reagan-Bush Era*, 125.

56. *Federalist* 51.

57. *Industrial Union Department v. American Petroleum Institute*, 448 U.S. 607 (1980), 675.

58. Antonin Scalia, "A Note on the Benzene Case," *Regulation* (July/Aug. 1980), 28.

59. *American Textile Manufacturers v. Donovan*, 452 U.S. 490 (1981); "Supreme Court Upholds OSHA's Cotton Dust Standard, Deals Setback to Cost-Benefit Analysis," *Environmental Law Reporter* 11 (1981), 10163.

60. *Motor Vehicle Manufacturers Association v. State Farm*, 463 U.S. 29 (1983); Jerry L. Mashaw, "The Story of *Motor Vehicle Manufacturers Association of the United States v. State Farm Mutual Automobile Insurance Co.*: Law, Science and Politics in the Administrative State," in *Administrative Law Stories*; Schiller, "An Unexpected Antagonist," 272.

61. Thomas W. Merrill, "The Story of *Chevron*: The Making of an Accidental Landmark," in *Administrative Law Stories*; Thomas W. Merrill, "Justice Stevens

and the *Chevron* Puzzle," *Northwestern University Law Review* 106 (2012), 551–66; Antonin Scalia, "Remarks," *Administrative Law Review* 66 (2014), 243–51.

62. Gary Lawson, *Federal Administrative Law*, 5th ed. (St. Paul, MN, 2009), 371–582.

63. William N. Eskridge Jr. and John Ferejohn, *A Republic of Statutes: The New American Constitution* (Yale, 2010), 177; Schiller, "An Unexpected Antagonist"; David McIntosh and William J. Haun, "The Separation of Powers in an Administrative State," in *Liberty's Nemesis: The Unchecked Expansion of the State*, ed. Dean Reuter and John Yoo (New York, 2016), 247; James R. Conde and Michael Greve, "*Yakus* and the Administrative State" (2015); Martin Shapiro, *Who Guards the Guardians? Judicial Control of Administration* (Georgia, 1988), 124. A similar double standard was apparent in the Roosevelt Court, whose liberals showed more deference to pro-labor than to pro-business agencies. This was in keeping with the spirit of the *Carolene Products* case— David H. Rosenbloom, "The Judicial Response to the Rise of the Administrative State," *American Review of Public Administration* 15 (1981), 29–51.

64. Speech, Elmira, NY, 3 May 1907, in *Papers and Addresses of Charles Evans Hughes* (New York, 1908), 139.

65. Alonzo L. Hamby, *Liberalism and Its Challengers: FDR to Bush* (Oxford, 1992), 385.

66. Stewart, "Administrative Law in the Twenty-First Century," 440; Elena Kagan, "Presidential Administration," *Harvard Law Review* 114 (2001), 2245–2385; Daniel A. Farber and Anne Joseph O'Connell, "The Lost World of Administrative Law," *Texas Law Review* 92 (2014), 1137–89.

67. Harris and Milkis, *The Politics of Regulatory Change*, 29; John A. Rohr, *To Run a Constitution: The Legitimacy of the Administrative State* (Kansas, 1986).

68. Reagan had made a similar gesture in 1976, proposing to adopt Richard Schweicker, the most liberal Republican in the Senate, as his running mate.

69. Harris and Milkis, *Politics of Regulatory Change*, 280–86; Mark Green and Mark A. Pinsky, "George Bush's Regulatory Flop," *Nation*, October 31, 1988, 414; E. J. Dionne, Jr., "The Democrats in Atlanta," *New York Times*, July 22, 1988.

70. Ed Rubenstein, "The Re-Regulation President," *National Review*, September 14, 1991, 16; Steven Waldman, "Regulation Comes Back," *Newsweek*, September 12, 1988, p. 44.

71. Weissmann, "Disability Insurance." The Social Security Disability system is the largest adjudicatory body in the world. Daytime television is filled with the advertisements of lawyers who promise to get your disability application approved.

72. Scott C. James, "Prelude to Progressivism: Party Decay, Populism, and the Doctrine of a 'Free and Unrestrained Competition' in American Antitrust Policy, 1890–1897," *Studies in American Political Development* 13 (1999), 288–336.

73. Robert W. Crandall, *Competition and Chaos: Telecommunications since the 1996 Telecom Act* (Washington, DC, 2005), 6, 16, 156.

74. Gerald P. O'Driscoll Jr., "Money and the Present Crisis," *Cato Journal* 29 (2009), 167–86.

75. Joffe-Walt, "Unfit for Work."

76. Patrick McGuinn and Frederick Hess, "Freedom from Ignorance? The Great Society and the Evolution of the Elementary and Secondary Education Act of 1965," in *The Great Society and the High Tide of Liberalism*, ed. Sidney Milkis and Jerome M. Mileur (Massachusetts, 2005), 310.

77. Sidney M. Milkis and Jesse H. Rhodes, "George W. Bush, the Republican Party, and the 'New' American Party System," *Perspectives on Politics* 5 (2007), 461–88; David H. Rosenbloom, "Reevaluating Executive-Centered Administrative Theory," in *The Oxford Handbook of American Bureaucracy*.

78. They had been so for the first few weeks of his administration, until Vermont Republican James Jeffords switched parties and gave the Democrats control of the Senate.

79. Kevin A. Hassett, "The Deregulation That Wasn't," *National Review*, August 16, 2010, 6; Katherine Mangu-Ward, "Is Deregulation to Blame?" *Reason*, January 2009, 37; Deidre Dawson, "Reluctant Warriors: When It Comes to Deregulation, Bush is No Reagan," *Legal Times*, December 24, 2001, 34; Rebecca Adams, "GOP, Business Rewrite the Regulatory Playbook," *CQ Weekly*, May 5, 2001; Rebecca Adams, "Regulating the Rule-Makers: John Graham at OIRA," *CQ Weekly*, February 23, 2002.

80. Jeffrey Goldberg, "Party Unfaithful," *New Yorker*, June 4, 2007; Christopher DeMuth, "The Regulatory State," *National Affairs* (Summer 2012), 74.

81. Morton Keller, *Obama's Time: A History* (Oxford, 2015), 36.

82. The midterm loss of Congress was also due to the exposure of lobbying by Jack Abramoff, who used his ties with congressional Republicans on behalf of his Indian-casino clients.

83. Christopher DeMuth, "The Regulatory State," *National Affairs* (Summer 2012).

84. Peter J. Wallison, "The Designation of Systemically Important Financial Institutions by the Financial Stability Oversight Council and the Financial Stability Board," in *Liberty's Nemesis*, 331.

85. Timothy A. Canova, "Legacy of the Clinton Bubble," *Dissent* (Summer 2008), 41–50; Peter Ferara, "Media Parrot Obama Financial Crisis Campaign Propaganda," *Forbes*, November 10, 2011.

86. M. Stanton Evans, "The Liberal Twilight," *Imprimis* 5 (1976), 1–6; Dale Steinreich, "The Savings and Loan Debacle Twenty-Five Years Later: A Misesian Re-Examination and Final Closing of the Books," *Quarterly Journal of Austrian Economics* 17 (2014), 154; F. A. Hayek, *The Constitution of Liberty* (Chicago, 1960), 338; Wallison, "The Designation of Systemically Important Financial Institutions," 332. Charles Norris Cochrane sees this phenomenon in the ancient

Roman historians Livy and Ammianus—*Christianity and Classical Culture* (Indianapolis, 2003 [1940]), 348.

87. *Federalist* 44.

88. Gretchen Morgenson and Joshua Rosner, *Reckless Endangerment* (New York, 2011); John A. Allison, *The Financial Crisis and the Free Market Cure* (New York, 2013).

89. The Freedmen's Savings Bank of the Reconstruction period provides a similar moral-hazard story.

90. Daniel C. L. Handy, "Regulatory Capture in Banking," International Monetary Fund (2006).

91. Steven M. Davidoff and David Zaring, "Regulation by Deal: The Government's Response to the Financial Crisis," *Administrative Law Review* 61 (2009), 463–541; Richard A. Epstein, "The Fannie/Freddie Fiasco: Executive Overreach in the Regulation of Financial Markets," in *Liberty's Nemesis*, 108.

92. Davidoff and Zaring, "Regulation by Deal"; Allison, *The Financial Crisis*; Stephen Gandel, "Did the Auto Bailouts Break the Constitution?" *Time*, December 8, 2010; John Schwartz, "Some Ask if Bailout Is Unconstitutional," *New York Times*, January 15, 2009; Keller, *Obama's Time*, 75.

93. Ironically, the universal mandate had been a conservative idea, like income-tax withholding and the negative income tax, and a feature of the Massachusetts health-insurance law signed by Obama's 2012 opponent, Mitt Romney. Avik Roy, "How the Heritage Foundation, a Conservative Think Tank, Promoted the Individual Mandate," *Forbes*, October 20, 2011.

94. Peter Suderman, "Unpacking Obamacare," *Reason* 47 (2105), 54; Keller, *Obama's Time*, 109.

95. Charles Kesler, *I Am the Change: Barack Obama and the Crisis of Liberalism* (New York, 2012).

96. Betsy McCaughey, "Obama's Health Rationer-in-Chief," *Wall St. Journal*, August 27, 2009; Pierre Lemieux, "The Dangers of 'Public Health,'" *Regulation* (Fall 2013), 30–35.

97. Philip J. Hamburger, *Is Administrative Law Unlawful?* (Chicago, 2014), 375.

98. Norbert Michel, "Dodd-Frank's Expansion of Federal Power: A Historical Perspective," *Cato Journal* 34 (2014), 557–67.

99. Earlier regulation, especially state bank regulation, had made the American banking system unusually decentralized.

100. Todd Zywicki, "The Consumer Financial Protection Bureau: Savior or Menace?" (2012).

101. Kagan, "Presidential Administration."

102. *Noel Canning v. NLRB*, 573 U.S. ___ (2014).

103. David J. Barron and Todd D. Rakoff, "In Defense of Big Waiver," *Columbia Law Review* 113 (2013), 265–345; Yair Sagy, "A Better Defense of Big Waiver: From James Landis to Louis Jaffe," *Marquette Law Review* 98 (2014), 697–761.

104. "Remarks by the President," 14 Jan. 2014, Office of the White House

Press Secretary, https://www.whitehouse.gov/the-press-office/2014/01/14/remarks
-president-cabinet-meeting (accessed 1 Aug. 2016).

105. Of course, those who adhere to the "nondelegation" principle will
make a similar argument against waivers.

106. Michael S. Greve, "The Rise of Executive Federalism," *RealClearPolicy
Blog* (May 26, 2015).

107. Keller, *Obama's Time*, 127.

108. Derek W. Black, "Federalizing Education by Waiver?" *Vanderbilt Law
Review* 68 (2015), 607–80.

109. Robert J. Delahunty and John C. Yoo, "Dream On: The Obama
Administration's Nonenforcement of Immigration Laws, the DREAM Act, and
the Take Care Clause," *Texas Law Review* 91 (2013).

110. Jonathan H. Adler, "The Ad Hoc Implementation of Health Care
Reform," in *Liberty's Nemesis*; Ted Cruz, "The Obama Administration's
Unprecedented Lawlessness," *Harvard Journal of Law and Public Policy* 38
(2014), 64–115.

111. *National Federation of Independent Business v. Sibelius,* 567 U.S. ___
(2012).

112. *King v. Burwell,* 576 U.S. ___ (2015).

Conclusion

1. As Allan Bloom put it in *The Closing of the American Mind: How Higher
Education Has Failed Democracy and Impoverished the Souls of Today's
Students* (New York, 1987), 152.

Select Bibliography

A Centennial History of the American Administrative State. Edited by Ralph C. Chandler. New York: Free Press, 1986.

Administrative Law Stories. Edited by Peter L. Strauss. New York: Foundation, 2006.

Alvis, J. David, Jeremy D. Bailey and F. Flagg Taylor IV. *The Contested Removal Power.* Lawrence: University of Kansas Press, 2013.

American Bar Association. "Report of the Special Committee on Administrative Law." *Annual Report of the American Bar Association* 63 (1938).

Balogh, Brian. *A Government Out of Sight: The Mystery of National Authority in Nineteenth Century America.* New York: Cambridge University Press, 2009.

Bernstein, Marver. *Regulating Business by Independent Commission.* Princeton, NJ: Princeton University Press, 1955.

Burns, Arnold I., and Stephen Markman. "Understanding Separation of Powers." *Pace Law Review* 7 (1987).

Carpenter, Daniel P. *The Forging of Bureaucratic Autonomy: Reputations, Networks, and Policy Innovation in the Executive Agencies, 1862–1928.* Princeton, NJ: Princeton University Press, 2001.

Chase, William C. *The American Law School and the Rise of Administrative Government.* Madison: University of Wisconsin Press, 1982.

Crenson, Matthew A. *The Federal Machine: Beginnings of Bureaucracy in Jacksonian America.* Baltimore, MD: Johns Hopkins University Press, 1975.

Cuellar, Mariano-Florentine. "Administrative War." *George Washington Law Review* 82 (2014).

Cushman, Robert E. *The Independent Regulatory Commissions.* New York: Oxford University Press, 1941.

De Tocqueville, Alexis. *Democracy in America.* Edited by Eduardo Nolla. Translated by James T. Schleifer. Indianapolis: Liberty Fund, 2010.

Derthick, Martha, and Paul J. Quirk. *The Politics of Deregulation*. Washington, DC: Brookings, 1985.

Dicey, A. V. *Introduction to the Study of the Law of the Constitution*. Indianapolis: Liberty Fund, 1982 [1885].

Dickinson, John. *Administrative Justice and the Supremacy of Law*. Cambridge, MA: Harvard University Press, 1927.

Ernst, Daniel R. *Tocqueville's Nightmare: The Administrative State Emerges in America, 1900–1940*. New York: Oxford University Press, 2014.

Eskridge, William N., and John Ferejohn. *A Republic of Statutes: The New American Constitutionalism*. New Haven, CT: Yale University Press, 2010.

Federal Administrative Law. Edited by Gary Lawson. 5th ed. St. Paul, MN: West, 2009.

Final Report of the Attorney General's Committee on Administrative Procedure. Washington, DC: U.S. Government Printing Office, 1941.

Fiorina, Morris P. *Congress: Keystone of the Washington Establishment*. 2nd ed. New Haven: Yale University Press, 1989.

Freedman, James O. *Crisis and Legitimacy: The Administrative Process and American Government*. New York: Cambridge University Press, 1978.

Goodnow, Frank J. *Politics and Administration*. New Brunswick, NJ: Transaction, 2003 [1900].

Goodnow, Frank J. *The Principles of the Administrative Law of the United States*. New York: G. P. Putnam's Sons, 1905.

Grisinger, Joanna L. *The Unwieldy American State: Administrative Politics Since the New Deal*. New York: Cambridge University Press, 2012.

Hamburger, Philip. *Is Administrative Law Unlawful?* Chicago: University of Chicago Press, 2013.

Harris, Richard A., and Sidney M. Milkis. *The Politics of Regulatory Change: A Tale of Two Agencies*. 2d ed. New York: Oxford University Press, 1996.

Hartog, Hendrik. "The Public Law of a County Court: Judicial Government in Eighteenth Century Massachusetts." *American Journal of Legal History* 20 (1976).

Hoogenboom, Ari. *Outlawing the Spoils: A History of the Civil Service Reform Movement, 1865–1883*. Westport, CT: Greenwood, 1961.

Hoogenboom, Ari, and Olive Hoogenboom. *A History of the Interstate Commerce Commission: From Panacea to Palliative*. New York: W. W. Norton, 1976.

Howard, Christopher. *The Hidden Welfare State: Tax Expenditures and Social Policy in the United States*. Princeton, NJ: Princeton University Press, 1997.

Huntington, Samuel P. "The Marasmus of the Interstate Commerce Commission: The Commission, the Railroads and the Public Interest." *Yale Law Journal* 61 (1952).

Iancu, Bogdan. *Legislative Delegation: The Erosion of Normative Limits in Modern Constitutionalism*. New York: Springer, 2012.

Kagan, Elena. "Presidential Administration." *Harvard Law Review* 114 (2001).

Karl, Barry D. *Executive Reorganization and Reform in the New Deal: The Genesis of Administrative Management, 1900–39.* Chicago: University of Chicago Press, 1963.

Kelly, Alfred H., Winfred A. Harbison, and Herman Belz. *The American Constitution: Its Origins and Development.* 7th ed. New York: W. W. Norton, 1991.

Landis, James M. *The Administrative Process.* New Haven, CT: Yale University Press, 1938.

Lawson, Gary. "The Rise and Rise of the Administrative State." *Harvard Law Review* 107 (1994).

Lessig, Lawrence, and Cass Sunstein. "The President and the Administration." *Columbia Law Review* 94 (1994).

Liberty's Nemesis: The Unchecked Expansion of the State. Edited by Dean Reuter and John Yoo. New York: Encounter, 2016.

Lilley, William III, and James C. Miller. "The New 'Social Regulation.'" *Public Interest* 47 (1977).

Lowi, Theodore J. *The End of Liberalism: The Second Republic of the United States.* 40th anniversary ed. New York: W. W. Norton, 2009.

Mashaw, Jerry L. *Creating the Administrative Constitution: The Lost One Hundred Years of American Administrative Law.* New Haven, CT: Yale University Press, 2012.

McCraw, Thomas K. *Prophets of Regulation: Charles Francis Adams, Louis D. Brandeis, James M. Landis, Alfred E. Kahn.* Cambridge, MA: Harvard University Press, 1984.

McNollgast. "The Political Origins of the Administrative Procedure Act." *Journal of Law and Economic Organization* 15 (1999).

Merriam, C. Edward. *A History of American Political Theories.* New York: Macmillan, 1920 [1903].

Merrill, Thomas W. "Article III, Adjudication and the Origins of the Appellate Model of Administrative Law." *Columbia Law Review* 111 (2011).

Merrill, Thomas W. "Capture Theory and the Courts, 1967–83." *Chicago-Kent Law Review* 72 (1997).

Milkis, Sidney M. "Remaking Government Institutions in the 1970s: Participatory Democracy and the Triumph of Administrative Politics." *Journal of Policy History* 10 (1998).

Milkis, Sidney M., and Jesse H. Rhodes. "George W. Bush, the Republican Party and the 'New' American Party System." *Perspectives on Politics* 5 (2007).

Nathan, Richard P. *The Plot that Failed: Nixon and the Administrative Presidency.* New York: Wiley, 1975.

Nelson, Michael. "A Short, Ironic History of American Bureaucracy." *Journal of Politics* 44 (1982).

Niskanen, William A. *Bureaucracy and Representative Government.* Chicago: Aldine Atherton, 1971.

Novak, William J. "The Myth of the 'Weak' American State." *American Historical Review* 113 (2008).

Penick, James L. Jr. "The Age of the Bureaucrat: Another View of the Ballinger-Pinchot Controversy." *Forest History* 7 (1963).

Polenberg, Ricard. *Reorganizing Roosevelt's Government: The Controversy over Executive Reorganization, 1936–1939*. Cambridge, MA: Harvard University Press, 1969.

Pound, Roscoe. "Executive Justice." *American Law Register* 46 (1907).

President's Committee on Administrative Management. *Report*. Washington, DC: U.S. Government Printing Office, 1937.

Rabin, Robert L. "Federal Regulation in Historical Perspective." *Stanford Law Review* 38 (1986).

Rabkin, Jeremy. "The Judiciary in the Administrative State." *Public Interest* 71 (1983).

Regulation in Perspective: Historical Essays. Edited by Thomas K. McCraw. Cambridge, MA: Harvard University Press, 1981.

Regulation in the Reagan Era: Politics, Bureaucracy, and the Public Interest. Edited by Roger E. Meiners and Bruce Yandle. New York: Holmes & Meier, 1989.

Robinson, Glen O. "The Federal Communications Commission: An Essay on Regulatory Watchdogs." *Virginia Law Review* 64 (1978).

Rohr, John A. *To Run a Constitution: The Legitimacy of the Administrative State*. Lawrence: University of Kansas Press, 1986.

Schiller, Reuel. "The Era of Deference: Courts, Expertise, and the Emergence of New Deal Administrative Law." *Michigan Law Review* 106 (2007).

Schoenbrod, David. *Power without Responsibility: How Congress Abuses the People Through Delegation*. New Haven, CT: Yale University Press, 1993.

Schwartz, Bernard. "The Administrative Agency in Historical Perspective." *Indiana Law Journal* 36 (1961).

Shapiro, Martin. *Who Guards the Guardians? Judicial Control of Administration*. Athens: University of Georgia Press, 1988.

Shepard, George B. "Fierce Compromise: The Administrative Procedure Act Emerges from New Deal Politics." *Northwestern University Law Review* 90 (1996).

Short, Lloyd M. *The Development of National Administrative Organization in the United States*. Baltimore: Johns Hopkins University Press, 1923.

Simon, William H. "Legality, Bureaucracy and Class in the Welfare System." *Yale Law Journal* 92 (1983).

Skowronek, Stephen. *Building a New American State: The Expansion of National Administrative Capacities, 1877–1920*. New York: Cambridge University Press, 1982.

Stigler, George J. "The Theory of Regulation." *Bell Journal of Economics and Management Science* 2 (1971).

The Great Society and the High Tide of Liberalism. Edited by Sidney Milkis and Jerome M. Mileur. Amherst: University of Massachusetts Press, 2005.

The Imperial Congress: Crisis in the Separation of Powers. Edited by Gordon S. Jones and John A. Marini. New York: Pharos, 1988.

The New American State: Bureaucracies and Policies Since World War Two. Edited by Louis Galambos. Baltimore, MD: Johns Hopkins University Press, 1987.

The Politics of Regulation. Edited by James Q. Wilson. New York: Basic, 1980.

The Reagan Regulatory Strategy. Edited by George C. Eads and Michael Fix. Washington, DC: Urban Institute, 1984.

Town and County: Essays on the Structure of Local Government in the American Colonies. Edited by Bruce C. Daniels. Middletown, CT: Wesleyan University Press, 1978.

Van Riper, Paul P. "The American Administrative State: Wilson and the Founders—An Unorthodox View." *Public Administration Review* 43 (1983).

Vile, M. J. C. *Constitutionalism and the Separation of Powers.* 2d ed. Indianapolis: Liberty Fund, 1998.

Vogel, David. "The Public-Interest Movement and the American Reform Tradition." *Political Science Quarterly* 95 (1981).

Waldo, Dwight. *The Administrative State: A Study of the Political Theory of American Public Administration.* New York: Ronald, 1948.

White, Leonard D. *The Federalists: A Study in Administrative History.* New York: Macmillan, 1948.

White, Leonard D. *The Jacksonians: A Study in Administrative History, 1829–61.* New York: Macmillan, 1954.

White, Leonard D. *The Jeffersonians: A Study in Administrative History, 1801–29.* New York: Macmillan, 1951.

White, Leonard D. *The Republican Era, 1869–1901: An Administrative History.* New York: Macmillan, 1958.

Wilson, James Q. "The Rise of the Bureaucratic State." *Public Interest* 41 (1975).

Wilson, Woodrow. *Congressional Government: A Study in American Politics.* New York: Meridian, 1956 [1885].

Wilson, Woodrow. "The Study of Administration." *Political Science Quarterly* 2 (1887).

Index

About the Author

PAUL D. MORENO holds the William and Berniece Grewcock Chair in Constitutional History at Hillsdale College. He has held visiting professorships at Princeton University and the University of Paris School of Law. He is the author of *From Direct Action to Affirmative Action* (LSU, 1997), *Black Americans and Organized Labor: A New History* (LSU, 2006), and *The American State from the Civil War to the New Deal: The Twilight of Constitutionalism and the Triumph of Progressivism* (Cambridge, 2013). He lives in Hillsdale, Michigan, with his wife, Lisa, and their four children, Judy, Mark, Ruth, and Gregory.